COMMUNITY ENGAGED
LEADERSHIP FOR SOCIAL JUSTICE

This book advocates for informed leaders who are aware of the larger historical, political-economic, sociological, and philosophical issues that surround the schools and communities they serve. Extending beyond mainstream conceptions of instructional leadership and broad social justice paradigms, *Community Engaged Leadership for Social Justice* offers a multidisciplinary framework that helps leaders better serve the needs of their students, teachers, and communities. Exploring issues of urban school reform as it relates to the principal, as well as priorities that are relevant to the process of school improvement and the promotion of social justice, this book provides a critical, equity-oriented set of best practices grounded in research and empirical cases. This is a must-have resource for building consciousness, offering hope, and engaging in dialogical and collaborative leadership practices to radically transform schools and communities.

David E. DeMatthews is Associate Professor of Educational Leadership and Policy at the University of Texas at Austin, USA.

COMMUNITY ENGAGED LEADERSHIP FOR SOCIAL JUSTICE

A Critical Approach in Urban Schools

David E. DeMatthews

Routledge
Taylor & Francis Group

NEW YORK AND LONDON

First published 2018
by Routledge
711 Third Avenue, New York, NY 10017

and by Routledge
2 Park Square, Milton Park, Abingdon, Oxon, OX14 4RN

Routledge is an imprint of the Taylor & Francis Group, an informa business

© 2018 Taylor & Francis

The right of David E. DeMatthews to be identified as author of
this work has been asserted by him in accordance with sections 77
and 78 of the Copyright, Designs and Patents Act 1988.

Library of Congress Cataloging-in-Publication Data
A catalog record for this title has been requested

ISBN: 978-1-138-04457-9 (hbk)
ISBN: 978-1-138-04458-6 (pbk)
ISBN: 978-1-315-17226-2 (ebk)

Typeset in Bembo
by Swales & Willis Ltd, Exeter, Devon, UK

I dedicate this book to my parents and family who invested in me, to Kara for keeping me grounded and focused, to the teachers and leaders who have inspired and mentored me throughout my career, to Hanne Mawhinney for providing me with the foundation to succeed in academia, and to all my students from Baltimore, Washington, DC, and El Paso.

CONTENTS

PREFACE

Much ink has been spilled discussing how principals might improve, lead, transform, or turnaround low-performing urban schools. Many principals work tirelessly to improve their schools and the lives of the students they serve, but often fall short of accomplishing any meaningful long-term improvement outcomes. Racial achievement and discipline gaps persist. Students of color are disproportionately identified into special education and educated in separate classrooms and schools. Culturally and linguistically diverse students are frequently viewed as testing liabilities in need of intervention, rather than students with unique and valuable assets. A hidden curriculum pervades classrooms and socializes low-income students of color in ways that maintain rather than transform the status quo. A broad consensus of researchers, policymakers, and educators recognize how important parents are to school improvement and student success. However, in practice, many schools perceive Black and Latina/o parents as deficient. They fail to recognize and take advantage of the community cultural wealth of families and communities of color (Yosso, 2005). Relatedly, as principals lead in ways that emphasize student achievement, they sometimes fail to understand how the broader social and political context of their communities impact students and negate any one-track approach to school improvement.

Principals are important to creating inclusive and high-performing schools that meet the needs of all students, but the enterprise of urban school leadership remains too focused on compliance and the narrow alignment of curriculum and instruction to state-mandated assessments. The principal frequently views herself or himself as an instructional leader who uses her or his positional authority, expertise, and culture shaping skillset to enhance teacher capacity and improve student achievement, but progress often comes at the expense of the physical, social, and emotional development of students. A powerful logic of consistency and neutrality pervades the practice of many principals. Too often, principals view schools as apolitical organizations to be managed using consistent and neutral management approaches. School leadership from this perspective emphasizes efficiency and the minimization of any disruption or variance. Many principals believe such an environment is best suited for preparing students to demonstrate mastery of curriculum on state-mandated assessments. They work to create this environment in the name of social justice and narrowing achievement gaps.

The field of educational administration and leadership's knowledge base and professional standards has provided an important foundation for conceptualizing the role of the principal and considering the essential practices for improving schools, but has also fostered this neutral organizational leadership approach. It has blinded many principals from understanding and working to address the diverse needs of urban students, families, and communities. The underlying problem and motivation for this book is to reconsider the role of the principal in light of the historic, economic, political, and social injustices that have operated in many urban communities, districts, and schools. My motivation is driven by a belief that if principals are knowledgeable about these injustices they will reconsider their approaches and practices in ways that are not neutral, but purposeful, community engaged, and culturally responsive. In other words, knowledge of school-community context allows principals to reconsider their priorities, recognize their communities as assets, and reframe parent and community involvement as a mechanism for school transformation and improvement (DeMatthews, Edwards, & Rincones, 2016; Watson & Bogotch, 2015).

I draw upon a range of traditions including history, sociology, political economy, and critical theory to support the need for leadership to be community engaged and grounded by school-community context. In my synthesis of these traditions, I situate urban school leadership not as an abstract set of practices focused on improving systems, processes and practices within schools, but as a dialogical, inquiry-oriented, and critical approach to school and community improvement. A community engaged leadership approach is centered on the real experiences and challenges confronting the students and families living in the enrollment boundaries of a school. While situating urban school leadership within communities, I acknowledge and engage with the real problems of practice principals confront as leaders working within and for school districts. Situating leadership in the real experiences and challenges confronting urban schools and communities requires fully recognizing the complicated, multifaceted, and political nature of the principalship as well as understanding the ways principals are constrained given their positions within the system.

This book is intended for education and education leadership scholars, specifically those interested in examining social justice, urban education, and school reform through critical perspectives. In addition, this book is written in an accessible language to engage a broader audience of principals, superintendents, school board members, activists, teachers, and education policymakers. I view this book as a tool for building consciousness, offering hope, and envisioning how principals might engage in community engaged leadership practices to transform their schools and communities. This is not a neutral book. While I see value in some of the traditional ways principals lead and think about improving their schools, I argue that dominant perspectives coupled with the current era of top-down education reform have hindered principals' ability to position schools in ways that meet the needs of their students and families. I believe urban schools can be radically transformed if principals are knowledgeable about the history of their communities and develop a critical consciousness, engage in ongoing dialogue and social analysis with families and other stakeholders to problem-pose and problem-solve, and lead with hope and humility. *Community Engaged Leadership for Social Justice* is premised on the notion that principals need to understand the historical and current contexts in which they live and lead others. That is why each chapter concludes with "principal takeaways." I strongly believe principals need to understand how racism and other forms of oppression have operated within their city, district, and school and they need to understand how to lead with others and in ways that bring about meaningful change in their schools and the lives of their students. I challenge the reader to determine if I have successfully made my case.

Summary of Chapters

The shortcomings confronting urban schools cannot be fixed with more of the same school type of school leadership that is focused on achievement, test scores, and district priorities. This is not to say that there are not valuable practices in traditional approaches to school leadership or that community engaged leadership alone will remedy all the challenges confronting urban schools. However, principals cannot afford to ignore the social and economic conditions around schools. Many of the sources of school failure reside in the social and economic conditions and policies that affect students and families (Berliner, 2013). Socioeconomic status (SES) and neighborhood context are well-known factors that influence the physical and mental health of children (Leventhal & Brooks-Gunn, 2000). SES and neighborhood context impact student achievement and have a lasting influence on social and economic indicators of health and well-being into adulthood (Miller, Chen, & Parker, 2011). Events during childhood have long-lasting effects on a child's ability to learn, listen, cooperate, and respect others (Currie & Almond, 2011). Diet, inadequate healthcare, exposure to pollutants and violence, and poor health habits contribute to a student's risk of physical illness and emotional distress. In other words, many of the most pressing problems in education exist outside schools. In many cases, families and community organizations are working to address these challenges and could benefit from greater collaboration with public schools. Principals must understand this context before considering their approaches to leadership.

In Part I, I examine the social, economic, and political aspects of urban neighborhoods and urban public schools. I explore the development of urban neighborhoods where few children escape poverty, provide a history of how racially explicit government policies created segregated, low-opportunity communities and unequal schools, and detail how past and current approaches to educational reform has made little meaningful progress. I also draw attention to how history informs social relations and conditions within schools, how these relations reproduce educational inequalities, and how principals can transform their schools by reconsidering the historical and social context in which they work. I hope that understanding the history of low-opportunity urban communities and schools creates opportunities for new frames of reference, identities, and aspirations for school leadership. This section of the book is about building racial, social, and political consciousness, which I view as an important foundation for community engaged leadership.

In Chapter 2, "Neighborhoods of (In)Opportunity," I identify some of the social and economic inequalities that negatively affect many urban, low-income communities of color. I discuss the implications of racial segregation, disinvestment and unemployment, unequal educational attainment outcomes, community violence, and public health challenges for the academic, physical, and emotional well-being of children and families. These social and economic inequalities shape and constrain the public schools embedded in these neighborhoods. I focus on urban schools and communities that are profoundly shaped by racism and poverty. I discuss pressing issues in urban education and in urban school districts, which include funding disparities, teacher quality and turnover problems, achievement and discipline gaps, and the less than adequate education often provided to many children of color also labeled as a student with a disability or an English language learner.

In Chapter 3, "Racial Segregation and Urban Schools," I describe in detail how racism and racial segregation created profound educational inequalities in many urban schools. I begin providing a 100-year history of racist government housing policies that created low-opportunity urban communities of color described in Chapter 2. In this chapter, I also describe, using case studies of Baltimore, Maryland, and El Paso, Texas, how racial segregation and other structural forms of racism contributed to unequal, underfunded, and underserving urban public schools. I provide this history and the linkages between racist housing policies and unequal urban schools to underscore the depth of inequality in America and its public schools.

In Chapter 4, "A History of Urban School Reform," I present an overview of urban educational reform over the course of four eras: The Common School era (1820–1860), the Progressive era (1890–1950), the Civil Rights era (1950–1980), and the Accountability and Market-Based Reform era (1980–present). I highlight several important historical events relevant to how economic and cultural changes in society influence urban school reform. I also describe how the principal's role was conceptualized and evolved over time. While urban school reform is not monolithic and varies by district, I discuss how dominant, business-like reforms driven by corporate elites have shaped urban public schools in the past and present and have failed at one of its primary intended purposes: closing racial and economic achievement gaps.

In Chapter 5, "Schools as Social Institutions," I utilize a sociological lens to critique dominant urban school reform policies and explore the possibilities of more critical and social justice oriented approaches to improving schools, curriculum, and relationships between the school, students, and families. Because principal preparation programs rarely consider the sociological nature of schools and their relationship with society, I begin with an overview of functionalist, conflict, and interactionist theories to consider the different roles public schools play in society. Next, I provide an overview of educational research in the field of sociology of education to identify how schools, as social institutions, reinforce or address the various social and educational injustices presented in the previous chapters. I conclude with a discussion of what many education scholars have called the "hidden curriculum" and how it reinforces rather than transforms the status quo in urban schools.

In Part II, I focus on the history of educational administration and leadership, how dominant and non-dominant perspectives inform preparation and practice, and how principals can practice a community engaged leadership directed at creating more inclusive, socially just and high-performing schools. I will explore the history of the field of educational administration and leadership and how dominant perspectives offer only a narrow view of creating the schools low-income students of color require. Then, I describe alternative ways of leading that are focused on community engagement, social justice, and the multifaceted needs of students and families. I emphasize the need for principals to shed their neutrality, learn about their communities and the needs of families and students, and lead in ways that are locally and culturally responsive. I also underscore the importance of critical reflection, because no leadership approach is perfect and any principal can make a decision that has harmful unintended negative consequences.

In Chapter 6, "The Science of Educational Administration," I critically analyze the dominant perspective in the field of educational administration and leadership as developed over the past 120 years. I begin with the rise of Taylorism and scientific management (1900–1935) and continue with human relations perspectives (1935–1950), the development of a "new" and more scientific perspective in administration focused on social science research and theory generation (1950–1980), and the current era where reform and accountability movements fostered a need for a knowledge base and professional standards (1980–present). I focus on the dominant perspective in the field because it has been central to discussions about the role and duties of the principal, but has also served as a significant distraction to addressing educational injustices and significant social problems external to the school but that negatively impact urban, low-income students of color. This chapter does not outright and entirely reject the dominant perspective and its contributions to the field, but, instead, it reveals its narrowness and inability to bring about meaningful change if it is not also supported with a community engaged approach.

In Chapter 7, "Alternative Ways of Knowing and Leading," I examine alternative perspectives in educational administration and leadership and how they contribute to new possibilities for the creation of the schools necessary in low-opportunity communities. I begin by tracing the development of major criticisms of the dominant perspective in educational administration that emerged in the 1970s and 1980s. I also consider the leadership of Black and Latina/o principals in the pre- and post-Jim Crow era to highlight the long history of social justice leadership that went mostly unrecognized by mainstream professors of educational administration. These principals are powerful examples of community engaged leaders for social justice. I conclude this chapter with a review of the literature on culturally responsive leadership centered on advocacy, community engagement, and an enhanced instructional leadership that builds on the assets of urban, low-income students of color and their families.

In Chapter 8, "Leading for Social Justice," I argue that we need principals in low-opportunity communities of color who recognize how families, students, and communities have been devalued. I begin with a review of the work of John Rawls, Nancy Fraser, and other political philosophers to unpack the meaning of social justice and how it relates to community. Then, I present a review of literature and a new framework for community engaged leadership for social justice in urban public schools. I draw here on the work of Paulo Freire, William Foster, Michael Dantley, Vanessa Siddle Walker, George Theoharis, and James Ryan to understand and develop each element of this framework, which consists of personal experiences and commitments, situational awareness, advocacy, critical reflection and praxis, and technical expertise and standards-based leadership practices.

In Chapter 9, "Critical Cases of Leadership in Low-Opportunity Communities," I present four case studies from my research in the Mid-Atlantic region of the USA and from along the USA–Mexico border. Each case study provides information about the district and school context, the principal's background and commitments, their leadership priorities and actions, and the outcomes and personal reflections about the nature of trying to create more inclusive, locally and culturally responsive, and socially just schools. The cases are not heroic narratives nor are they shining examples of fully transformed schools. Instead, these are cases of principals working with teachers, families, and students to undo, address, and rectify educational and social injustices while struggling with the demands of being a principal within a public school system. In the concluding chapter, I summarize community engaged leadership as well as the book's main points. I also offer practical recommendations for urban principals seeking to apply a community engaged approach.

References

Berliner, D. C. (2013). Effects of inequality and poverty vs. teachers and schooling on America's youth. *Teachers College Record, 115*(2), 1–26.

Currie, J., & Almond, D. (2011). Human capital development before age five. *Handbook of Labor Economics, 4*, 1315–1486.

DeMatthews, D. E., Edwards Jr., D. B., & Rincones, R. (2016). Social justice leadership and family engagement: A successful case from Ciudad Juárez, Mexico. *Educational Administration Quarterly, 52*(5), 754–792.

Leventhal, T., & Brooks-Gunn, J. (2000). The neighborhoods they live in: The effects of neighborhood residence on child and adolescent outcomes. *Psychological Bulletin, 126*(2), 309.

Miller, G. E., Chen, E., & Parker, K. J. (2011). Psychological stress in childhood and susceptibility to the chronic diseases of aging: Moving toward a model of behavioral and biological mechanisms. *Psychological Bulletin, 137*(6), 959.

Watson, T. N., & Bogotch, I. (2015). Reframing parent involvement: What should urban school leaders do differently? *Leadership and Policy in Schools, 14*(3), 257–278.

Yosso, T. J. (2005). Whose culture has capital? A critical race theory discussion of community cultural wealth. *Race, Ethnicity and Education, 8*(1), 69–91.

ACKNOWLEDGMENTS

My family, friends, mentors, colleagues, and students worked with me and inspired me to write this book. I truly thank all of them for their belief in and support for my work. My thinking and development as a leader, scholar, and human being has been shaped by my experiences working with amazing educators and students, and from the ideas of many of the authors I reference in this book. Friends, colleagues, and mentors who read and critiqued former drafts of this manuscript include Gary Anderson, Roderick Carey, Robert Donmoyer, Julia Duncheon, D. Brent Edwards Jr., Elena Izquierdo, Stephen Kotok, David Knight, Arturo Pacheco, Rebecca Tarlau, and Terri Watson. Special thanks to my former graduate students and research assistants, including James Coviello, Becca Gregory, Kevin Moussavi-Saeedi, and Timothy Nelson. Others who assisted in many ways include Floyd Beachum, Juan Cabrera, Paul Carrola, Elke Chen, Kevin Cox, Sonia Denis, Maria Garcia, Donald Hackmann, Rodrick Hobbs, Patricia Lowe-Gould, Delphine Lee, Katherine Cumings Mansfield, Richard Nyankori, Gustavo Reveles, Rodolfo Rincones, Richard Sorenson, Shaneka Stewart, Leman Tarawaly, Tyhquan Walker, and Anjale Welton.

1

INTRODUCTION

History, as nearly no one seems to know, is not merely something to be read. And it does not refer merely, or even principally, to the past. On the contrary, the great force of history comes from the fact that we carry it within us, are unconsciously controlled by it in many ways, and history is literally present in all that we do. It could scarcely be otherwise, since it is to history that we owe our frames of reference, our identities, and our aspirations. And it is with great pain and terror that one begins to realize this. In great pain and terror, one begins to assess the history which has placed one where one is, and formed one's point of view. In great pain and terror, because, thereafter, one enters into battle with that historical creation, oneself, and attempts to recreate oneself according to a principle more humane and more liberating; one begins the attempt to achieve a level of personal maturity and freedom which robs history of its tyrannical power, and also changes history.

— James Baldwin (1965, p. 47)

In the quote above, James Baldwin exposes how history shapes our frames of reference, our identities, and what we believe is possible for ourselves, our communities, our social institutions, and for others. Principals can learn a great deal from how Baldwin understood history and the social world. In fact, principals need to be historians and have knowledge and respect for the communities they serve. Unfortunately, it has been my experience that few principals have this depth of knowledge or even recognize the need to further explore their personal history or the histories of their schools and communities. I frequently talk with urban principals in a variety of cities, but I rarely find a principal who sees their role within the historical context of a community. While many of these principals are highly intelligent and all have graduate degrees, most cannot see how history has shaped their identities, frames of reference, beliefs and priorities, and approaches to school leadership. Most principals I talk to believe they must always remain neutral, keep politics out of their school and out of their decisions, and lead in ways that promote student achievement as measured by state assessments and continuous improvement goals. The past is always behind these principals and they are always looking forward without reflection. They are often driven by compliance, competition with other principals in their district, and a desire to ensure each day runs smoothly and without controversy. This way of thinking and leading cuts across principals from diverse backgrounds.

Two Constrained Administrators

As a middle school assistant principal in the District of Columbia Public Schools (DCPS), I was a student of history and a voracious reader. I took great effort to learn about the communities I served. I worked in the Shaw and U Street neighborhoods of Washington, DC. In the 1920s, the U Street neighborhood was one of the largest urban Black communities in the USA and in its heyday, was known as "Black Broadway" because of the famous performers who played in the area, such as Cab Calloway, Louis Armstrong, Sarah Vaughan, and Billie Holliday. In 1968, following Dr. Martin Luther King's assassination, the neighborhood was at the epicenter of the 1968 Washington, DC riots. U Street became blighted, many residents and businesses fled, and those left behind began to struggle with the effects of poverty, drug trafficking, and other public health problems. In the 1990s and 2000s, gentrification began to significantly change the racial and economic dynamics of neighborhoods across the city. By 2010, most of my students lived in nearby housing projects because public housing was increasingly the only part of the U Street and Shaw neighborhoods that long-term residents could afford.

I was aware of the rich history of the U Street community. A museum sat across the street from my school and numerous historical markers were nearby. I frequently talked to students about U Street's history and exposed them to the music and artistry that dominated the neighborhood's past. We painted murals of Black civil rights leaders on our school's walls and most of the teachers were proud to work in such a historic community. We studied the history and prominent scholars and alumni of nearby Howard University. After work, I played basketball with students in neighborhood recreational centers and housing projects. I walked the nearby streets and introduced myself to church leadership, local businesses, community-based organizations, and non-profits. I invited neighborhood police officers out for drinks after work to establish rapport and help them see how police can be partners with the school, rather than as adversaries. I loved U Street and the community. I made lifelong friends with students, families, and residents.

I was also aware of how DCPS and the DC City Government had failed to support its residents. Numerous class action lawsuits against the city were active while I was working at Shaw. Young Black men were being murdered at an alarming rate, including one of my middle school students. Despite my passion for history and my connection to the U Street neighborhood, I too felt a need to lead in ways that narrowly promoted student achievement. I worked hard to eliminate any form of disruption so teachers could complete their daily lessons. I prioritized the compliance expectations my district emphasized. I became frustrated with students who continually engaged in misconduct and even though I knew that much of their behavior was a function of a lack of experienced and culturally conscious teachers, at times, I suspended students feeling I had no other option. As a school, we worked hard to understand the issues confronted by families and students. We engaged in the community and advocated for our students. We had many community partnerships. Yet, upon reflection, I still see the many ways I contributed to the school-to-prison pipeline and how I fell short of leading in ways that promoted a meaningful education. In other words, I knew better and I cared deeply but struggled to shake the constraints of a history that has manipulated school leaders into being neutral and focused narrowly on prescribed objectives. I was not entirely prepared to critically reflect on my practice and battle with myself about what I genuinely valued. I was not mature enough to be an authentic individual that could lead in ways that truly served my community.

Perhaps, I fell short because I was not from the U Street community. I was a White man from New Jersey working in Washington, DC. While I was committed and wholehearted in my efforts, maybe I was not meant to lead a school in a Black community. I do not believe this, but I recognize that our racial identity is a dominant force in shaping our frames of reference. Recently, I began working with a Mexican-American graduate student who is also a principal. Juan has been a principal for more than three years, and I have visited his school on occasion. He works very hard, he cares about his teachers and students, and he wants to see all his students be successful. The community he serves includes many families who recently immigrated to the USA from Mexico. Many families are struggling financially and most parents speak only Spanish. When I first met Juan, he told me about how his family moved to the USA from Mexico not speaking English and with little money. He said his parents inspired him to get an education and how they are so proud that he is now a principal in the same district he attended as a student. Juan works in the El Paso Independent School District (EPISD) in Texas.

In November 2016, I invited Juan into one of my graduate courses for aspiring principals to talk about curriculum development. Donald Trump had just been elected president and many students and teachers were upset given the president's statements about Mexican immigrants, immigration policy, and the border wall. A graduate student preparing to be a principal asked Juan, "Would you encourage your teachers to engage in a protest with students over a civil rights issue or a public policy that seemed threatening to the community?" I could tell Juan felt uncomfortable answering the question and ultimately, he said, "It's impractical for a principal to be political. You must focus on student achievement. It's your job to improve your school and not be distracted by other issues, even if they are important." Some students nodded in agreement with Juan and appreciated his businesslike focus while others looked on with disgust.

I knew Juan was a good man and a caring principal, but I wondered how much he knew about El Paso's history. It was hard for me to imagine the caring and dedicated man I knew not taking a stance on a political issue impacting students, teachers, and families. El Paso is a border city and has long been the site of racial injustice. In 1976, a federal court concluded that for nearly 80 years EPISD operated two separate, racially segregated, and unequal districts (see *Alvarado et al. v EPISD*). One set of schools was for Mexican-American students, and another for White students. As a child, Juan and his siblings attended schools in the "Mexican District," although he was not knowledgeable about the court case or the fact that his district had a history of segregation. More than 40 years later many of these schools remain segregated and unequal.

In 2011, the district's former superintendent and several district administrators, principals, and assistant principals inappropriately kept low-performing students out of tested grade levels by improperly promoting or holding back students, preventing them from enrolling in school, or forcing them to drop out (DeMatthews, Izquierdo, & Knight, 2017). The cheating scandal was a daily headline in local newspapers and national media. Juan was well-aware of the story and how these students were Mexican-American English language learners (ELLs) from low-income families just like his own. So, why would an intelligent, hardworking principal in a district that historically marginalized Mexican Americans and just recently targeted its most vulnerable students feel his job was always to be "neutral" or that taking a political stance on an issue was "impractical" for a principal?

While it may seem hard to believe that Juan would commit to being neutral in such an unjust context, I cannot say I am surprised by his stance. I know many will say Juan was merely trying to keep his job and not risk his employment. However, Juan was often outspoken as a principal and was not afraid to challenge his superintendent and district on an issue he felt impacted his school. Juan, like many principals, took calculated risks. He spoke out publicly concerning a curricular reform adopted by the district. His stance took courage and he took stands because he cared about his students and teachers. After class, I talked to Juan and asked why he felt it was impractical for a principal to be political under certain circumstances. He restated that a principal's job was to focus on school improvement and raising student achievement. He said, "The principal has to be the one person who holds everything together, he sets the expectations, he ensures consistency, and makes sure everyone is on the same page. Otherwise, things won't get done." Juan viewed the principalship as a management position and felt he needed to ensure teachers were all "rowing in the same direction" and consistent with all students. He felt without consistent management, teachers would receive mixed signals about what was appropriate behavior and what was inappropriate behavior. It was clear to me that Juan believed schools should be frictionless organizations that run efficiently and smoothly. He saw himself as a middle-manager between the district and the classroom. Juan felt that by creating this efficient and smoothly run school where all teachers were working together to raise student achievement, his students would receive a quality education enabling them to escape poverty and make a new life, just as he did.

Many educators and citizens believe public schools are the "great equalizers" in our society and that the "American Dream" is alive and well. Appropriating civil rights era jargon for racial and economic equality, many principals firmly believe if they focus their efforts and attention on raising test scores, their schools will provide their students with social mobility. I also learned another reason why many principals working within districts that have long maintained racial inequalities can be so naïve and so narrowly focused on the district's mandate to improve test scores. In my conversation with Juan, he never learned about the federal court case decision in 1976 that declared EPISD was operating two separate districts. He was prepared to be a principal in El Paso. His coursework was focused on instructional leadership, budgeting, law, administration, and supervision. All he knew was to follow the rules, ensure consistency, and get teachers to work together to improve student achievement. His clinical internship before receiving his certification was focused on following orders. Later, as an assistant principal, Juan was groomed by his principal and district to follow orders.

Rejecting Neutrality and Acknowledging Racism

I believe it is impractical for a principal to remain neutral when schools that serve urban, low-income students of color are so frequently unequal and when neutral approaches have continually failed to close achievement gaps or improve other important educational outcomes. I also believe it is negligent to lead a public school without in-depth history and knowledge of the surrounding community or its needs. A principal's lack of historical awareness is not an indictment of the individual, but rather how they have been prepared and mentored. It is also reflective of how certain standardized and generic leadership practices and ideologies have been peddled by "reformers" and social scientists as magic bullet solutions to school improvement. The issues I described in DCPS and EPISD have been documented in New York City, Detroit, Newark, and other urban school districts serving high proportions of students of color. I am not surprised that so many principals who are deeply committed to improving the lives of their students maintain such frames of reference and pursue such extraneous avenues of reform. It is difficult for any of us to see how history controls our thoughts, actions, priorities, and aspirations. The dominant perspectives in the field of educational administration and leadership have viewed schools as ahistorical and abstract organizations, not as social institutions embedded within communities with rich histories and dynamic needs. Most programs that prepare principals narrowly adopt the field's knowledge base and state and national professional standards, which tend to ignore the historical, social, and political forces that shape schools, communities, teachers, students, and families.

This book is intended to challenge the underlying assumptions about the role of the principal, especially in communities that are struggling with the pervasive effects of poverty, and racial and economic segregation. The normality of racism allows many principals to believe they are acting fairly and consistently, despite historic and current evidence that suggests otherwise. Too many principals continue to describe Black boys and girls, in particular, as more threatening, disruptive, and disrespectful than their White peers (Morris, 2005). Black boys continue to be deemed as "unsalvageable," viewed as mannish, and disproportionately punished (Ferguson, 2001). Some principals and their teachers share a belief that low-income Black and Latina/o families are culturally deficient and do not want to be involved in their children's education (DeMatthews, Carey, Olivarez, & Moussavi-Saeedi, 2017; Yosso, 2005). The pervasiveness of racism has even led educators to believe that low-income children of color need to be "walled out" from their communities and families because of perceptions that the child's home and community are potentially harmful (Lipman, 1997). We cannot afford to have principals who lack an awareness of the historical situation in which they work and lead.

We cannot afford to have principals who are not critically reflective and able to find new avenues for improving their schools. We cannot afford to have principals who do not understand how racism operates in schools and society. Principals must be knowledgeable about the meaning and pervasiveness of racism. When I use the word race or racism in this book, I do so with full recognition that race is socially constructed and is not an objective reality nor a biological one (Omi & Winant, 1994). I draw on the assumptions of critical race theory (CRT) that suggest racism is normal and appears natural to the point it goes unquestioned (Delgado & Stefancic, 2012). CRT challenges traditional claims of racial neutrality, colorblindness, and objectivity. These ideologies are understood to be camouflage for self-interest, power, and the privilege imbued in the master narratives of dominant groups (Solórzano & Yosso, 2002). In the first section of this book, I highlight more indirect forms of racism that reflect discrimination that privileges White people over non-Whites. Kwami Ture (formerly known as Stokley Carmichael) and Charles Hamilton (1967/1992) defined institutional racism as "the predication of decisions and policies on considerations of race for the purpose of subordinating a racial group and maintaining control over that group" (p. 10). Institutional racism reflects subtle forms of discrimination that can be purposeful, conscious or unconscious, and actualized by well-intended educators. Institutional racism also exists in the large social and economic policies that create and shape communities. Principals must not only be prepared to recognize overt racism and be willing to intercede, but also be willing and able to undo institutionally racist school and district policies, address misunderstandings about race and class, and work within communities to take on educational and public policy issues that marginalize students and families.

Unpacking Urban and Low-Opportunity

I use the word "urban" frequently in this book. Scholars from many disciplines (anthropology, economics, geography, history, political science, psychology, sociology, etc.) have not produced a consensus definition of "urban." Sometimes, "urban" is utilized by educators to discuss multifaceted problems related to poverty, race, public health and crime, family, and student achievement. New York City, Chicago, and Los Angeles come to mind as urban because they are large, densely populated metropolitan areas with significant infrastructure and substantial disparities between wealthy and low-income residents. Cities are often racially and economically segregated and represent a duality of urban life. On the one hand, cities are sources of cultural, social, and economic resources including significant transportation systems, large research universities, museums, historic landmarks, financial centers, and a wealthy class of people. On the other hand, cities are places of unequal resources, services, and opportunities for minority, immigrant, and low-income residents.

I use the word urban with some hesitancy because I recognize words like "urban" generalize places as well as people and their humanity. Urbanites are people with families, hopes, and dreams and there is no one objective "urban reality." Each city and neighborhood has a unique history with multiple realities, although similarities indeed exist. The size of a city, its history, status, and its cultural, financial, and human resources are important factors that are relevant to public education. In urban communities, it is essential to recognize that children and families have agency, are conscious beings, and make meaningful choices that shape their futures. Too often urbanites are viewed as deviants, long-term welfare recipients, and street criminals (Wilson, 2012) or as lacking capacity to take control of their lives due to historic and structural injustice. This characterization is bogus and neglects the indigenous assets and the dynamic networks of residents, activists, organizations, and institutions that work together to benefit children and families. Urban public schools and their principals also have agency and can powerfully impact their communities.

I define neighborhoods and communities in spatial terms and recognize that many have their boundaries imposed on them by outsiders (Sampson, 2012). I speak to the power of these outsiders in subsequent chapters with attention to how racial segregation in government housing policy created unequal access to resources and opportunities. I also use the term "low-opportunity" to describe some urban communities. Each time I use the term I cringe, because I recognize how it devalues a community and suggests that a place and group of people lack resources and opportunities that can help children and families live happy and healthy lives. I believe that it is important to acknowledge that all families and communities have assets and resources. I also think that a historical analysis of any low-opportunity community will reveal a legacy of powerful resistance and solidarity that has challenged harmful social and economic policies. However, it is undeniable that there are certain neighborhoods where few families escape poverty, and where children have little access to adequate housing and healthcare, quality schools, high-nutrition foods, and safe places to play (Tate, 2008). When I discuss low-opportunity communities and urban schools in this book, I do so because I recognize how socioeconomic status (SES) and neighborhood context are well-known facts that influence the physical and mental health of children (Leventhal & Brooks-Gunn, 2000) and that these factors have a lasting influence on the health and well-being of students as they transition into adulthood (Miller, Chen, & Parker, 2011).

Why Are Principals So Important?

I choose to focus on principals in this book because principals are essential to creating urban schools that meet the diverse needs of students and because many principals overlook or are naïve to the alternative possibilities and avenues they might take for building more socially just schools. Mainstream research in the field of educational administration and leadership confirms that principal leadership is an essential element to a high-performing, inclusive, and caring school (Klar & Brewer, 2013; Leithwood, Harris, & Hopkins, 2008). The Professional Standards for Educational Leadership (National Policy Board for Educational Administration (NPBEA), 2015) are based on an extensive knowledge base and identify several vital actions and practices of effective principals, which include:

- collaborating with faculty to develop a shared mission and vision;
- recognizing and addressing policies and practices that marginalize groups of students;
- developing organizational conditions and systems that promote teacher inquiry and professional growth;
- engaging families and communities and recognizing the community's multiple forms of capital (e.g., cultural, social, intellectual, linguistic, political).

The standards also call for principals to "Institute, manage, and monitor operations and administrative systems" (NPBEA, 2015, p. 17) and utilize methods of continuous improvement that are situationally appropriate. Principals can be very successful at improving their schools when they recognize there is no single model for achieving success, appreciate how context affects the nature and direction of leadership, and commit to finding a balance between "top-down" and "bottom-up" approaches that are responsive to context and shifting landscapes within schools and communities (Day et al., 2011). Principals are in a conspicuous position to lead such work, and it is hard to imagine any school serving its students well without a principal engaging in such efforts.

Alternative perspectives in the field of educational administration and leadership do not outright reject many of the so-called "effective practices" summarized in standards and the knowledge base but call for a more critical, locally responsive, activist- and socially justice-oriented approach to leadership. From this perspective, principals learn together with teachers, students, and families to become knowledgeable about how history informs practice. Through collaborative work, principals and teachers become more racially, socially, and politically conscious. A Freirean-like approach to dialogue and collaborative learning are essential leadership activities. School goals and priorities are not externally imposed, but instead collectively generated (DeMatthews & Izquierdo, 2017). Likewise, principals collaborate with others to engage in a social analysis that deconstructs and then reconstructs priorities, policies, practices, and pedagogies in ways that create more equitable outcomes. In other words, principals work with people, not on people. They work and engage with a profound love for others and with a deep faith that, together, educators and families can collectively transform their current realities. They embody a critical hope that refuses to accept the history of injustice and inequality as unalterable despite present conditions because they have a deep belief in humanity, and democratic practices. Lastly, and perhaps most importantly, these principals have humility and know that they do not have all the answers. They do not engage in dialogue and collaborate with others to gain consent or manipulate, but instead they do so out of an authentic belief that the school community is stronger together than the sum of each of its parts.

Takeaways for Principals

Principals need to thoughtful, educated, and informed individuals. They need to be able to look introspectively and recognize how their own past experiences inform their frames of reference. Principals also need to understand the context in which they work and acknowledge that racism and other forms of discrimination play an important role in maintaining educational and social inequalities. Principals are leaders within their communities because schools are vital social institutions. If they fail to educate themselves on the historical context and current challenges confronting families and students, they will be unable to lead in ways that help students find success. No place in this book will I offer a remedy for success or a roadmap for school improvement. Instead, I will provide an examination of urban schools and communities and detail how principals might work collaboratively with communities and others to improve the lives of students. I will not suggest that principals can change the world on their own or even promise that being conscious of injustice and trying to make a difference will be enough to create and maintain change. The challenges confronting many schools in low-opportunity urban communities are significant and highly complex. However, principals can play an important role with families, teachers, and communities to catalyze change.

References

Baldwin, J. (1965). The white man's guilt. *Ebony, 20*(1), 47–51.

Day, C., Sammons, P., Leithwood, K., Hopkins, D., Gu, Q., Brown, E., Ahtaridou, E. (2011). *Successful school leadership: Linking with learning and achievement.* Maidenhead, UK: McGraw Hill Open University Press.

Delgado, R., & Stefancic, J. (2012). *Critical race theory: An introduction.* New York: NYU Press.

DeMatthews, D. E., Carey, R. L., Olivarez, A., & Moussavi Saeedi. (2017). Guilty as charged? Principals' perspectives on disciplinary practices and the racial discipline gap. *Educational Administration Quarterly, 53*(4), 519–555.

DeMatthews, D. E., & Izquierdo, E. (2017). The role of principals in developing dual language education: Implications for social justice leadership and preparation. *Journal of Latinos and Education.* DOI: 10.1080/15348431.2017.1282365

DeMatthews, D. E., Izquierdo, E., & Knight, D. (2017). Righting past wrongs: A superintendent's social justice leadership for dual language education along the US–Mexico border. *Education Policy Analysis Archives, 25*(1), 1–28.

Ferguson, A. A. (2001). *Bad boys: Public schools in the making of Black masculinity.* Ann Arbor: University of Michigan Press.

Klar, H. W., & Brewer, C. A. (2013). Successful leadership in high-needs schools: An examination of core leadership practices enacted in challenging contexts. *Educational Administration Quarterly, 49*(5), 768–808.

Leithwood, K., Harris, A., & Hopkins, D. (2008). Seven strong claims about successful school leadership. *School leadership and management, 28*(1), 27–42.

Leventhal, T., & Brooks-Gunn, J. (2000). The neighborhoods they live in: The effects of neighborhood residence on child and adolescent outcomes. *Psychological Bulletin, 126*(2), 309.

Lipman P. (1997). Restructuring in context: A case study of teacher participation and the dynamics of ideology, race, and power. *American Educational Research Journal, 34*(1), 3–38.

Miller, G. E., Chen, E., & Parker, K. J. (2011). Psychological stress in childhood and susceptibility to the chronic diseases of aging: Moving toward a model of behavioral and biological mechanisms. *Psychological Bulletin, 137*(6), 959.

Morris, E. W. (2005). "Tuck in that shirt!" Race, class, gender, and discipline in an urban school. *Sociological Perspectives, 48*, 25-48.

NPBEA. (2015). *Professional standards for educational leaders 2015.* Reston, VA: Author.

Omi, M., & Winant, H. (1994). *Racial formation in the United States: From 1960s to 1990s.* New York, NY: Routledge.

Sampson, R. J. (2012). Neighborhood inequality, violence, and the social infrastructure of the American city. In W. F. Tate (Ed.). *Research on schools, neighborhoods, and communities: Toward civic responsibility* (pp. 11–28). Plymouth, UK: Rowman & Littlefield.

Solórzano, D. G., & Yosso, T. J. (2002). Critical race methodology: Counter- storytelling as an analytical framework for education research. *Qualitative Inquiry, 8*, 23–44.

Tate IV, W. F. (2008). "Geography of opportunity": Poverty, place, and educational outcomes. *Educational Researcher, 37*(7), 397–411.

Ture, K., & C. Hamilton (1967/1992). *Black Power: The politics of liberation in America.* New York: Vintage Books.

Wilson, W. J. (2012). *The truly disadvantaged: The inner city, the underclass, and public policy.* Chicago, IL: University of Chicago Press.

Yosso, T. J. (2005). Whose culture has capital? A critical race theory discussion of community cultural wealth. *Race, Ethnicity and Education, 8*(1), 69–91.

PART I

Exploring Urban Communities, Schools, and Reform

2

NEIGHBORHOODS OF (IN)OPPORTUNITY

A group of researchers led by Stanford economist Raj Chetty recently investigated if the USA was indeed a "land of opportunity." What Chetty and his colleagues (Chetty, Hendren, Kline, & Saez, 2014) found was that the USA was "better described as a collection of societies, some of which are 'lands of opportunity' with high rates of mobility across generations, and others in which few children escape poverty" (p. 1554). In other words, not all neighborhoods in which children live, grow up, and go to school are places of opportunity (Chetty, Hendren, & Katz, 2016; Sampson, Morenoff, & Gannon-Rowley, 2002). In this book, I focus on low-opportunity urban communities of color and their schools. I define low-opportunity urban communities as places that have been racially segregated by racist government housing policies, where few families escape poverty, and where children have limited access to adequate housing and healthcare, high-quality schools, healthy foods, and safe spaces to live and play. I have spent my career working in Baltimore, Washington, DC, and El Paso public schools and I have seen how limited opportunities within communities stifled the potential of students, especially when schools and principals are not understanding and responsive to the issues that arise from unequal opportunities. For schools to be responsive to the needs of students, principals need to recognize and understand the challenges within communities in which they work.

The chapter that follows describes how certain neighborhoods and schools provide both assets and opportunities as well as challenges and difficulties for children and families. In this chapter, I begin with a discussion of the often-untapped assets and resources that exist within urban communities. I emphasize that these communities are places of tremendous potential opportunity on which schools can capitalize. The reader should recognize that all communities have assets and resources that are valuable, regardless of the social and economic challenges that may also exist. This is of central importance to the purpose of this book. Next, I provide an overview of urban demographics and economic and educational challenges within cities. I conclude with a discussion of problems confronting urban districts and schools.

Places of Opportunity

In the USA, opportunities and resources are not evenly dispersed across communities. A long history of racism, discriminatory housing policies, and disinvestment and unequal development has created a significant inequality between communities with different racial and class characteristics. Researchers have long referred to patterns of spatial inequality as "geography of opportunity" to reveal how neighborhood context impacts access to opportunities and resources (Galster & Killen, 1995). As I will discuss later in this chapter, researchers and historians have continually documented how the geographic structure of opportunity is related to racism, access to quality schools, adequate healthcare, affordable housing, and employment opportunities. However, before reviewing this landscape, I want to emphasize how urban spaces are not just places of inequalities, but places of opportunity and transformation. Sutton and Kemp (2011) described a tension in low-opportunity communities between inequality and "a context of transformation and possibility" (p. 5). In other words, challenges can provide an opportunity for transformation.

A small group of critical educational researchers has suggested that educational reforms must expand beyond school-based remedies to address the school's social and community context (Berliner, 2013; Horsford & Heilig, 2014; Miller, 2012; Milner, 2013; Noguera & Wells, 2011). Tate (2008) called for educational researchers to "recognize the importance of geography in the research process" (p. 408). Tate also found that low-opportunity communities of color often do not change despite well-intentioned development efforts. The difficulty of improving these communities has called some to question if external investments can make a difference to schools and in the lives of children and families. Green (2015) acknowledged the challenges within low-opportunity communities, but also reframed them as "places of possibility" by mapping nearby assets and considering how schools can effectively partner with community-based organizations to improve both school and community outcomes. Green's research in racially segregated Detroit identified numerous indigenous assets, including churches and church stakeholders with a rich array of resources and networks, universities, and community-based organizations. These assets can provide schools and families with important assets, information, and support as well as serving as locations to build solidarity and resistance against harmful social and economic policies. An important lesson from this research and the reframing of "low-opportunity" to "opportunity" is the rejection of binary discussions of urban communities. A more nuanced understanding of the realities and assets of all communities is necessary.

Lack of Opportunity in Racially Segregated Urban Neighborhoods

Before any discussion of school leadership can take place in this book, the challenges confronting students, families, and schools in low-opportunity communities must be well understood. SES and neighborhood context are well-known factors that influence the physical and mental health of children (Leventhal & Brooks-Gunn, 2000). These factors impact student achievement and have a lasting influence on multiple social and economic indicators of health and well-being into adulthood (Miller, Chen, & Parker, 2011). Specifically, events during childhood have long-lasting effects on a child's ability to learn, listen, cooperate, and respect others (Currie & Almond, 2011). Diet, inadequate healthcare, exposure to pollutants and violence, and poor health habits contribute to the risk of illness. Patterns of racial segregation, limited employment and educational opportunities, and community violence and public health concerns are clustered in parts of cities where most low-income students of color live. Thus, some of the most pressing problems in urban education exist outside schools.

Racial Segregation and Gentrification

Racial segregation is one significant factor that contributes to the development of low-opportunity communities. Segregation has been increasing since the late 1980s, while race and poverty continue to be more concentrated geographically (Orfield & Lee, 2005). Black–White segregation rates remain high in Northeast and Midwest rustbelt cities. Gentrification is a phenomenon where decades of decline and disinvestment in urban communities draws the attention of artists and professionals seeking an urban lifestyle. Their demand for housing creates instabilities within neighborhoods, the cost of housing rises, and many long-time residents are forced to leave (Freeman & Braconi, 2004). Although gentrifying neighborhoods can appear racially diverse in the short-term, gentrification often adds to racial segregation in the long-term while negatively disrupting local schools (DeMatthews & Mawhinney, 2014; Lipman, 2013). Table 2.1 shows the degree of racial segregation in five reference cities. Cities like New York City, Chicago, Baltimore, and Washington, DC continue to have highly segregated neighborhoods where most Black people live in majority Black communities despite making up just a small fraction of the overall population (Frey, 2015). While the total population of Latina/os continues to rise, their geographic dispersion remains significantly higher in major metropolitan areas and cities like Los Angeles, New York City, Houston, and Miami.

Economic and educational resources have gone missing from many cities with large populations of racial minorities. The consequences are diminished community structures that alleviate the effects of poverty and related inequalities. In gentrifying communities, additional resources are often deployed by

TABLE 2.1 Percent of Blacks in Neighborhood of the Average Black Resident, 2010–2014

Metropolitan area	Metropolitan area percent Black	Percent of Blacks in neighborhood of average Black resident
New York City	16%	51%
Chicago	17%	64%
Los Angeles	7%	27%
Baltimore	29%	61%
Washington, DC	25%	54%

Source: U.S. Census Bureau (n.d.)

city governments, but this typically happens as lower-income households are displaced. Student achievement is usually depressed in segregated low-income communities of color (Leventhal & Brooks-Gun, 2000). Perhaps this is because racial segregation and other forms of systemic racism are public health stressors, which include a myriad of neighborhood conditions that impact student achievement (e.g., lack of healthy foods, exposure to crime, violence, and pollution, and limited healthcare facilities) (Phelan & Link, 2015).

Race, Poverty, and Unemployment

Poverty and unemployment are also characteristic of low-opportunity communities. Many racially segregated communities have higher rates of unemployment and poverty. Faulty governance and business disinvestment contribute to unemployment and poverty. The Great Recession of the late 2000s and early 2010s exacerbated previous divestments in many low-opportunity communities of color. An analysis of recent data from the American Community Survey, which consist of five-year estimates (2005–2009, 2010–2014), concluded that:

- The number of impoverished neighborhoods grew by over 40%, 13.5% of people were poor in impoverished neighborhoods (i.e., census tracts where 40% or more of the population is below the federal poverty line).
- Poverty rose more sharply than the national average for Latina/os and Blacks, and concentrated poverty increased in 67 of the 100 largest metropolitan areas in the nation between the two surveys (Kneebone & Holmes, 2016).
- Large cities were home to appropriately three-quarters of the major metropolitan area poor population living in impoverished neighborhoods (Kneebone & Holmes, 2016).

Poverty rates are related to unemployment rates. Table 2.2 provides unemployment data for reference cities. These cities have significant populations living

TABLE 2.2 City Unemployment Rates by Race (2014 Averages)

City	Total unemployment rate	White	Black	Hispanic/ Latino	Asian	Women who maintain families
New York City	7.3%	5.6%	10.9%	8.6%	6.4%	9.3%
Chicago	8.4%	5.7%	14.7%	7.5%	7.3%	9.7%
Los Angeles	8.4%	7.6%	15.8%	8.2%	7.4%	13.1%
Baltimore	11.2%	5.2%	16.2%	2.0%	–	13.9%
Washington, DC	7.8%	2.9%	15.4%	3.9%	3.0%	18.8%
United States	6.2%	5.3%	11.3%	7.4%	5.0%	–

Source: U.S. Department of Labor (n.d.)

below the poverty line, and racial disparities are unmistakable. In Baltimore and Washington DC, 16.2% and 15.4% of Black residents are unemployed while single women maintaining families are unemployed at similar rates (13.9% and 18.8% respectively). Many of these Black and Latina/o residents live in racially segregated neighborhoods where few jobs exist due to disinvestment and a lack of transportation systems that lead from communities to job sites. Consequently, significant percentages of households struggle financially even for those who are employed.

In 2017, federal poverty guidelines were updated. The poverty line was set at $12,060 a year for one person or $20,420 for a single parent raising two children (Families USA, 2017). Poverty line thresholds were developed in the 1960s based on dated research that considered how families spent income on food, housing, and other items. Table 2.3 provides household income data in reference cities with the median gross rent and median housing price disaggregated by race. It seems evident that the federal poverty line is understated as the cost of housing coupled with food, transportation, childcare, healthcare, taxes and other expenses extend beyond these thresholds. Consider life in Los Angeles, where 42% and 32% of Black and Hispanic households earn less than $30,000 annually, and gross median rent is approximately $1,271 a month ($15,252 annually). Poverty and unemployment contribute to the proportion of people living in unstable neighborhoods with lower quality housing. Families struggling with rent and mortgages may move from home to home or crowd into homes with other relatives. Crowding and moving often affect a child's ability to sleep, cope with stress, and maintain healthy relationships with parents, friends, and family (Cutts et al., 2011).

Families slightly above the poverty line lose access to public assistance, public housing, heat subsidies, free and reduced meals, and Medicaid for children (Allegretto, 2006). Individuals living below or slightly above the poverty line and in impoverished communities are also more likely to exhibit poor physical and mental health outcomes (Ogden, Lamb, Carroll, & Flegal, 2010). These individuals are

TABLE 2.3 Percentage of Households with Annual Income under 30,000 Dollars

	Total	White	Black	Hispanic	Asian	Median gross rent	Median housing price
New York City	30.3%	23.4%	37.6	41.9%	27.5%	$1,317	$650,046
Chicago	32.6%	22.4%	50.4%	32.7%	30.9%	$985	$321,158
Los Angeles	29.6%	25.6%	42%	32.2%	28.2%	$1,271	$744,781
Baltimore	36.6%	21.2%	45.4%	32.3%	38.0%	$981	$202,441
Washington, DC	24.2%	8.9%	40.4%	21.7%	17.3%	$1,417	$648,661
El Paso	25.6%	31.6%	26.1%	36.1%	24.7%	$752	$141,056

Source: U.S. Department of Labor (n.d.)

often forced to deal with higher community crime rates (Hipp, 2007), have weaker job-seeking networks (Hamm & McDonald, 2015), and lack access to education and job training over the course of their lifetimes (Chetty et al., 2016). They are also more likely to struggle with periods of unemployment, underemployment, low wages, housing and food insecurity, and a perpetual cycle of poverty. Without sufficient funds and opportunities, most families will rent and be unable to own a home. Home ownership is important, because it helps build a stronger sense of community, increases the likelihood of voting, and decreases mobility (Manturuk, Lindblad, & Quercia, 2009).

Educational Attainment

Educational attainment is important to a community because it is related to future employment, income, health status, and access to housing in a safe community (Belfield & Levin, 2007). Parents' education and their expectations also affect their children's academic outcomes, partly because parents with more education have experience with academic success and can help navigate their children through K–12 schools and higher education (Davis-Kean, 2005). Higher levels of family income also reduce a student's financial burden of participating in important extracurricular activities that build confidence and help with university admissions. Not surprisingly, disparities in educational attainment across low- and high-opportunity communities are consistently reported (Henig, Hula, Orr, & Pedescleaux, 2001). Table 2.4 provides national educational attainment data of employed people across the USA and Table 2.5 provides educational attainment disaggregated by race in the reference cities listed. Glaring differences between the percent of Black and Latina/o adults receiving a bachelor's degree or higher are apparent. In Washington, DC, almost 90% of White residents have at least a bachelor's degree in comparison to 24.4% of Blacks and 41.8% of Latina/os. These data further underscore the significant and negative effects of racial segregation.

TABLE 2.4 Educational Attainment of Labor Force by Race in 2014

Educational attainment	White	Black	Asian	Latina/o
Less than a high school diploma	8.0	8.2	6.2	27.7
High school graduate	26.7	31.3	17	30.3
Some college, no degree	16.3	21.8	9.8	15.2
Associate's degree	11.3	11.3	6.8	8.2
Bachelor's degree and higher	37.7	27.3	60.1	18.6

Source: Bureau of Labor Statistics, U.S. Department of Labor (2015)

TABLE 2.5 Population Age 25 or Older Educational Attainment in Reference Cities

	Percent total population	White	Black	Latina/o	Asian
New York City					
Less than a high school graduate	14.4%	13%	18.7%	35.0%	25.2%
High school graduate or higher	85.6%	92.5%	81.3%	65.0%	74.8%
Bachelor's degree and higher	34.2%	55.5%	22.4%	16.4%	41.2%
Baltimore					
Less than a high school graduate	17.0%	13.0%	20.0%	34%	8.0%
High school graduate or higher	83%	87%	80%	66.0%	92.0%
Bachelor's degree and higher	12.3%	52.3%	14.3%	25.1%	70.6%
El Paso					
Less than a high school graduate	21.9%	4.3%	6.7%	26.8%	10.7%
High school graduate or higher	78.1%	95.7%	93.3%	73.2%	89.3
Bachelor's degree and higher	23.3%	40.1%	29.1%	18.9%	49.4%
Washington, DC					
Less than a high school graduate	10.7%	2.8%	16.0%	29.4%	8.7%
High school graduate or higher	89.4%	97.2%	84.0%	70.6%	91.3%
Bachelor's degree and higher	54.6%	87.0%	24.4%	41.8%	76.7%

Source: U.S. Department of Labor (n.d.)

Community Violence

Some, but not all low-opportunity communities struggle with community violence. Childhood exposure to violence is a significant health concern and urban, low-income Black and Latina/o children are exposed to chronic school and community violence at higher rates than their White and Asian suburban peers (Buka, Stichick, Birdthistle, & Earls, 2001). For example, in 2016 in Baltimore, 322 adults and 22 juveniles were murdered (Baltimore Police Department, 2017). The *Baltimore Sun* reported, "Many victims were gunned down in the street, often in broad daylight. Others were innocent bystanders struck by bullets" (Rector, 2016). Police departments often respond to community violence in communities of color by ramping up "crime-fighting strategies" in specific neighborhoods, such as stop-and-frisk, which escalates racial tensions between communities and police, stops some citizens from sharing information with investigators, and can incite further violence (e.g., Baltimore Riots following the death of Freddie Gray). Community violence (including police violence) is as an important "bellwether of urban livability, sustainability, and overall well-being . . . [and] has been shown to undermine the social fabric of urban communities by inducing outmigration, fear, and moral cynicism" (Sampson, 2012, p. 13).

Chronic exposure to violence places children at significant risk of developing stress-related problems, including anxiety and depressive disorders. Stress can be viewed as a process, holding "that when stimuli, commonly referred to as stressors, are appraised as threatening and unmanageable, they elicit a psychological state that is experienced as stress, as well as a cascade of behavioral and biological adjustments, commonly referred to as responses" (Miller et al., 2011, p. 962). Violence is not only isolated to a single violent event, but part of overlapping experiences where violence occurs in multiple contexts, within homes, schools, and neighborhoods (Margolin et al., 2009). Horowitz, McKay, and Marshall (2005) have termed this "compounded community trauma," because youth often experience multiple traumatic events inside and outside of their home on a regular basis. Looking again at Baltimore, neighborhood violence had a direct and indirect impact on depressive symptoms of adults (Curry, Latkin, & Davey-Rothwell, 2008). Baltimore City students' self-reported school and neighborhood safety results were strongly associated with their academic performance (Milam, Furr-Holden, & Leaf, 2010). Neighborhood violence was associated with statistically significant decreases in math and reading achievement. Comparable studies in Chicago, New York City, and Los Angeles yielded similar results (Chen, 2007; Schwartz & Gorman, 2003). Children exposed to violence, stress, and long-term mental health issues are also more likely to have "difficulty concentrating, impaired memory, anxious attachments to caregivers, aggression, truncated oral development, and academic difficulties" (Lang, Brown, Hodges, & Chaplin, 2012, p. 285–286). These studies provide direct evidence that school reform focused only on improving teaching and curriculum will produce limited results for students in low-opportunity communities.

Public Health

Low-opportunity communities may also lack vital public health resources, which in turn have significant implications on children and families. Adults with higher income levels can afford appropriate housing, provide healthy food to their families, and ensure their children attend safe and high-quality schools while those with fewer means cannot. Accordingly, socioeconomic inequalities produce significant racial/ethnic disparities in morbidity (e.g., heart disease, smoking- and alcohol-related illnesses, hypertension, stroke, obesity, diabetes, cancer) and mortality rates, particularly for low-income Black and Latina/o communities.

Black and Latina/o youth in urban communities are also more likely to have elevated blood lead levels (Lanphear & Roghmann, 1997). Elevated blood lead levels affect all systems of the body, including the neurological and cardiovascular systems. It is also related to a decline in IQ, vocabulary, hand–eye coordination, impulse control and long-term outcomes, such as reduced academic performance, higher absenteeism, and lower class rank (Schuch, Curtis, & Davidson, 2017). Chronic lead exposure has been described as a poverty trap: "There is greater likelihood of exposure in troubled neighborhoods, and life course implications produce barriers for upward mobility" (Schuch et al., 2017, p. 607).

Health issues that impact Black and Latina/o youth extend beyond blood lead levels. Untreated tooth decay and cavities in children ages 2 through 8 are twice as high for Latina/o and Black children compared with White children and are also found to impact student performance (Dye, Thornton-Evans, Li, & Iafolla, 2015). A recent study of 1,495 elementary and high school students in Los Angeles revealed that students with toothaches were almost four times more likely to have a lower grade point average and were more likely to miss additional days of school each year due to dental problems (Seirawan, Faust, & Mulligan, 2012).

Children in urban, low-income communities are also likely to miss days of school due to complications of asthma. Basch (2011) found that "poor urban minority children not only have higher rates of asthma and more severe forms of disease, but are much less likely to receive contiguous high-quality medical care and to consistently use appropriate, efficacious medications" (p. 607). Children may, therefore, be less likely to engage in physical activity and more likely to spend higher amounts of time watching television and playing video games. Sedentary behavior increases the risk for obesity, diabetes, and other diseases. Overweight children are more likely to stay overweight into adulthood and develop self-esteem problems, which can produce a trend across generations within families.

Limited affordable and proximal healthcare services deny many children and adults access to treatment, education, and strategies to improve their health, diet, and exercise routines. Environmental factors also influence a child's physical activity and lifestyle. For example, Black boys and girls in urban communities typically have less access to programs, facilities, and safe play areas (Annesi, Faigenbaum, Westcott, & Smith, 2008; Vigo- Valentín, Hodge, & Kozub, 2011). Parent and child perceptions of crime and safety may limit outside play or walking to school (Rossen et al., 2011). Parents may also be concerned with their children witnessing or engaging in high-risk behavior, such as smoking cigarettes, drinking alcohol, or using illegal drugs (Atav & Spencer, 2002). The local food environment and access to affordable, healthy, and nutritious foods also hinder physical health. Some urban neighborhoods are characterized as "food deserts" because they lack access to a supermarket with healthy food. In place of supermarkets, many low-opportunity and racially segregated neighborhoods have fast-food restaurants, liquor stores, and corner/convenient stores (Lucan, Barg, & Long, 2010). It should be no surprise that many youths in these communities consume dangerously high amounts of fat, sodium, sugar, cholesterol, and calories (Sweeney, Glaser, & Tedeschi, 2007).

Urban Schools

Urban schools within low-opportunity communities are expected to ensure all students achieve at the same levels as children from opportunity-rich communities, but the students that arrive at their door each day may be struggling with many external issues that must first be addressed. Thus, many urban schools are expected to not only educate students based on state standards to the same level as schools in high-opportunity communities, but also make up for the lack of opportunity that can negatively impact the social, emotional, physical, and cognitive development of students. Unfortunately, many urban districts and schools have significant organizational challenges of their own and are not positioned to address outside-of-school problems. District governance instability, racially segregated schools, funding and teacher quality disparities, and other equity issues do not position most urban schools to meet the academic, social, and emotional needs of urban youth of color.

District Governance and (In)stability

District governance and instability may limit a principal's ability to make up for a lack of opportunity in a student's community. Many urban districts are guilty of a constant reform churn that is at least partly responsible for burning out principals while failing to address the social and emotional needs of students and families (DeMatthews & Mawhinney, 2013; Ravitch, 2016). Reform in urban districts remains elusive partly because superintendent turnover is frequent and does not support long-term planning or the development of coherent systems across various government agencies. The typical superintendent lasts about three to four years on the job. While democratically elected school boards control most districts, 11 large urban districts are under some degree of control by the city's mayor, which represents a power shift that allows mayors increased authority over schools and the selection of, and influence over, the superintendents. Researchers have struggled to find the degree to which districts account for student achievement, particularly when considering the variety of factors that contribute to it, such as student demographics, teacher capacity, and school leadership quality (Whitehurst, Chingos, & Gallaher, 2013).

Racially and Economically Segregated Schools

Urban schools are often as racially and economically segregated as the surrounding neighborhoods. The Council of the Great City Schools (CGCS) is composed of 69 large school districts in cities with populations of over 250,000 and district enrollment over 35,000. These districts enroll about 7.3 million children mostly from diverse racial and linguistic backgrounds (40% Hispanic, 29% Black, 20% White, 8% Asian/Pacific Islander, 17% English language learners (ELLs)). They also serve higher than average populations of students with disabilities (14%) and students receiving free and reduced meals (70%). Table 2.6 provides student demographic data on select reference urban districts.

Many urban schools are steadily becoming more racially and economically segregated. The Civil Rights Project at the University of California at Los Angeles (UCLA) conducted extensive research on school segregation and highlighted alarming trends. Between 1990 and 2013, the population of White students has fallen from 69% to 50% (Orfield, Ee, Frankenberg, & Siegel-Hawley, 2016). During the same time-period, the Latina/o student population grew from 11% to 25% while Black student enrollment held steady at about 15%. Despite this growth, beginning in 1991 and continuing to present day, Black and Latina/o students are increasingly enrolled in segregated non-White schools (defined as less than 10% White student enrollment). Between 1988 and 2013, the percent of non-White schools more than tripled from 5.7% to 18.6% of all public schools. Black and Latina/o students are increasingly attending schools with both high percentages of minorities and where two-thirds of students or more are considered poor (Orfield et al., 2016). The proportion of students in poverty in the school of the typical Black and Latina/o student increased from 37% and 45.6% in 1993 to 67.9% in 2013 for both groups respectively (Orfield et al., 2016).

Funding and Teacher Quality

It is hard to imagine a school making a difference for students without adequate funding. Disparities in local property wealth and taxes profoundly impact how schools in low-opportunity communities are funded. Districts raise between 62% and 75% from property taxation, but in some states, those numbers are as high as 95% (Baker & Corcoran, 2012). Districts serving high proportions of low-income students of color receive roughly 15% less than districts serving the fewest (Ushomirsky & Williams, 2015). State finance systems that utilize a combination of state aid and local taxes to fund public school costs (federal aid makes up a small percent) can create these inequalities. Baker and Corcoran (2012) identified "stealth inequalities" or "often-overlooked features of school funding systems that tend to exacerbate inequities in per-pupil spending rather than reduce them, and that do so in a way that favors communities with the least needs" (p. 1). Schools located in low-opportunity communities of color have a limited wealth and tax base and therefore must rely on states to provide additional aid to help

TABLE 2.6 Number and Percent Distribution of Urban District Students, by Race/Ethnicity and Poverty, Special Education, and Limited English Proficiency

Agency name	Total	LEP	IEPs	FARM	Latino	Black	White	Asian
*New York City DOE	972,325	114,849	235,770	690,484	397,424	243,268	151,022	162,859
	(100%)	(11.1%)	(24.2%)	(1.4%)	(40.1%)	(25%)	(15.5%)	(16%)
Los Angeles USD	646,683	164,349	82,337	487,818	476,507	56,863	63,385	36,879
	(100%)	(25.4%)	(12.7%)	(75.4%)	(73.4%)	(10.12%)	(11.38%)	(1.57%)
Chicago Public Schools	392,558	69,091	52,502	340,273	179,535	154,826	37,563	14,112
	(100%)	(17.6%)	(13.3%)	(86.6%)	(45.7%)	(39.4%)	(10.46%)	(1.3%)
Baltimore City PS	84,976	3,460	13,608	71,402	6,284	70,234	6,820	849
	(100%)	(1.4%)	(16%)	(84%)	(1.89%)	(82.7%)	(2.1%)	(0.9%)
District of Columbia Public Schools	46,155	4,882	7,547	46,054	8,042	30,386	5,861	886
	(100%)	(10.5%)	(16.3%)	(99.7%)	(17.4%)	(65.8%)	(12.6%)	(0.19%)
El Paso ISD	60,852	12,451	6,047	41,279	50,598	2,286	6,102	700
	(100%)	(20.5%)	(1.9%)	(67.8%)	(83.15%)	(1.37%)	(2.5%)	(0.1%)

*New York City DOE enrollment data is based on combing New York City geographic districts 1–32.

LEP = Limited English Proficiency; IEP = Individualized Educational Program; FARM = Free and Reduced Meals; DOE = Department of Education; USD = Unified School District; PS = Public Schools; ISD = Independent School District

Source: U.S. Department of Education, National Center for Education Statistics (2018)

overcome a shortfall in the resources necessary to meet the needs of their students, but in many instances, state funding systems exacerbate inequalities rather than reduce them.

States also set up different rules for how districts can raise taxes as well as establish rules for how wealth is measured and assessed. For example, Ohio and Minnesota are progressive, and their low-income districts receive about 22% more dollars per student from state and local sources than wealthier districts. Illinois is the nation's most regressive, as high-poverty districts receive nearly 20% less state and local funding than the lowest poverty districts (Ushomirsky & Williams, 2015). Even within urban districts, racial and class composition (e.g., low-income neighborhood of color versus gentrified or historically wealthy neighborhood) is associated with funding inequalities (Condron & Roscigno, 2003). With fewer resources, many urban schools are physically decaying and underperforming.

Schools with high populations of low-income and Black and Latina/o students often employ the least skilled and experienced teachers (Lankford, Loeb, & Wyckoff, 2002). For example, in Washington state, "virtually every measure of teacher quality . . . experience, licensure exam scores, and value added—is inequitably distributed across every indicator of student disadvantage—free/reduced-price lunch status, underrepresented minority, and low prior academic performance" (Goldhaber, Lavery, & Theobald, 2015, p. 293). The cultural mismatch between teachers and low-income students of color adds to achievement, discipline, and teacher turnover problems (Goldenberg, 2014; Stearns, Banerjee, Mickelson, & Moller, 2014). Teacher turnover is exceedingly costly and further reduces district budgets. For example, in Chicago Public Schools and Milwaukee Public Schools the costs of turnover were substantial (average cost per teacher–leaver was $17,872 in school year 2002–2003 and $15,325 in school year 2003–2004) (Barnes, Crowe, & Schaefer, 2007).

Academic Achievement

The National Assessment of Educational Progress (NAEP) in partnership with the CGCS created the Trial Urban District Assessment (TUDA) in 2002 to measure educational progress in large urban districts. TUDA results from the 21 participating CGCS districts revealed how urban districts underperform on fourth- and eighth-grade NAEP mathematics and reading assessments. Racial and economic student achievement gaps also persisted (National Center for Education Statistics (NCES), 2013). Figure 2.1 shows the average scores for eighth-grade public school students in NAEP reading in Baltimore City Public Schools (BCPS), Chicago Public Schools, the District of Columbia Public Schools (DCPS), and New York City Department of Education in comparison to national averages. A closer look at urban performance within districts reveals additional concerns. For example, Figure 2.2 shows within-district racial achievement gaps in those same districts.

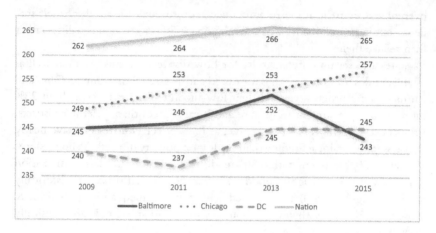

FIGURE 2.1 NAEP Eighth-Grade Reading Average Scores between 2009 and 2015 by District and Nation

Source: NCES (2015)

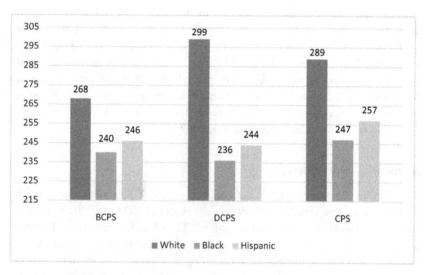

FIGURE 2.2 2015 NAEP Eighth-Grade Reading Average Scores by Race in Baltimore, District of Coumbia and Chicago Schools

Source: NCES (2015)

Discipline

Many urban schools also struggle with student discipline, which led Gregory, Skiba, and Noguera (2010) to ask: is the racial achievement gap and the racial discipline gap "two sides of the same coin?" They argued that student characteristics related to race, income, and achievement need to be further investigated regarding discipline and suspension. In 2014, the U.S. Department of Justice and U.S. Department of Education (2014) issued a joint *Dear Colleague* letter to help public schools meet obligations under federal law to administer student discipline without discriminating based on race, color, or country of origin. The letter highlighted how Black students were three times as likely as their White peers to be expelled and suspended. The letter also noted that Black and Latina/o students were more likely to be arrested by law enforcement for similar offenses than White students, which in turn contributed to long-term educational, economic, and social problems.

Losen and Skiba (2010) analyzed school and district suspension data from the U.S. Department of Education Office of Civil Rights and focused on understanding the frequency of suspension across subgroups of children by race/ethnicity and gender. They found that while the average suspension rate was 11.2% for middle schools, the average suspension rate for Black boys and girls was 28.3% and 18% respectively. The researchers then looked at 18 of the nation's largest districts and calculated a suspension risk index. In 11 of the 18 districts, over one in three Black males were suspended and in Palm Beach County and Milwaukee, the district-wide suspension rate for Black males was over 30%. Across all 18 large districts, 84 middle schools were suspending Black males at a rate of at least 50% per year. They also found that the 50% suspension rate was met or exceeded in 31 schools for Black females, 13 schools for Latino males and 22 schools for White males.

Special Education and English Language Learners

Black students are presently 1.4 times more likely to be identified for special education in general, 2.08 times more likely to be identified with an emotional disturbance, 2.22 times more likely to be identified with an intellectual disability, and 1.51 times as likely to be identified with a specific learning disability than all other racial/ethnic groups combined (U.S. Department of Education, Office of Special Education and Rehabilitative Services, 2014). Black and Latina/o students with disabilities are also less likely to be included in the general education classroom for more than 80% of the day than their White and Asian peers. The overrepresentation of Black students and the increased likelihood of segregated placements is particularly problematic given that students with disabilities are more likely to drop out of school and less likely to earn a regular high school diploma than their peers. Moreover, many urban districts have been subject to special education class action lawsuits for a broad variety of systemic special education failures.[1] For example, in Baltimore, city schools were involved in federal litigation in *Vaughn G v Mayor and City Council of Baltimore* for failing to meet the needs and deliver appropriate services to students with disabilities. The case remained open, and the district was under federal supervision between 1984 and 2010. Many of the problems and issues identified within these cases are also more likely to occur in low-opportunity communities, where schools lack the necessary resources and staff continuity to efficiently implement high-quality special education programs.

ELLs are among the fastest-growing demographic groups in the USA and now make up 9.4% of all public school students. A significant portion of ELLs are enrolled in urban public schools and approximately 77% are native-Spanish speakers (NCES, n.d.). Nearly 1.2 million ELLs (or almost 24% of all ELLs) attend CGCS member districts (Uro & Barrio, 2013). Considerable variation between state policies for teaching ELLs exist. In some states, cultural and linguistic heritage is viewed as an asset and built upon by teachers and not denigrated, rejected, and replaced with English and other Eurocentric values and norms. Differences in state policies mean urban schools serving high proportions of Latina/o and ELLs might be constrained in adopting the most effective practices. Problematic state policies become even more complex where schools have historically struggled to build meaningful relationships with families and communities. Principals and teachers can view these families and communities through a deficit lens and miss an opportunity to work together to advocate for necessary state policies (Baquedano- López, Alexander, & Hernández, 2013).

Takeaways for Principals

The purpose of this chapter was to familiarize the reader with the assets and challenges within low-opportunity communities. The research and statistics presented in this chapter describe an unfortunate set of economic and political circumstances that place many urban students of color at a significant disadvantage to their White and Asian suburban peers. I am outraged by these conditions and inequalities, but I believe urban public schools and their principals can reduce these disadvantages. First, they must be knowledgeable about why these conditions exist. Knowledge is crucial for principals seeking to improve their schools and is a prerequisite for action. The next chapter provides a more in-depth history of how such unequal and unjust circumstances came into existence and how it has influenced urban education.

Note

1 See: Baltimore City Public Schools: *Vaughn G. v. Mayor and City Council of Baltimore* (1996); Chicago Public Schools: *Corey H. v. Board of Education of Chicago* (1998); District of Columbia Public Schools: *Blackman/Jones v. District of Columbia* (2005); Newark Public Schools: *M.A. v. Newark Public Schools* (2003).

References

Allegretto, S. A. (2006). Basic family budgets: Working families' incomes often fail to meet living expenses around the United States. *International Journal of Health Services, 36*(3), 443–454.

Annesi, J., Faigenbaum, A., Westcott, W., & Smith, A. (2008). Relations of self-appraisal and mood changes with voluntary physical activity changes in African American preadolescents in an after-school care intervention. *Journal of Sports Science and Medicine, 7*(2), 260–268.

Atav, S., & Spencer, G. A. (2002). Health risk behaviors among adolescents attending rural, suburban, and urban schools: A comparative study. *Family & Community Health, 25*(2), 53–64.

Baker, B. D., & Corcoran, S. P. (2012). *The stealth inequities of school funding: How state and local school finance systems perpetuate inequitable student spending.* Washington, DC: Center for American Progress. Retrieved from http://www.statewideonline.org/111312/files/StealthInequities%20Rutgers.pdf

Baltimore Police Department. (2017). *Crime center: Baltimore police department's open data.* Retrieved from: http://www.baltimorepolice.org/content/crime-statistics

Baquedano-López, P., Alexander, R. A., & Hernández, S. J. (2013). Equity issues in parental and community involvement in schools: What teacher educators need to know. *Review of Research in Education, 37*(1), 149–182.

Barnes, G., Crowe, E., & Schaefer, B. (2007). *The cost of teacher turnover in five school districts: A pilot study.* Washington, DC: National Commission on Teaching and America's Future. Retrieved from http://files.eric.ed.gov/fulltext/ED497176.pdf

Basch, C. E. (2011). Asthma and the achievement gap among urban minority youth. *Journal of School Health, 81*(10), 606–613.

Belfield, C. R., & Levin, H. M. (Eds.). (2007). *The price we pay: Economic and social consequences of inadequate education.* Washington, DC: Brookings Institution Press.

Berliner, D. (2013). Effects of inequality and poverty vs. teachers and schooling on America's youth. *Teachers College Record, 115*(12), 1–26.

Blackman-Jones v. District of Columbia, 401 F.3d. 516, 522 (D.C. 2005).

Buka, S. L., Stichick, T. L., Birdthistle, I., & Earls, F. J. (2001). Youth exposure to violence: prevalence, risks, and consequences. *American Journal of Orthopsychiatry, 71*(3), 298.

Bureau of Labor Statistics, U.S. Department of Labor (2015). *The Economics daily: Educational attainment and occupation groups by race and ethnicity in 2014.* Retrieved from https://www.bls.gov/opub/ted/2015/educational-attainment-and-occupation-groups-by-race-and-ethnicity-in-2014.htm

Chen, G. (2007). School disorder and student achievement: A study of New York City elementary schools. *Journal of School Violence, 6*(1), 27–43.

Chetty, R., Hendren, N., & Katz, L. F. (2016). The effects of exposure to better neighborhoods on children: New evidence from the Moving to Opportunity experiment. *The American Economic Review, 106*(4), 855–902.

Chetty, R., Hendren, N., Kline, P., & Saez, E. (2014). Where is the land of opportunity? The geography of intergenerational mobility in the United States. *The Quarterly Journal of Economics, 129*(4), 1553–1623.

Condron, D. J., & Roscigno, V. J. (2003). Disparities within: Unequal spending and achievement in an urban school district. *Sociology of Education, 76*(1), 18–36.

Corey H v. The Board of Education of the City of Chicago, 995 F. Supp. 900 (N.D. Ill. 1998).

Currie, J., & Almond, D. (2011). Human capital development before age five. *Handbook of Labor Economics, 4*, 1315–1486.

Curry, A., Latkin, C., & Davey-Rothwell, M. (2008). Pathways to depression: The impact of neighborhood violent crime on inner-city residents in Baltimore, Maryland, USA. *Social Science & Medicine, 67*(1), 23–30.

Cutts, D. B., Meyers, A. F., Black, M. M., Casey, P. H., Chilton, M., Cook, J. T. . . . Frank, D. A. (2011). US housing insecurity and the health of very young children. *American Journal of Public Health, 101*(8), 1508–1514.

Davis-Kean, P. E. (2005). The influence of parent education and family income on child achievement: The indirect role of parental expectations and the home environment. *Journal of Family Psychology, 19*(2), 294.

DeMatthews, D. E., & Mawhinney, H. B. (2013). Addressing the inclusion imperative: An urban school district's responses. *Education Policy Analysis Archives, 21*(61), 1–30. Retrieved from http://epaa.asu.edu/ojs/article/view/1283

Dye, B. A., Thronton-Evans, G., Li, X., & Iafolla, T. J. (2015). *Dental caries and sealant prevalence in children and adolescents in the United States, 2011–2012.* NCHS data brief, no 191. Hyattsville, MD: National Center for Health Statistics.

Families USA. (2017, February). *Federal poverty guidelines.* Washington, DC: Author. Retrieved from http://familiesusa.org/product/federal-poverty-guidelines

Freeman, L., & Braconi, F. (2004). Gentrification and displacement New York City in the 1990s. *Journal of the American Planning Association, 70*(1), 39–52.

Frey, W. H. (2015, December 8). Census shows modest declines in black-white segregation. *Washington, DC: Brookings.* Retrieved from https://www.brookings.edu/blog/the-avenue/2015/12/08/census-shows-modest-declines-in-black-white-segregation/

Galster, G., & Killen, P. (1995). The geography of metropolitan opportunity: A reconnaissance and conceptual framework. *Housing Policy Debate, 6*(1), 10–47.

Goldhaber, D., Lavery, L., & Theobald, R. (2015). Uneven playing field? Assessing the teacher quality gap between advantaged and disadvantaged students. *Educational Researcher, 44*(5), 293–307.

Goldenberg, B. M. (2014). White teachers in urban classrooms: Embracing non-white students' cultural capital for better teaching and learning. *Urban Education, 49*(1), 111–144.

Green, T. L. (2015). Places of inequality, places of possibility: Mapping "opportunity in geography" across urban school-communities. *Urban Review, 47*(4), 717–741.

Gregory, A., Skiba, R. J., & Noguera, P. A. (2010). The achievement gap and the discipline gap: Two sides of the same coin? *Educational Researcher, 39*(1), 59–68.

Hamm, L., & McDonald, S. (2015). Helping hands: Race, neighborhood context, and reluctance in providing job-finding assistance. *Sociological Quarterly, 56*(3), 539–557.

Henig, J. R., Hula, R. C., Orr, M., & Pedescleaux, D. S. (2001). *The color of school reform: Race, politics, and the challenge of urban education.* Princeton, NJ: Princeton University Press.

Hipp, J. R. (2007). Income inequality, race, and place: Does the distribution of race and class within neighborhoods affect crime rates? *Criminology, 45*(3), 665–697.

Horowitz, K., McKay, M., & Marshall, R. (2005). Community violence and urban families: Experiences, effects, and directions for intervention. *American Journal of Orthopsychiatry, 75*(3), 356.

Horsford, S. D., & Heilig, J. V. (2014). Community-based education reform in urban contexts. *Urban Education, 49*(8), 867–870.

Kneebone, E., & Holmes, N. (2016). *U.S. concentrated poverty in the wake of the great recession*. Washington, DC: Brookings. Retrieved from https://www.brookings.edu/research/u-s-concentrated-poverty-in-the-wake-of-the-great-recession/

Lang, C. M., Brown, E. J., Hodges, E. V., & Chaplin, W. F. (2012). Children's responses to community violence: The roles of avoidant and confrontive coping. *Journal of Child & Adolescent Trauma*, 5(4), 285–302.

Lankford, H., Loeb, S., & Wyckoff, J. (2002). Teacher sorting and the plight of urban schools: A descriptive analysis. *Educational Evaluation and Policy Analysis*, 24(1), 37–62.

Lanphear, B. P., & Roghmann, K. J. (1997). Pathways of lead exposure in urban children. *Environmental Research*, 74(1), 67–73.

Leventhal, T., & Brooks-Gunn, J. (2000). The neighborhoods they live in: The effects of neighborhood residence on child and adolescent outcomes. *Psychological Bulletin*, 126(2), 309.

Lipman, P. (2013). *The new political economy of urban education: Neoliberalism, race, and the right to the city*. New York: Routledge.

Losen, D. J., & Skiba, R. J. (2011). *Suspended education: Urban middle schools in crisis*. Los Angeles, CA: UCLA Civil Rights Project. Retrieved from https://www.civilrightsproject.ucla.edu/research/k-12-education/school-discipline/suspended-education-urban-middle-schools-in-crisis

Lucan, S. C., Barg, F. K., & Long, J. A. (2010). Promoters and barriers to fruit, vegetable, and fast-food consumption among urban, low-income African Americans—a qualitative approach. *American Journal of Public Health*, 100(4), 631–635.

M.A. v. Newark Public Schools (2003). 2003 Decisions. 232. Retrieved from http://digitalcommons.law.villanova.edu/thirdcircuit_2003/232

Manturuk, K., Lindblad, M., & Quercia, R. G. (2009). Homeownership and local voting in disadvantaged urban neighborhoods. *Cityscape*, 11(3), 213–230.

Margolin, G., Vickerman, K. A., Ramos, M. C., Serrano, S. D., Gordis, E. B., Iturralde, E., . . . & Spies, L. A. (2009). Youth exposed to violence: Stability, co-occurrence, and context. *Clinical Child and Family Psychology Review*, 12(1), 39–54.

Milam, A. J., Furr-Holden, C. D. M., & Leaf, P. J. (2010). Perceived school and neighborhood safety, neighborhood violence and academic achievement in urban school children. *The Urban Review*, 42(5), 458–467.

Miller, G. E., Chen, E., & Parker, K. J. (2011). Psychological stress in childhood and susceptibility to the chronic diseases of aging: Moving toward a model of behavioral and biological mechanisms. *Psychological Bulletin*, 137(6), 959.

Miller, P. (2012). Mapping educational opportunity zones: A geospatial analysis of neighborhood block groups. *Urban Review*, 44(2), 189–218.

Milner, R. (2013). Analyzing poverty, learning, and teaching through a critical race lens. *Review of Research in Education*, 37, 1–53.

NCES. (2013). *The nation's report card: A first look: 2013 mathematics and reading trial urban district assessment* (NCES 2014-466). Washington, DC: Author. Retrieved from https://nces.ed.gov/nationsreportcard/subject/publications/main2013/pdf/2014466.pdf

NCES. (2015). *2015 reading trial urban districts snapshot report: Baltimore, grade 8, public schools*. Washington, DC: Author. Retrieved from https://nces.ed.gov/nationsreportcard/subject/publications/dst2015/pdf/2016048XM8.pdf

NCES. (n.d.). *EDFacts* file 141, Data Group 678, extracted May 30, 2017; Common Core of Data (CCD), "State Nonfiscal Survey of Public Elementary and Secondary Education," 2014–15. See *Digest of Education Statistics 2016*, table 204.27.

Noguera, P., & Wells, L. (2011). The politics of school reform: A broader and bolder approach for Newark. *Berkeley Review of Education, 2*(1), 5–25.

Ogden, C. L., Lamb, M. M., Carroll, M. D., & Flegal, K. M. (2010). *Obesity and socioeconomic status in children and adolescents: United States, 2005–2008.* NCHS Data Brief. Number 51. Washington, DC: National Center for Health Statistics.

Orfield, G., Ee, J., Frankenberg, E., & Siegel-Hawley, G. (2016). *Brown at 62: School segregation by race, poverty and state.* Los Angeles, CA: Civil Rights Project. Retrieved from https://www.civilrightsproject.ucla.edu/research/k-12-education/integration-and-diversity/brown-at-62-school-segregation-by-race-poverty-and-state/Brown-at-62-final-corrected-2.pdf

Orfield, G., & Lee, C. (2005). *Why segregation matters: Poverty and educational inequality.* Cambridge, MA: The Civil Rights Project. Retrieved from https://www.civilrightsproject.ucla.edu/research/k-12-education/integration-and-diversity/why-segregation-matters-poverty-and-educational-inequality/orfield-why-segregation-matters-2005.pdf

Phelan, J. C., & Link, B. G. (2015). Is racism a fundamental cause of inequalities in health? *Annual Review of Sociology, 41*, 311–330.

Rector, K. (2016, Jan 1). Deadliest year in Baltimore history ends with 344 homicides. *Baltimore Sun.* Retrieved from: http://www.baltimoresun.com/news/maryland/baltimore-city/bs-md-ci-deadliest-year-20160101-story.html

Ravitch, D. (2016). *The death and life of the great American school system: How testing and choice are undermining education.* New York: Basic Books.

Rossen, L. M., Pollack, K. M., Curriero, F. C., Shields, T. M., Smart, M. J., Furr-Holden, C. D. M., & Cooley-Strickland, M. (2011). Neighborhood incivilities, perceived neighborhood safety, and walking to school among urban-dwelling children. *Journal of Physical Activity and Health, 8*(2), 262–271.

Sampson, R. J. (2012). Neighborhood inequality, violence, and the social infrastructure of the American city. In W. F. Tate (Ed.). *Research on schools, neighborhoods, and communities: Toward civic responsibility* (pp. 11–28). Plymouth, UK: Rowman & Littlefield.

Sampson, R. J., Morenoff, J. D., & Gannon-Rowley, T. (2002). Assessing "neighborhood effects": Social processes and new directions in research. *Annual Review of Sociology, 28*(1), 443–478.

Schuch, L., Curtis, A., & Davidson, J. (2017). Reducing lead exposure risk to vulnerable populations: A proactive geographic solution. *Annals of the American Association of Geographers, 107*(3), 606–624.

Schwartz, D., & Gorman, A. H. (2003). Community violence exposure and children's academic functioning. *Journal of Educational Psychology, 95*(1), 163.

Seirawan, H., Faust, S., & Mulligan, R. (2012). The impact of oral health on the academic performance of disadvantaged children. *American Journal of Public Health, 102*(9), 1729–1734.

Stearns, E., Banerjee, N., Mickelson, R., & Moller, S. (2014). Collective pedagogical teacher culture, teacher–student ethno-racial mismatch, and teacher job satisfaction. *Social Science Research, 45*, 56–72.

Sutton, S. E., & Kemp, S. P. (Eds.). (2011). *The paradox of urban space: Inequality and transformation in marginalized communities.* New York, NY: Palgrave Macmillan.

Sweeney, N. M., Glaser, D., & Tedeschi, C. (2007). The eating and physical activity habits of inner-city adolescents. *Journal of Pediatric Health Care, 21*(1), 13–21.

Tate, W. F. (2008). "Geography of opportunity": Poverty, place, and educational outcomes. *Educational Researcher, 37*(7), 397–411.

Ushomirsky, N., & Williams, D. (2015). *Funding gaps 2015: Too many states still spend less on educating students who need the most*. Washington, DC: Education Trust. Retrieved from https://edtrust.org/wp-content/uploads/2014/09/FundingGaps2015_TheEducation Trust1.pdf

Uro, G., & Barrio, A. (2013). *English language learners in America's great city schools: Demographics, achievement, and staffing*. Washington, DC: Council of the Great City Schools. Retrieved from http://files.eric.ed.gov/fulltext/ED543305.pdf

U.S. Census Bureau. (n.d.). *American fact finder*. Retrieved from https://factfinder.census. gov/faces/tableservices/jsf/pages/productview.xhtml?src=CF

U.S. Department of Education, National Center for Education Statistics. (2018). *Common core of data*. Washington, DC: Author. Retrieved from https://nces.ed.gov/ccd/elsi/ tableGenerator.aspx?savedTableID=55260

U.S. Department of Education, Office of Special Education and Rehabilitative Services, Office of Special Education Programs (2014). *36th annual report to Congress on the implementation of the Individuals with Disabilities Education Act, 2016*. Washington, D.C. Author.

U.S. Department of Justice & U.S. Department of Education. (2014, January 8). *Notice of language assistance: Dear colleague letter on the nondiscriminatory administration of school discipline*. Retrieved from http://www.justice.gov/crt/about/edu/documents/dcl.pdf

U.S. Department of Labor. (n.d.). *Local area unemployment statistics*. Retrieved from https:// www.bls.gov/lau/

Vaughn G. et al. v. Mayor and City Council et al. (U.S. Dist. Ct., Dist. Maryland, Case No. 84–1911–MJG). (1996).

Vigo-Valentín, A., Hodge, S. R., & Kozub, F. M. (2011). Adolescents' dietary habits, physical activity patterns, and weight status in Puerto Rico. *Childhood Obesity*, 7(6), 488–494.

Whitehurst, G. J., Chingos, M. M., & Gallaher, M. R. (2013). *Do districts matter?* Washington, DC: Brookings Institute. Retrieved from https://www.brookings.edu/ wp-content/uploads/2016/06/Districts_Report_03252013_web.pdf

3

RACIAL SEGREGATION AND URBAN SCHOOLS

The neighborhood a child lives in matters. I demonstrated in Chapter 1 that some children live in low-opportunity communities, which impact their well-being and academic achievement. In this chapter, I describe the history of racially explicit government policies that have segregated metropolitan areas and public schools. While government agencies and businesses no longer practice many (but not all) of these policies, long-term effects have not been remedied. After presenting a history of these policies, I provide two case studies to link racist government policies of the past to current challenges confronting urban public schools. I am outraged to tell this story, but no urban principal should go to work without knowledge of how explicitly racist government policies created segregated neighborhoods and unequal schools. Today's segregation is not the product of individual preferences of homeowners or happenstance, but instead explicit and racist public policies that have intentionally segregated every metropolitan area in the USA. This ugly history began more than 100 years ago and is why zip codes and neighborhoods matter so much for children and schools today. This history implores principals to think about how their schools can work with and for communities, rather than for pursuing narrow school reform agendas. This history is the fodder for community engaged leadership.

Racial Segregation in American Cities

Zoning

In 1899 Washington, DC was one of the first cities to enact zoning laws, which regulated the heights of buildings. In 1908, Los Angeles adopted zoning laws to protect residential areas from industrial development. In 1916, New York City developed zoning for residential, commercial, and industrial zones. Policymakers, developers, and special interest groups began zoning to alleviate congestion, address public health concerns, and destroy or improve existing slum neighborhoods (Haar & Kayden, 1989), but zoning soon evolved to "protect" White neighborhood home values from people of color. Baltimore enacted one of the nation's first racial zoning ordinances in 1910 making it illegal to sell a house on a majority White block to a Black person, or vice versa.

In 1917, the U.S. Supreme Court unanimously agreed in *Buchanan v Warley* that a Louisville, Kentucky city ordinance prohibiting the sale of property to Blacks in a White-majority neighborhood violated the Fourteenth Amendment. City planners and local government officials tweaked racial zoning policies, which allowed them to argue that their ordinance was different from that of *Buchanan* decision (Rothstein, 2017). Planners and politicians used various techniques to maintain segregation without mentioning race. Zoning was then used to place toxic and industrial areas in or nearby Black and Latina/o neighborhoods. For example, in 1919, St. Louis purposefully designated land for industrial development in or near Black neighborhoods but not in or near White neighborhoods. Today, geographic studies show a relationship between environmental hazards and community demographics. Blacks and Latina/os are still more likely to live in more polluted cities and neighborhoods than Whites (Zimring, 2016). In rare instances when Blacks moved into White neighborhoods, they were often subjected to extreme violence. In Chicago, between 1917 and 1921, 58 firebombings of Black homes on White neighborhood border areas were reported with no arrests or prosecutions (Rothstein, 2017). As previously noted in Chapter 2, the impact of violence on children is significant and has long-lasting effects.

Great Depression and the New Deal

The Great Depression created an opportunity for federal government involvement in housing policy. Unfortunately, federal policies sponsored segregation and exacerbated racial inequalities with President Franklin Delano Roosevelt's New Deal. In 1933, Roosevelt created the Home Owner's Loan Corporation (HOLC) to purchase mortgages in foreclosure and issue new mortgages with inexpensive repayment options. HOLC quickly created "redlining maps" to detail the level of security for real estate investment in 239 cities across the USA. Black neighborhoods were outlined in red (hence redlining) and considered to be the riskiest for investment.

The Public Works Administration (PWA) began in 1933 to address a national housing shortage and to create construction jobs. PWA housing projects were segregated even in integrated neighborhoods. In 1934, the Federal Housing Administration (FHA) was formed to set standards for home construction, underwriting, and loan insurance made by banks and private lenders. FHA set guidelines to steer investors away from Black and Latina/o communities. Many residential housing developments approved by the FHA upheld a Whites-only clause. Early underwriting manuals included explicit instructions that racial integration created instability and home value losses. Between 1945 and 1959, only 2% of Blacks received federally insured home loans (Hanchett, 2000). Whites could purchase new homes in the suburbs using more affordable FHA-backed mortgages allowing them to move from cities while Blacks and Latina/os remained left behind.

In 1940, Congress passed the Defense Housing and Community Facilities and Services Act to fund housing for workers in defense industries. Worker housing was also segregated in most cities and frequently shoddier in Black and Latina/o neighborhoods. President Roosevelt saw highways as essential to putting people back to work during the depression. The Federal-Aid Highway Act (FAHA) of 1944 included provisions for the creation of a 40,000-mile national highway system to connect major cities and industrial areas. In 1956, FAHA was reauthorized by President Eisenhower and became one of the largest public works projects in American history. State, local, and federal governments conspired to design interstate highways purposefully destroying Black and Latina/o neighborhoods or further isolating them from White communities, business districts, and employment opportunities (Bayor, 1988; Rothstein, 2017). The director of the American Association of State Highway Officials in the 1950s even claimed: "some city officials expressed the view in the mid-1950's that the urban Interstates would give them a good opportunity to get rid of the local 'niggertown'" (Schwartz, 1976, p. 485). Today, one can quickly use Google Maps to investigate how major highways cut through cities and isolate specific communities.

Post World War II and Civil Rights Movement

After World War II, the Veterans Administration (VA) and the G.I. Bill's mortgage program continued to sponsor racial segregation. The VA demanded properties use race-based restrictive covenants which forbid the sale of property in majority White neighborhoods to Blacks and other families of color. Non-Whites received fewer than 100 of the first 67,000 mortgages insured by the VA through the G.I. Bill (Hanchett, 2000). In 1945, the Shelleys, a Black family in St. Louis purchased a house with a restrictive covenant. Louis Kraemer, a nearby White resident, sued the Shelleys to prevent them from moving in (*Shelley v. Kraemer*, 1947). The Supreme Court of Missouri held that the covenant was enforceable, but the U.S. Supreme Court ultimately decided that states could not enforce racially based restrictive covenants. The decision did not invalidate racially based restrictive covenants altogether, but rather only their enforcement by the government. Housing developers created community associations requiring membership before purchase. Community associations regularly denied membership to Blacks and Latina/os families.

Real estate developers lobbied Congress after World War II to cut subsidized housing projects for middle- and working-class families. Already racially segregated neighborhoods became prime locations for housing units exclusively for the most impoverished residents. A loss of middle-class residents in public housing eliminated an influential voting constituency to advocate for upkeep and amenities (Rothstein, 2017). These policies helped to concentrate poverty within Black and Latina/o neighborhoods. Racially segregated, low-opportunity communities of color were created.

The overall inability of Blacks and Latina/os to find homes also created opportunities for unethical real estate practices, such as blockbusting. Blockbusting is a real estate scheme where speculators buy property in borderline Black–White neighborhoods, rent or sell property to Black families at above market prices given their desire to access property, and then persuade White residents to sell their homes at a discounted rate because the area would soon turn into a "Black slum." Real estate agents later sold homes at inflated prices. Since the FHA did not certify loans for Blacks in these neighborhoods, many families purchased homes using unfair, deceptive, or fraudulent practices. These loans were frequently costlier. Loan provisions sometimes stipulated a family could be evicted for a single late monthly payment. The higher costs of homes and more expensive mortgages contributed to foreclosures and neighborhood deterioration.

In 1962, President John F. Kennedy issued an executive order prohibiting federal funds to support racial housing discrimination. The 1968 Fair Housing Act rejected the legality of racial discrimination by any financial institutions. By the 1970s, the federal government had a clear understanding of how federal, state, and local government policies created a concentrated disadvantage in every American city. A 1973 report from the U.S. Commission on Civil Rights noted:

> Like other social problems that have deep roots in history, fair housing cannot be understood without understanding what that history has been. Segregated patterns of residency have not developed spontaneously. They have been influenced by a variety of public and private forces . . . Federal, State, and local governments have been active participants.
>
> *pp. 1–2*

The report further noted that:

> Segregated residential patterns in metropolitan areas undermine efforts to assure equal opportunity in employment and education. While centers of employment have moved from the central cities to suburbs and outlying parts of metropolitan areas, minority group families remain confined to the central cities, and because they are confined, they are separated from employment opportunities . . . In addition, lack of equal housing opportunity decreases prospects for educational opportunity.
>
> *p. 1*

Unfortunately, the federal government's recognition of racial discrimination did little to change the next 45 years.

White Flight, Decay, and Renewal

The federal government began restructuring in the early 1970s in ways that limited federal funding to social programs and cities. Cities started borrowing large amounts of money and after several cities failed to repay loans, rating agencies like Standard and Poor's and Moody's closely monitored cities and exerted increasing pressure to cut city expenditures. The pressure from rating agencies created a shift in how municipal governments behaved. Municipal governments began to focus on being "economically efficient, business-friendly, anti-deficit entities" (Hackworth, 2007, p. 39).

New business coalitions emerged for the redevelopment of downtown areas. City governments collaborated and supported major research universities and research centers to expand and provide high-paying jobs to well-trained, white-collar professionals. Cities pursued upscale shopping centers and promoted tourism in downtown areas. They offered tax breaks to keep or lure large corporations and sought to attract the defense industry and military bases, mainly as Reagan built up the military in the 1980s. Many cities benefitted financially from these coalitions, but development was uneven across neighborhoods. New resources, amenities, and jobs were placed in downtown areas, but low-opportunity communities of color remained neglected.

Commercial redevelopment and a renewed position of cities in a global economy fostered a revaluation of previously disinvested and racially segregated neighborhoods in the 1990s and 2000s, particularly those near downtown. Gentrification is associated with redevelopment and the arrival of hipsters, yuppies, and professionals in downtowns and previously disinvested neighborhoods. Gentrification often causes residential displacement via housing demolition, ownership conversion of rental units, increased housing costs (rent and taxes), and evictions (Newman & Wyly, 2006). Black and Latina/o residents in gentrifying low-income neighborhoods often find their community networks destroyed and at times are forced to move further away from jobs and other community resources.

In cities like Washington, DC and New York City, gentrification created a mixing of people from different socioeconomic strata, which at times led to conflict and unequal power dynamics. Clashes between youth of color and new White and professional residents can lead to increased police surveillance and even police violence (Freeman, 2011). While gentrification can bring about modern amenities and services for low-income residents, it may be unwelcome because of existing residents' cynicism toward government based on a long history of redlining, discrimination, and police violence.

The recent Great Recession had a negative impact on most cities, which disproportionately impacted low-opportunity communities. One contributing factor was "reverse redlining," or excessive marketing of exploitative and predatory loans in Black and Latina/o neighborhoods. Racially segregated metropolitan areas were more likely to have borrowers with subprime loans than borrowers in less segregated areas (Hyra, Squires, Renner, & Kirk, 2013). In 2011, Secretary of Housing and Urban Development (HUD) Shaun Donovan described how Countrywide Financial Corporation:

> charged more than 200,000 African American and Latino families more for their loans because of their race or ethnicity . . . [and] put more than 10,000 of those families who had qualified for safe loans in the prime market into risky, subprime mortgages—at the same time white borrowers with similar credit histories were steered into safer, prime loans.
>
> *U.S. Department of Housing and Urban Development, 2011*

Donovan asked the American public to consider the effects of Countrywide's wrongdoing, stating that: "between 2005 and 2009, fully two-thirds of median household wealth in Hispanic families were wiped out. From Jamaica, Queens, New York, to Oakland, California, strong, middle-class African American neighborhoods saw nearly two decades of gains reversed in a matter of not years—but months" (U.S. Department of Housing and Urban Development, 2011). City governments were forced to increase spending in tough financial times to secure abandoned and foreclosed buildings and address additional issues related to poverty, crime, and homelessness because of massive foreclosures rather than work to improve their schools and social service agencies.

Cases of Segregation and Unequal Schools: Baltimore and El Paso

The brief history of how explicit government policies created segregated neighborhoods is relevant to urban schools and principals because it helped create low-opportunity communities and numerous conditions that impact the lives of students and families. In this section, I focus on Baltimore and El Paso as case studies to show how racism and housing discrimination created unequal school districts and schooling experiences for Black and Latina/o children over the past 100 years. I focus on Baltimore and El Paso because of my own personal and professional experience in these cities, although most American cities have similar histories. As a high school teacher in Baltimore, I taught my students the history of racial segregation in their city and neighborhood. In El Paso, as a professor, I helped the aspiring principals I worked with understand the context in which they work. Knowledge of history is important to building consciousness and commitments to community engaged leadership.

Baltimore, Maryland

Racial Segregation and Discriminatory Practices

Baltimore, Maryland is one of America's most racially segregated cities. Baltimore has a population of about 614,000 people (29.5% White, 63.7% Black, 4.2% Hispanic) (U.S. Census Bureau, 2017b). Real estate discrimination and unequal development are part of Baltimore's past and present. Maryland was a slave state until the end of the Civil War and until 1817 free Blacks in Baltimore convicted of petty crimes could be sold as slaves. During the 1800s, Baltimore maintained a community of free Blacks. In 1910, Baltimore established an ordinance of block-by-block segregation. Real estate agents were barred from introducing Black families into neighborhoods that were White (Pietila, 2010). HOLC developed redlining maps in Baltimore to support existing racial biases. Black neighborhoods were isolated from employment opportunities to benefit White workers. Numerous protests occurred throughout the city, such as the "Don't Buy Where You Can't Work Campaign" of 1933, which targeted the A&P supermarkets for not hiring Blacks but depending heavily on their business (Orr, 1999).

Baltimore's public housing was established in the 1930s as an officially segregated program. Between 1940 and 1954, HUD and the Housing Authority of Baltimore City (HABC) constructed 14 racially segregated public housing projects serving roughly equal numbers of Black and White families. In 1939, the HABC developed Gilmor Homes in the Sandtown neighborhood after initially planning to build the Black housing project in a cheaper, less developed, and more racially integrated area. However, White opposition caused HABC to build Gilmor Homes in a racially segregated Black neighborhood and to do the project for the highest possible density because of the difficulty in acquiring land for Black public housing.

During the city's economic boom years in the 1940s and 1950s, thousands of Black families moved to the city for work. Between 1955 and 1970, seven of the eight new HUD/HABC projects were opened in Black neighborhoods and populated by Black residents. Between 1971 and 1995, seven out of nine new housing projects were placed in majority Black neighborhoods and had maintained almost 100% Black residency since opening. HUD and HABC have frequently been accused of consistently pursuing "slum clearance and the actual siting of public housing projects to foster, shape and reinforce patterns of housing segregation" (*Thompson et al. v U.S. HUD*, 1995, p. 12).

Plaintiffs from Baltimore City's public housing filed a class action lawsuit against HUD in 1995. The action, known as *Thompson v HUD* (1995), noted that Black residents in racially segregated Baltimore housing projects "suffered segregation and discrimination on the basis of their race and minority status" and have "been denied safe, affordable and integrated housing and have suffered the loss of social, economic and educational advantages from interracial associations produced by living in an integrated neighborhood" (p. 50). Plaintiffs described how they have "been restricted to racially segregated neighborhoods where they are subjected to concentrated poverty, unemployment, drug trafficking and criminal violence . . . [and] have suffered and will continue to suffer irreparable harm for which no monetary damages or other legal remedy could compensate them" (p. 51). In 1996, the parties entered a consent decree where HUD pledged to desegregate public housing. In 2004, a federal court found HUD violated terms of the consent decree.

Despite discriminatory policies, many Black neighborhoods thrived from the early 1900s through the 1960s. They flourished because residents organized to address their concerns with the National Association for the Advancement of Colored People (NAACP), the National Urban League, and local advocacy groups, such as the Baltimore Citizens Housing Committee (McDougall, 1993). Schools were often served as community hubs and meeting sites for residents and organizations. One of the only positive outcomes of racial segregation and other discriminatory practices was how Black neighborhoods and community organizations developed close bonds and trust among each other (Orr, 1999). However, the 1968 Baltimore Riots following the assassination of Dr. Martin Luther King disrupted many thriving Black neighborhoods.

The riots resulted in the death of six people, 700 injuries, almost 6,000 arrests, and approximately 1,000 damaged or robbed buildings. Governor Spiro Agnew criticized Black city leaders for failing to control their residents, a move that further raised tensions between White and Black residents. He described Black civic and religious rights leaders as "Circuit riding, Hanoi visiting, caterwauling, riot inciting, burn America down type of leaders" (Witcover, 2007, p. 13). His words reflected how the state government felt about the Black community in Baltimore. Between 1950 and 1970, thousands of White families left the city using federal government support while the predominately White city government remained in place. Local officials took efforts to marginalize the city's Black neighborhoods by giving city jobs to White Democrats rather than equitably distributing them to Black residents. Corruption with Baltimore renewal projects would eventually force Spiro Agnew out of the vice presidency of the USA.

After 1968, manufacturers scaled back production in Baltimore, invested in new technologies, and moved thousands of jobs to the suburbs and later to developing countries. Baltimore lost more than quarter of a million people between 1950 and 2000 (949,708 to 648,654). Financial institutions also left:

> Banks closed branches in the inner city and minority areas, leaving financial services to check-cashing outfits, payday loan offices, and other assorted loan sharks. When whites applied for money to buy homes, they were offered conventional mortgages . . . when blacks and Hispanics applied, even big-name lenders offered only higher-priced or predatory loans.
>
> *Pietila, 2010, p. 257*

Baltimore was increasingly viewed as the state's greatest liability because its population loss made it politically vulnerable and the city's poverty caused the state to spend more than it could afford. Many Black families were trapped in a withering city. To make matters worse, "Slum clearance, urban renewal, and expressway construction demolished many black neighborhoods, displacing 75,000 people between 1951 and 1971" (McDougall, 1993, p. 100).

Since the 1970s, most Baltimore neighborhoods are at least 90% Black or 90% White. Unemployment rates, median income, high school graduation, health, and other socioeconomic indicators vary greatly across neighborhoods. Neighborhoods with the highest percentage of children with elevated blood lead levels are in predominately low-income Black neighborhoods, such as Sandtown-Winchester (7.4%) and Edmondson Village (5.3%) (Baltimore Neighborhood Alliance (BNA), 2017). Policing is also different by neighborhood. A recent U.S. Department of Justice (2016) report on Baltimore Police Department found:

> Community members living in the City's wealthier and mostly white neighborhoods told us that officers tend to be respectful and responsive to their needs, while many individuals residing in the City's largely African-American communities informed us that officers tend to be disrespectful and do not respond promptly to their calls for service. Members of these mostly African-American communities often felt they were subjected to unjustified stops, searches, and arrests, as well as excessive force.
>
> *p. 5*

The same Justice Department report documented how officers consistently treated Black residents differently. Their report detailed unconstitutional arrests, excessive force producing severe and unjustified disparities in rates of arrests in Black neighborhoods, and retaliation against Black residents engaging in constitutionally protected activities. The report detailed an anal cavity search of a Black woman in broad daylight after being pulled over for a broken headlight. Excessive physical force was consistently used against Black youth and training protocols prompted officers to point their guns at unarmed citizens. Per the report (U.S. Department of Justice, 2016), "BPD officers frequently used unreasonable force against juveniles without implementing widely accepted techniques and tactics for engaging with youth . . . BPD officers engage in unnecessary and excessive force with youth and fail to adjust their tactics to account for the age and developmental status of the youth they encounter" (pp. 85–86). The report logged instances where officers punched a Black male youth in the face for sitting on the front steps of his home, using a taser on a 5'2", 85-pound Black female youth for not complying with directions, and the arrest of a 7-year-old Black boy for sitting on a dirt bike.

Baltimore now has the least upward mobility of the nation's largest 100 municipalities (Chetty & Hendren, 2015). The median income for White families and

Black families are $60,550 and $33,610 respectively. For Black and White men between the ages of 20 and 24, the unemployment is rate is 37% and 10% respectively (U.S. Census Bureau, 2017b). Life expectancy differed as much as 20 years across neighborhoods. One-third of children live below the federal poverty line, one in three youth are either obese or overweight, and more than 12% of babies are born with low birthweight compared to a national average of 6% (Baltimore City Health Department, n.d.). Baltimore also has one of the highest heroin use and overdose rates in the nation with over 192 heroin-related deaths in 2014 and more than 60,000 people with drug or alcohol addictions.

Baltimore City Public Schools

Baltimore City Public Schools (BCPS) reflects the city's ugly history with racial segregation and inequality. BCPS enrollment peaked in the 1970s at almost 200,000 students, but in 2015–2016 the district enrolled just 84,000 students. Approximately 82% of students are Black, 5% Latina/o, 85% low income, 5% English language learners (ELLs), and 15% students with disabilities. BCPS has 181 schools, which includes 34 charter schools and additional schools operated under an "alternative governance" contract. The district has a 1.3-billion-dollar annual budget and 5,000 teachers. Teacher turnover has been a persistent and costly challenge. Almost half of BCPS teachers have been employed for less than five years and less than 30% have been employed in BCPS for more than ten years. More than a quarter (26.8%) of teachers and students felt unsafe in their own school buildings per school surveys. Recent scores from the Partnership for Assessment of Readiness for College and Careers (PARCC) show that only 14% and 5.7% percent of BCPS students met or exceeded standards in grade 8 English language arts and mathematics.

BCPS became part of the city government in 1829 and maintained separate facilities for Black students for more than a century. The Baltimore school board did not hire any Black teachers until 1888 after decades of protest. BCPS desegregated its schools following *Brown v. Board of Education* in 1954, although the district already admitted Black students at its engineering-oriented selective Baltimore Polytechnic Institute because no "Black schools" offered equal or equivalent coursework at the time. In 1971, Roland N. Patterson was appointed as the city's first Black superintendent, but his appointment created friction with White Democrats and power brokers. He repeatedly clashed with Mayor William Donald Schaefer, a powerful political boss who long represented White Democratic interests in the city and state.

Patterson recognized how the White patronage system marginalized Black neighborhoods and school reform efforts. He developed ties with Black community leaders, decentralized power, gave community leaders greater access to the system, and removed patronage jobs and hired more Black principals and district administrators. Patterson battled the mayor and city council for teacher pay raises following a teacher strike in 1974. He also addressed a federal desegregation order that many White Democrats in the city and state believed would upset White families and contribute to the city's White flight.

Patterson's tenure is representative of the challenges confronting systemic reform in a historically segregated city with powerful White elites maintaining a patronage system.

> Insofar as Patterson's reforms went against the grain of the predominant political culture, he met resistance from black school leaders and city officials who had long developed a mode of cooperation centered on patronage. Baltimore's political culture spawned the expectation that the public school system functions principally as a major source of jobs and patronage . . . these ingrained experiences became barriers to [future] systemwide school reform.
>
> *Orr, 1999, p. 62*

The continued White middle-class departure from the city through the 1990s led politicians to prioritize downtown urban renewal projects instead of education and social reforms that would help racially segregated low-opportunity communities. High unemployment rates during a two-year recession beginning in 1989 spawned rapid increases in poverty, welfare dependency, violence associated with the drug trade, and other symptoms of neighborhood distress. Baltimore of the 1980s and 1990s "presented the school system with an unprecedented challenge. Never before, in so many schools in the system, had so large a portion of the student population come from such conditions of economic and social havoc" (Orr, 1999 p. 71). The 1990s and early 2000s saw a rapid turnover of superintendents with seven appointed between 1990 and 2005 (Stringfield & Yakimowski-Srebnick, 2005). In 2017, BCPS confronted an approximate $130 million budget gap from shrinking school enrollment, decreasing state funding, school construction projects for old buildings, and teacher salaries. In 2017, the district cut more than $40 million, which resulted in the layoff of librarians, guidance counselors, assistant principals and 75 core subject teachers (Prudente, 2017).

Edmondson Village and Local Schools

Edmondson Village is a neighborhood in southwestern Baltimore along the Edmondson Avenue corridor. I worked in "The Village" as a Social Studies teacher and boys' basketball coach at Edmondson-Westside High School. Most of my students were from the Village and previously attended nearby elementary schools. My students struggled academically and often read between a fourth- and seventh-grade level. The Village had a history of racial segregation and continues to suffer from social inequities stemming from blockbusting in the 1950s. Edmondson Village was once a White lower-middle-class neighborhood, but blockbusting tactics created a low-opportunity community of color. Blockbusting in the Village had a powerful, negative destabilizing effect because many Black homeowners found their homes were not worth what they initially paid and were subject to faulty and unfair mortgages (Orser, 2015).

Edmondson Village now has 7,900 residents and is the city's most racially segregated Black neighborhood (98% of students are Black) (BNA, 2017). The median household income is less than $40,000 a year and has been decreasing in the last decade. About 30 percent of households earn less than $25,000 a year and more than half of the neighborhood's children live below the poverty line (51.9%) (BNA, 2017). A quarter of the residents receive some form of housing voucher and fewer than 50% of mothers received prenatal care (BNA, 2017). Edmondson Village also suffers from persistent crime and a lack of access to healthy food. The neighborhood does not have a bank, many residents report dirty streets, and the unemployment rate is about 17% (Ames et al., 2011; BNA, 2017). The neighborhood had a higher than city average youth and adult arrest rate, non-fatal shootings rate, and homicide rate (Ames et al., 2011). Energy cut off rates were 40% higher than the city average (Ames et al., 2011). Residents must travel approximately 29 minutes by bus or 43 minutes by foot to access a supermarket (Baltimore Neighborhood Alliance, 2017). It is not surprising that vacant lots and abandoned homes are common and most occupied homes are worth less than $100,000.

In the school year 2015–2016, Lyndhurst Elementary School (ES) enrolled approximately 340 students with a student mobility rate of 33.2%. More than 80% of students received free and reduced meals and 16.9 % students were identified as having a disability (Maryland State Department of Education, 2016). Approximately 15% of teachers at Lyndhurst ES had a conditional teaching certificate and 20% of classes were not taught by a highly qualified teacher (Maryland State Department of Education, 2016). This high rate is shocking in comparison to nearby White suburban districts. Students frequently miss more than 20 days per year at the neighborhood middle school (15.2% of students) and high school (40.5 % of students) (BNA, 2017). ES students from Edmondson Village struggled on the Maryland State Assessment (MSA), as only 50.6% and 55.3 % of third graders passed mathematics and reading assessments. The approximately 1,200 students at Edmondson-Westside High School had courses taught by teachers who were not highly qualified (26.2%). High school students from the Village struggle on state assessments, as only 27.7% and 45.5% of students passed the Maryland High School Assessment (HSA) in Algebra and English.

El Paso, Texas

Racial Segregation and Inequality in a Border City

El Paso is a large geographically isolated city at the western tip of Texas located along the USA–Mexico border more than 500 miles west of San Antonio and 700 miles west of Houston. El Paso has 683,000 residents (80% Hispanic, mostly of Mexican descent; 14.2% White; 3.1% Black; 1.4% Asian) (U.S. Census Bureau, 2017a) and is part of a large metropolitan area of 2.7 million people (El Paso–Las Cruces, New Mexico–Ciudad Juarez, Mexico). A quarter of El Paso's residents were born outside the country, mostly in Mexico. Spanish conquistador Don Juan de Onate, who was responsible for the murder and enslavement of indigenous people in what is now the American Southwest, celebrated a Thanksgiving Mass in 1598 in the El Paso area. The village of El Paso was later settled in 1680 and served as a Spanish government outpost. Few Anglo settlers appeared in the region before the Treaty of Guadalupe Hidalgo in 1848, which gave the USA the Rio Grande as the southernmost boundary of Texas among other land areas and financial settlements. Mexicans were given the option to receive American citizenship and full civil rights—most stayed. However, dark-skinned Mexicans were rarely granted any rights and their legal status was exploited to maintain a source of cheap labor. El Paso grew rapidly after the Civil War, growing from 736 people in 1880 to 10,338 people by 1890. With railroad construction, El Paso became connected with Mexico and the USA, and subsequently transformed into a violent Wild West boomtown.

Mexican-Americans consistently earned lower wages in a dual-wage system with separate pay scales with whites. They were also routinely denied access to higher paying jobs (St. John, 2011). The American Smelting and Refining Company's (ASARCO) giant smelting smokestacks in El Paso—one of the largest in the country—was a conspicuous symbol of the effects of globalization in the early 20th century. Most of the workers were of Mexican descent and lived amid the plant's toxic pollution. Into the 1960s, an entirely segregated Mexican-American neighborhood known as Smeltertown or "La Esmelda" lacked paved streets, streetlights, and updated sewage systems (Perales, 2010). ASARCO's presence was pervasive and problematic because residents were forced to deal with "contamination and pollution, the years of corporate intrusion into many aspects of their lives, the grueling labor, and the myriad of other hardships" (Perales, 2010, p. 3). Children in Smeltertown had dangerous amounts of lead blood levels and a broad range of health concerns from pollution. By the 1980s, many jobs were in factories producing clothing or on the city's outskirts where migrant workers grew chili peppers, cotton, and pecans. Given the low wages and transient nature of farm work, farm owners consistently took efforts to prevent the organization of Mexican-American and migrant workforce (Shirley, 1997). Wages remained low in the region and offered minimal opportunity for upward mobility.

Jim Crow segregation also existed in Texas through the 1960s, especially for the city's small Black population. Theaters, medical services, bars, restaurants, schools, and hotels were just some of the places segregated in the city. Langston Hughes visited El Paso in 1932 and recalled an El Paso/Ciudad Juarez, Mexico observation:

It was strange to find that just by stepping across an invisible line into Mexico, a Negro could buy a beer in any bar, sit anywhere in the movies, eat in any restaurant, so suddenly did Jim Crow disappear, and Americans visiting Juarez, who would not drink beside a Negro in Texas, did so in Mexico. Funny people, Southerners!

San Antonio Express, *1932*

Also in 1932, El Paso doctor and civil rights activist Lawrence Nixon won two U.S. Supreme Court rulings making it unconstitutional for all White primaries (*Nixon v Condon*, 1932). It was not until El Paso elected Raymond Telles Jr., the first Mexican-American mayor in 1957, did Blacks and Mexican begin to access jobs in the police, fire department, and other city jobs.

The lives of El Pasoans are tied to the political ebb and flow of Washington, DC and Mexico City as well as considerations about border security. During the Mexican Revolution, American leaders secured the border from spillover violence. In the 1980s, the border was militarized in response to Reagan's immigration reform, the War on Drugs, and heightened tensions between the USA and Mexico. In 1994, political leaders agreed to the North American Free Trade Agreement (NAFTA), which eliminated barriers to trade and investment between Canada, the USA, and Mexico. Maquiladoras (or twin assembly plants that import components to assemble or vice versa) grew rapidly in Ciudad Juarez as U.S. businesses moved manufacturing jobs to Mexico, including thousands of working-class jobs in El Paso.

After September 11th, 2001, the border again became a place of concern and insecurity. In 2006, Congress passed the Secure Fence Act to gain "operational control" of the border and prevent unlawful entry. Increased security created a host of social problems for families split between Ciudad Juarez and El Paso. Many El Paso children lost access to grandparents, family, and their native culture and language. A violent drug war in Mexico beginning in 2006 claimed the lives of more than 100,000 people, triggered significant political and economic destabilization, and displaced more than a million people in Mexico. The instability led to the immigration of Mexicans seeking asylum in El Paso.

The city's long history of racism, segregation, and tumultuous relationship with Washington, DC contributes to many present-day inequalities. Latina/os earn 55% of what Whites earn and the city has a severe lack of access to affordable housing (Southwest Fair Housing Council, 2011). Racial and economic segregation is particularly problematic because approximately 20% of households earn less than $25,000 per year (Southwest Fair Housing Council, 2011). Foreign-born and low-income families primarily live in segregated neighborhoods, predominately between Interstate 10 and the border. A recent housing report noted, "there are significant minority concentrations in El Paso that contradict the residential patterns that could be expected in a free housing market . . . Anecdotal data suggest lending discrimination and other fair housing violations have been occurring" (Southwest Fair Housing Council, 2011, pp. 43–44).

El Paso Independent School District

The El Paso Independent School District (EPISD) is a large urban school district that enrolled more than 62,000 students in the 2012–2013 school year (83% Hispanic; 11% White; 70% economically disadvantaged; 25% ELLs). EPISD was created in 1882 and teachers were discouraged from using Spanish with students after the district's inception. Between 1882 and 1892, there was no school in El Paso for Mexican-American students. In 1892, a private school for Mexican-American students previously established by Olivius Aoy was incorporated by EPISD and renamed "The Mexican Preparatory School." In 1899, a second "Mexican School" was established to address overcrowding on the Aoy/Mexican Preparatory School campus. By 1922, schools located south of the train tracks and adjacent to the Mexican border were known to be part of EPISD's "Mexican District," while those north of the tracks and further from the border were known as the "American District." EPISD also operated Douglass Grammar and High School for Black children. After the *Brown* decision, federal attention was rarely directed toward integrating Mexican-American students and many EPISD alumni recall the fear of being caught speaking Spanish and subsequent punishment as late as the 1970s (Rippberger & Staudt, 2003).

In 1970, plaintiff parents filed a class action suit known as *Alvarado v EPISD* alleging racial and ethnic discrimination by operating a dual, segregated, and unequal school system for children of Mexican descent. The court reviewed EPISD's history of racial segregation as well as immigration patterns, residential segregation, school construction and attendance boundaries, bus routes, and school infrastructure. In 1976, a U.S. District Court held that "the parents had successfully demonstrated that the school district had effectuated intentionally segregation policies against Mexican-Americans" (*Alvarado et al. v. El Paso Independent School District*, 1976). The court also noted that EPISD had historically and intentionally maintained "inferior facilities for Mexican-American students," which included unequal funding, poor building maintenance, overcrowding, inadequate playground and sports facilities, poor lighting conditions, significant physical deterioration of facilities, and constructing new schools in predominantly White areas before correcting deterioration elsewhere. The court also found gerrymandering of attendance zones to maintain racial segregation. A 1974 U.S. Commission on Civil Rights (1974) report described conditions and practices in five Southwestern border states, which included evidence from El Paso. The report concluded that the educational system in the region ignored the language and culture of Mexican-American students, which led to placing Mexican-American students in lower academic tracks. Also, the report noted that Mexican-American students were often taught by teachers with different cultural backgrounds whose "training leaves them ignorant and insensitive to the students' needs" (p. iii).

EPISD also maintained ineffective, segregated transitional bilingual programs for ELLs that failed to prepare students to be successful in general classrooms or support the development of their family's language. The marginalization of

Mexican-American ELLs extended into the current decade. Former EPISD superintendent Lorenzo Garcia pled guilty in 2012 to two counts of conspiracy to commit mail fraud associated with high-stakes test rigging. One significant aspect of the alleged cheating scandal was associated with district administrators and some principals inappropriately keeping students out of classrooms by improperly promoting, holding back, or preventing potentially low-performing students from arriving for the test or enrolling for school (Weaver & Tidwell, 2013).

An independent evaluation of the cheating scandal found "systemic non-compliance with both District policy and state law at the campus level" (Weaver & Tidwell, 2013, p. 80). The evaluation concluded that numerous district officials either encouraged cheating or looked the other way. The report noted the following:

> It is important to remember that for a period of some five and a half years, the District was run by a criminal. Garcia insulated and surrounded himself with willing accomplices, and his influence and reach were vast. The District has since suffered from a culture that has put desires and egos of adults over the needs of students. The culture has manifested in many forms, including the intentional manipulation of recognized subpopulations to avoid consequences . . . Long after Garcia's arrest and departure on August 1, 2011, many of these practices continued unabated . . . In the rush to avoid accountability consequences for inadequate graduation rates, many District high schools became credit mills and, eventually, diploma mills, as unearned credits resulted in the graduation of ill-prepared students. These students are the victims of the culture Garcia promulgated, and it is not a culture easily undone.
>
> *pp. 2–3*

Juan Cabrera, a former school law attorney, was hired as superintendent in September 2013 after more than a yearlong transitional period that employed three interim superintendents. Early in his tenure as superintendent, it appeared he was focused on supporting all students. EPISD is still struggling to regain trust in the community and change the perceptions of teachers and principals. Promising signs are emerging after Cabrera and the school board unanimously decided to implement dual language education for all ELLs across the district (DeMatthews, Izquierdo, & Knight, 2017).

Segundo Barrio and Neighborhood Schools

Segundo Barrio is one of the oldest and most historic neighborhoods in El Paso. It is situated along the USA–Mexico border and next to one of the city's oldest and primary ports of entry, making it a community where newly arriving immigrants have restarted their lives during three different centuries. Segundo Barrio is a cultural center for food, entertainment, social consciousness, political activism, and art as well as the birthplace or home of famous and successful Mexican-Americans. Segundo Barrio has historically been a tight-knit community of families immigrating from Mexico, uprooted by turmoil and violence. Peasant farmers settled the area in the 1830s. The Mexican Revolution in 1910 brought immigrants fleeing violence and instability. Impoverished immigrants who could not continue to migrate north remained in Segundo Barrio for generations. By the 1930s the neighborhood became overcrowded and filled with tenements. In the 1940s, El Paso received federal assistance to build the 349-unit Alamito Housing Project to help address many of the housing and slum-like conditions in Segundo Barrio.

Segundo Barrio continues to be a low-opportunity neighborhood that is racially segregated and without access to adequate healthcare and healthy food sources. A report by El Paso Children's Hospital (EPCH) (2014) found that poverty, a lack of insurance, and high rates of unemployment contribute to public health problems in the region. The census tract in which Segundo Barrio is located also has the highest Community Need Index (CNI) risk score (EPCH, 2014). More than 11,000 people live in Segundo Barrio, the clear majority of which identify as Latina/o and Mexican (95.2% and 91%) (U.S. Census Bureau, 2017a). The median household income in 2014 was $14,302 per year, the unemployment rate within the community was about 18%, almost 35% of families did not have any form of health insurance, and more than 70% of children live below the poverty line (US Census Bureau, 2017b). The median value of a home in Segundo Barrio is about $63,500 although most households rent (86.1%). Only about 40% of residents obtained a high school diploma or equivalency. Less than 15% of residents are monolingual English speakers and most households primarily speak Spanish (87.9%) (U.S. Census Bureau, n.d.).

Aoy ES, Hart ES, Guillen Middle School, and Bowie High School are the public schools serving the neighborhood. Aoy ES enrolled more than 550 students in the school year 2014–2015. At Aoy ES, 97% of students are Hispanic, 87.2% are economically disadvantaged, 78.5% of students are ELLs, and 15.6% of students have disabilities. Aoy ES students perform well across all grades subjects on the state assessments in relation to their peers in the district and state: 62% of all students and 63% of ELLs have met or exceeded standards. However, few students meet the state's more rigorous post-secondary readiness standards in reading and writing (14%, and 21%). Students continue to underperform when they enroll a Guillen MS as only 12% and 32% meet the state's post-secondary readiness standard in reading and mathematics by eighth grade. Bowie High School students struggle meeting post-secondary readiness standards as only 19% and 12% meet standards in reading and mathematics.

Bowie High School was part of the EPISD cheating scandal. In August 2009, a school counselor noticed 77 student transcripts had been altered to remove courses improperly. The school counselor and EPISD's director of guidance reported these issues to numerous district administrators. The allegations eventually led to a Texas Education Authority (TEA) review. The review concluded: "EPISD disappeared 55% of students entering Bowie High School in 2007 through such means as transfers, deportation, sending students to charter schools, holding students back in the 9th grade, or promoting students to the 11th grade" (Weaver & Tidwell, 2013, p. 10). More than 130 students had their grade reclassified to avoid state exams, and 17 students had 45 passing grades changed to failing grades to avoid exams. The evaluation found that the school's assistant principal falsified attendance forms to manipulate records. A 2010 audit of Bowie student transcripts revealed evidence that the improper changes in student transcripts were sufficient to impact accountability ratings for the school. The FBI became involved an investigation in December 2010, and the principal and other administrators were removed.

Takeaways for Principals

Racial segregation in America has created low-opportunity communities of color in cities like Baltimore and El Paso. Schools within these communities have been placed at a disadvantage given how districts have often struggled to provide adequate funding and support to majority Black and Latina/o serving schools. I am outraged by this history, and I hope that by principals knowing about the history of racial segregation and injustice within their cities they, too, will be outraged. Outrage is especially crucial for urban principals. As Jean Anyon (2014) noted:

> In order for injustice to create an outrage that can ultimately be challenged into public demands, knowledge of the facts is necessary, and an appreciation of the consequences must be clear . . . knowledge is crucial to an accurate understanding of what plagues urban education. We must know where the problem lies in order to identify workable solutions.
>
> *pp. 26–27*

Outrage and the response it provokes must be thoughtful. The next chapter critically considers the history of urban school reform. I argue that the last things principals working in low-opportunity communities should do is to narrowly adhere to top-down school reform efforts.

References

Alvarado et al. v. El Paso Independent School District, 426 F. Supp. 575 (W.D.Tex., 1976).

Ames, A., Evans, M., Fox, L., Milam, A., Petteway, R., & Rutledge. (2011, December). *Neighborhood health profile: Edmondson village*. Baltimore, MD: Baltimore City Health Department. Retrieved from http://health.baltimorecity.gov/sites/default/files/15%20Edmondson.pdf

Anyon, J. (2014). *Radical possibilities: Public policy, urban education, and a new social movement*. New York: Routledge.

Baltimore City Health Department (n.d.). *Baltimore city community health survey 2014: Summary results report.* Baltimore, MD: Author. Retrieved from http://health.baltimor ecity.gov/sites/default/files/BCHD%20CHS%20Report%20Sept%2016%202015.pdf

Baltimore Neighborhood Alliance. (2017). *Vital signs 15: Measuring progress toward a better quality of life in every neighborhood.* Baltimore, MD: Jacob France Institute. Retrieved from http://bniajfi.org/wp-content/uploads/2017/04/VS15_Compiled-04-12-17-08-41.pdf

Bayor, R. H. (1988). Roads to racial segregation: Atlanta in the twentieth century. *Journal of Urban History, 15*(1), 3–21.

BNA. (2017). *Vital signs 15: Measuring progress toward a better quality of life in every neighborhood.* Baltimore, MD: Jacob France Institute. Retrieved from http://bniajfi.org/wp-content/uploads/2017/04/VS15_Compiled-04-12-17-08-41.pdf

Brown v. Board of Education of Topeka, 347 U.S. 483 (1954).

Buchanan v. Warley, 245 U.S. 60 (1917).

Chetty, R., & Hendren, N. (2015). *The impacts of neighborhoods on intergenerational mobility: Childhood exposure effects and county-level estimates.* Cambridge, MA: National Bureau of Economic Research. Retrieved from http://scholar.harvard.edu/files/hendren/files/nbhds_paper.pdf

DeMatthews, D., Izquierdo, E., & Knight, D. S. (2017). Righting past wrongs: A super-intendent's social justice leadership for dual language education along the US–Mexico border. *Education Policy Analysis Archives, 25,* 1.

EPCH. (2014). *Community health needs assessment.* El Paso, TX: Author. Retrieved from http://elpasochildrens.org/wp-content/uploads/2014/09/EPCH-CHNA-Report-FINAL-9-29-14-V3.pdf

Freeman, L. (2011). *There goes the hood: Views of gentrification from the ground up.* Philadelphia, PA: Temple University Press.

Hackworth, J. (2007). *The neoliberal city: Governance, ideology, and development in American urbanism.* Ithaca, NY: Cornell University Press.

Hanchett, T. W. (2000). The other subsidized housing: Federal aid to suburbanization 1940s–1960s (pp. 163–179). In J. F. Bauman, R. Biles, and K. M. Szylvian (Eds.), *From tenements to the Taylor homes: In search of an urban housing policy in twentieth century America.* University Park, PA: Pennsylvania State University Press.

Haar, C., & Kayden, J. S. (1989). *Zoning and the American dream: Promises still to keep.* Chicago, IL: Planners Press.

Hyra, D. S., Squires, G. D., Renner, R. N., & Kirk, D. S. (2013). Metropolitan segregation and the subprime lending crisis. *Housing Policy Debate, 23*(1), 177–198.

Maryland State Department of Education. (2016). *2016 Maryland report card.* Annapolis, MD: Author. Retrieved from http://reportcard.msde.maryland.gov/

McDougall, H. A. (1993). *Black Baltimore: A new theory of community.* Philadelphia, PA: Temple Press.

Newman, K., & Wyly, E. K. (2006). The right to stay put, revisited: Gentrification and resistance to displacement in New York City. *Urban Studies, 43*(1), 23–57.

Nixon v. Condon, 286 U.S. 73 (1932).

Orr, M. (1999). *Black social capital: The politics of school reform in Baltimore, 1986–1998. Studies in government and public policy.* Lawrence, KA: University Press of Kansas.

Orser, W. E. (2015). *Blockbusting in Baltimore: The Edmondson village story.* Lexington, KY: University Press of Kentucky.

Perales, M. (2010). *Smeltertown: Making and remembering a southwest border community.* Chapel Hill: University of North Carolina Press.

Pietila, A. (2010). *Not in my neighborhood.* Chicago, IL: Ivan R. Dee Publisher.

Prudente, T. (2017, May 23). Baltimore school board approves budget; Administrators prepare list of layoffs. *Baltimore Sun*. Retrieved from http://www.baltimoresun.com/news/maryland/education/k-12/bs-md-ci-school-budget-vote-20170523-story.html

Rippberger, S. J., & Staudt, K. A. (2003). *Pledging allegiance: Learning nationalism at the El Paso-Juarez border*. New York: Routledge.

Rothstein, R. (2017). *The color of law: A forgotten history of how our government segregated America*. New York: Liverlight.

San Antonio Express. (1932, April 8). Negro poet to appear. *San Antonio Express*.

Schwartz, G. T. (1976). Urban freeways and the interstate system. *Southern California Law Review, 49*(3), 406–513.

Shelley v. Kraemer, 334 U.S. 1. (1947).

Shirley, D. (1997). *Community organizing for urban school reform*. Austin, TX: University of Texas Press.

Southwest Fair Housing Council. (2011). *Analysis of impediments to fair housing choice: El Paso*. Tucson, AZ: Author. Retrieved from https://docs.google.com/viewer?url=https%3A%2F%2Fjay-young.squarespace.com%2Fs%2FEl-Paso-AI-2011.pdf

St. John, R. (2011). *Line in the sand: A history of the western U.S.–Mexico border*. Princeton, NJ: Princeton University Press.

Stringfield, S. C., & Yakimowski-Srebnick, M. E. (2005). Promise, progress, problems, and paradoxes of three phases of accountability: A longitudinal case study of the Baltimore City public schools. *American Educational Research Journal, 42*(1), 43–75.

Thompson v. U.S. HUD, Civil Action No. MJG 95-309. (1995).

U.S. Census Bureau. (2017a). *American fact finder: Community facts*. Retrieved from https://factfinder.census.gov/faces/nav/jsf/pages/index.xhtml

U.S. Census Bureau. (2017b). *Quick facts: Baltimore city, Maryland*. Retrieved from https://www.census.gov/quickfacts/table/INC110215/2404000,00

U.S. Census Bureau. (n.d.). *American fact finder*. Retrieved from https://factfinder.census.gov/faces/tableservices/jsf/pages/productview.xhtml?src=CF

U.S. Commission on Civil Rights. (1973, February). *Understanding fair housing*. Washington, DC: Author. Retrieved from https://www.law.umaryland.edu/marshall/usccr/documents/cr11042.pdf

U.S. Commission on Civil Rights. (1974, February). *Toward quality education for Mexican Americans: Report VI: Mexican American education study*. Washington, DC: Author. Retrieved from https://www.law.umaryland.edu/marshall/usccr/documents/cr12m573rp6.pdf

U.S. Department of Housing and Urban Development. (2011, December 21). *Prepared remarks of secretary Shaun Donovan during the countrywide settlement press conference*. Washington, DC: Author. Retrieved from https://archives.hud.gov/remarks/donovan/speeches/2011-12-21.cfm

U.S. Department of Justice. (2016, August 10). *Investigation of the Baltimore city police department*. Washington, DC: Author. Retrieved from https://www.justice.gov/crt/file/883296/download

Weaver & Tidwell. (2013, April 1). *Final report of investigation into alleged cheating scandal at El Paso Independent School District*. Retrieved from http://extras.mnginteractive.com/live/media/site525/2013/0401/20130401_045446_weaver_audit.pdf

Witcover, J. (2007). *Very strange bedfellows: The short and unhappy marriage of Richard Nixon and Spiro Agnew*. New York: Public Affairs.

Zimring, C. A. (2016). *Clean and white: A history of environmental racism in the United States*. New York: NYU Press.

4

A HISTORY OF URBAN
SCHOOL REFORM

History influences what gets noticed and neglected, priorities and assumptions, and how decisions are made about what is just and unjust. As Tyack and Cuban (1995) noted, "History provides a whole storehouse of experiments on dead people. Studying such experiments is cheap . . . and it does not use people (often the poor) as live guinea pigs" (p. 6). In this chapter, I explore the development of school reform in urban school districts with a specific focus on four eras: the Common School era (1820–1860), the progressive era (1890–1950), the Civil Rights Era (1950–1980), and the accountability and market-based reform era (1980–present). In each period, social and economic issues influenced reform agendas. The role of the principal evolved and became a middle management position used by superintendents to implement top-down reform.

The history of urban school reform is not monolithic and varies by district, region, community, and groups served. A universal urban district or school does not exist. I highlight several critical historical events that are relevant to how economic and cultural changes in society have influenced school reform and principals. I want to point out that some of what is presented here can seem discouraging because urban schools in low-opportunity communities have mostly fallen short at providing students with the education they require. I point to these shortcomings not to disparage urban schools or principals, but to build a recognition that traditional, top-down approaches to school reform rarely work and often maintain inequalities. My intention is not to suggest principals are agents of oppression or minions of policy elites, but instead to underscore that principals are regular people influenced by mainstream narratives about race and class, worried about steady employment, and working in an imperfect society. To transform their schools, they must have a critical awareness of mainstream reform's shortcomings.

The Common Schools Movement (1820–1860)

Northern cities were the focal point for social change following the American Revolution. Cities housed artists, writers, bankers, and wealthy merchants as well as those in poverty, including immigrants viewed by native-born White Americans as uncivilized and racially inferior. Like today, cities were contradictions: "Symbols of both economic growth and moral degradation, cities contained millionaires and paupers, demonstrating the widening gap between extremes of wealth and poverty" (Reese, 2011, p. 16). A new and expanding market economy produced great wealth, but also class divisions. The opening of the Erie Canal in 1825 and railroad expansion created a national market that pushed young adults from close-knit towns and villages into cities in search of factory work. Irish Catholic immigrants escaped famine and entered American cities in droves, which kept wages low and generated ethnic and religious tensions. Declining wages and working conditions led to union organizing and class conflict. Crime, disease, riots, vagrancy, domestic violence, and unemployment became common in cities.

Native-born White Protestant men with commitments to the market economy dominated the school reform agenda. They believed in the promise of individual reformation through principles of Christianity (Reese, 2011). Most reformers attributed urban social ills to personal defects and concluded a cure was in teaching discipline and self-control. New institutions were established to reform individuals along these lines (e.g., penitentiaries, hospitals, insane asylums, public schools) (Labaree, 2012).

Horace Mann (1796–1859), the Secretary of the Massachusetts State Board of Education, was perhaps the most recognized reformer during the Common School era. He advocated for a taxpayer-funded, locally controlled, universal, and non-sectarian system of public schools in Massachusetts. Age grading and a moral, democratic, and discipline-oriented curriculum were developed to prepare all White students regardless of gender, ethnicity, or social class. Mann wrote that he did not want a school system that was "necessarily cheap, ordinary, inferior, or which was intended for one class of the community; but such an education as was common in the highest sense, as the air and light were common . . . not only accessible to all, but, as a general rule, enjoyed by all" (Reese, 2011, p. 11). In Mann's *Twelfth Annual Report* in 1848, he stated his rationale for public schools: "Education, then, beyond all other devices of human origin, is the great equalizer of the conditions of men—the balance wheel of the social machinery" (Cremin, 1957, p. 87). Teacher certifications and teacher preparatory schools were created to ensure teachers taught self-control, positive social values, and the benefits of the new national market economy (Labaree, 2012).

The Common School movement solidified universal enrollment for boys and girls, the importance of local democratic control in educational decisions, age grading, curriculum centered on civic engagement, and teacher training and certification. However, the movement failed to produce meaningful change for communities of color. After the Civil War (1861–1865), many reformers ignored the education of free Blacks in Northern and Southern states as well as American Indians, Chinese, Mexicans, and other racial groups. In San Francisco, public schools did not enroll Chinese children through the 1870s. In El Paso, Mexican children remained in segregated communities, unable to access public schools, and forced into English language preparatory schools. Blacks vigorously fought to gain access to public education but were either denied schools altogether or forced into unequal schools.

When reformers created a publicly funded school system, they realized a need for a managerial authority to supervise teachers and report school progress. In 1865, Boston Superintendent John Philbrick stated that schools needed a manager to "keep all subordinates in their proper place and at their assigned tasks" (Katz, 1968). Principals reported on attendance and punctuality. Time-consciousness became a primary concern of principals. Principals kept records on daily attendance, enrollment, and punctuality (Reese, 2011). Principals became lead disciplinarians, which was important as reformers desired orderly students who could mature into compliant workers. Teacher training, new expectations for student conduct, and district oversight led to outlawing violent forms of student discipline (shaking children, blows to the head). Principals organized courses of study, administered discipline, and supervised classrooms and teachers (Rousmaniere, 2013).

The position of principal in this era also became a "man's job." Reformers viewed women as good candidates for teaching given their "maternal instincts" and the fact that they did not command high wages. Many superintendents like John Philbrick believed men of "high character" would be perfect for overseeing and closely supervising female faculty. Principals were given formal authority over administrative work, public relations duties, managerial tasks, and operating a chain of command within the school. Principals had little power over district policies, especially in urban districts.

The Progressive Era (1890–1920)

By the 1890s, corporations dominated industry and consolidated power into monopolies which often ruthlessly destroyed labor unions, kept wages low, and ensured workers were compliant. A new wave of poor and unskilled immigrants from southern and eastern Europe flocked to cities. Cities were hotbeds for activism, as poor immigrants and activists challenged politicians to improve living and working conditions. A severe economic depression during the 1890s increased the public's demand for more government intervention. Upton Sinclair's controversial 1906 novel *The Jungle* portrayed the harsh working conditions and exploitations of immigrants living in Chicago and other industrialized cities as well as the unsanitary conditions of the meatpacking industry. The novel and journalists known as muckrakers exposed social and political problems in cities and helped bring about government intervention. President Woodrow Wilson implemented several progressive policies, including the Sixteenth Amendment to the U.S. Constitution, which allowed Congress to levy a federal income tax. Federal taxes provided a new source of money for the government to involve itself with and improve public schools.

During this era, two groups of reformers debated whether schools should be more democratic, student-centered, and focused on issues of social justice or be governed by the efficiency logic of modern corporations, social science research, and principles of scientific management (Reese, 2011). Reformers concerned more with social justice wanted to connect schools with local neighborhoods and organize grassroots campaigns against the rising power of corporate interests. John Dewey, a professor and public intellectual, and other child-centered progressives viewed schools as social institutions and wanted to shift teaching to a student-centered approach that tapped students' natural interests and allowed them to experiment and experience the world. Another group of reformers known as administrative progressives was more successful at gaining control of the reform agenda. They further centralized districts and believed they could engineer schools to maximize efficiency and improve society altogether.

Administrative progressives built a hierarchical system of control headed by a chief executive/superintendent, who relayed information and directives to principals acting as middle managers between the district and classroom. Administrative progressives did not trust democracy or the judgment of low-income citizens elected to school boards. Thus, administrative progressives utilized their media connections to reshape public opinion about political machines, ward-boards, and the benefits of having business leaders and management experts operate districts rather than local communities. Critics of centralization argued that influential superintendents eliminated community influence and subjected immigrant students to racial and religious prejudices. There was evidence to suggest critics were correct.

Many administrative progressives subscribed heavily to eugenics and the lore that White ethnic minorities (e.g., Irish-Catholics, Italians, Russian Jews) as well as Blacks, Latina/os, American Indians, and Asians were inferior (Selden, 1999). Ellwood Cubberley, a pioneer professor in the field of educational administration and later the dean of the Stanford Graduate School of Education (1909) stated:

> These southern and eastern Europeans are of a very different type from the north Europeans who preceded them. Illiterate, docile, lacking in self-reliance and initiative, and not possessing Anglo-Teutonic conceptions of law, order, and government, their coming has served to dilute tremendously the national stock, and to corrupt civic life.
>
> *p. 15*

Cubberley argued that the task of education would be to "break up these groups . . . to assimilate and amalgamate these people as part of our American race . . . so far as can be done" (p. 15). He compelled states and districts to consider public education as a tool for preparing students for the economic and family roles they would fulfill in adulthood and to "give up the exceedingly democratic idea that all are equal, and that our society is devoid of classes" (p. 57).

Cubberley also promoted a system of accountability and tracking in his popular school administration textbooks. Social scientists developed a series standardized tests, which were adapted for public schools. These tests were used to move "slower" students into vocational programs, which disproportionately placed poor and culturally diverse students into lower academic programs. Most students held back were immigrants and ethnic minorities, which reinforced a belief that not all students could reach the same level of academic performance. The purpose of schooling shifted toward creating divisions based on perceived student potential while also prioritizing workforce preparation. Testing, tracking, vocational curriculum, and racially biased administrative processes became ingrained in urban public schools (Reese, 2011).

The principal's role became more narrowly administrative during this era. Administrative progressives often compared principals to the factory foreman in that they were responsible for daily operations and not strategic policy decisions (Rousamaniere, 2013). A new and more efficient system required principals to assume a middle management role with greater accountability. Superintendents and reformers criticized and fired principals who did not follow direct orders. Principals had little say over district policies but received blame for student achievement and any other shortcomings. The White male principal became the face of the profession and an "Education Trust" of university professors, state superintendents, and other officials formed a powerful network that served their interests and groomed White men to move from principal, to the superintendency, and into the professoriate (Tyack, 1974; Tyack & Hansot, 1982). This career ladder further incentivized principals to adhere to superintendent orders. While many women reached the elementary school principal position (for significantly less pay than their male counterparts), few women rose to the coveted position of high school principal, superintendent, or professor of educational administration because of the "Trust." Principals gained more training, authority, and professional stature during this era, but found themselves with increased responsibilities and expectations from above. Most principals understood that district priorities were more important than working with and meeting the needs of families and communities.

The Civil Rights Era (1945–1980)

The Civil Rights Era was a time of remarkable change and conflict. Between 1920 and 1945 the USA suffered through the Great Depression and World War II, but by the 1950s the USA had the world's strongest military and a booming economy. Soldiers returned from World War II and used the G.I. Bill to receive low-cost mortgages in new suburban communities. In 1952, Senator Joseph McCarthy underwrote the "Red Scare," where left-leaning activists, professors, teachers, and actors were targeted and investigated by Congress and other federal authorities. The paranoia of communism was aligned with the persecution of gays and lesbians. The launch of *Sputnik* by the Soviet Union in 1957 led to an immediate crisis in the USA. The National Defense Education Act of 1958 (NDEA) was enacted almost immediately, which increased federal funding for science, technology, engineering, mathematics, and foreign language education. Blacks and Latina/os were educated in separate schools, lived in different neighborhoods, were punished in separate prisons, and buried in separate cemeteries. Youth activism, civil rights movements and anti-war protests occurred in cities across the nation.

"White Flight" or migration of middle-class White people and working-class jobs began in the late 1950s. Redlining, neighborhood blockbusting, lending discrimination, and racial covenants blocked Black and Latina/o families from moving to the suburbs. Political power within states shifted from cities to suburbs, which left communities of color without influential elected voices. Riots broke out in cities across the country between 1965 and 1969 because of ongoing racial oppression, police brutality, lack of opportunity, and the assassination of Dr. Martin Luther King Jr. (e.g., 1964 Harlem; 1964 Philadelphia; 1965 Watts; 1967 Newark; 1967 Detroit; 1968 Chicago; 1968 Baltimore; 1968 Washington, DC). Cities were increasingly viewed as dangerous. The media vilified urban communities of color. Urban districts struggled with a shrinking tax base while city governments raised taxes. Many city governments funneled resources into White neighborhoods to stem White Flight and keep the remaining White middle-class families in cities (Orr, 1999).

Brown v Board of Education

Civil rights activists, lawyers, and policymakers played a prominent role in urban school reform in this era. Activists and lawyers utilized a longstanding struggle against Jim Crow segregation to improve public education. They highlighted the inequities in the segregated public school systems throughout the South. For example, in Atlanta during the 1940s, overcrowding of Black elementary schools caused the school day to be limited to just three hours to allow for multiple cohorts of students. The average annual per-pupil investment in segregated facilities in the city was $228 for Blacks and $570 for Whites (Bayor, 2000). In 1950, about 2% of Black Mississippians earned a high school diploma while the state invested about $122 for each White student annually as compared to only $32 for each Black student (Dittmer, 1994). Northern Whites maintained their own biases evidenced by gerrymandered districts and discriminatory housing. This

North–South racial narrative is captured in an old saying: "In the South, white people don't mind how close a Negro gets to them as long as he doesn't rise too high, while in the North people don't mind how high a Negro gets as long as he doesn't get too close" (Patterson, 2001, p. xxi).

Thurgood Marshall, a lawyer leading the National Association for the Advancement of Colored People's (NAACP) Legal Defense and Educational Fund challenged school segregation in the Supreme Court by merging five suits in what is known collectively as *Brown v. Board of Education* (1954).[1] The Supreme Court was a conservative force at the time and had previously preserved racial segregation.[2] In 1952, however, Thurgood Marshall and his colleagues concluded that state-imposed segregation "was inherently discriminatory and therefore a denial of the Equal Protection Clause of the Fourteenth Amendment" (Patterson, 2001, p. 53). The Court wrestled with Marshall's arguments, which articulated how segregated schools were unequal and negatively affected the psyche of Black children. In 1954, Chief Justice Warren read the Court's unanimous decision and "separate but equal" was rejected. In the opinion of the court, Warren noted that public education had changed since the Plessy decision: "Today, education is perhaps the most important function of state governments . . . Today it is a principal instrument in awakening the child to cultural values, in preparing him for later professional training, and in helping him to adjust normally to his environment." A widely quoted section of the decision described the Court's thinking: "To separate them [Black children] from others of similar age and qualifications solely because of their race generates a feeling of inferiority as to their status in the community that may affect their hearts and minds in a way unlikely ever to be undone." Several cities along the Mason–Dixon line quickly integrated (e.g., Washington, DC, Baltimore, St. Louis). In other places, progress was slow, non-existent, or violently charged.

The War on Poverty and Other Federal Interventions

The *War on Poverty* initiated by President Lyndon Johnson during his 1964 State of the Union address further expanded the federal government's role in education and poverty reduction. The pioneering Elementary and Secondary School Act (ESEA) was enacted in 1965 and provided additional funding to schools with high proportions of students from low-income families. The following year, the influential 1966 *Equality of Educational Opportunity Report* (often referred to as the Coleman report (Coleman et al., 1966)) provided evidence that students' background and socioeconomic status was a significant factor in determining educational outcomes. In 1968, the Bilingual Education Act mandated districts provide bilingual education services for English language learners (ELLs).[3] Federal intervention on civil rights issues continued in the 1970s. In *Mills v Board of Education of District of Columbia* (1972), the Supreme Court established the right to a free public education regardless of cost after parents filed a lawsuit against the

District of Columbia Public Schools for refusing to educate students with disabilities because of the financial burden. In 1975, Congress enacted the Education for All Handicapped Children Act (EAHCA) requiring all public schools to deliver a free and appropriate public education to all children with disabilities and provided federal funds to help states pay for the implementation costs.

Federal courts and Congress provided additional funds and new civil rights mandates but offered little guidance on how to enact these orders. Principals would have to be the builders of more inclusive schools. Unfortunately, the *Brown* decision had negative consequences as newly integrated districts pushed out veteran Black principals who were highly skilled at working with the Black community. "The firings threatened the livelihood of Black educators, the structure, values, and cultural norms of the Black community, and ultimately the social, emotional, and academic success of Black children" (Tillman, 2004, p. 281). Black principals had historically been community-oriented and culturally responsive leaders that did twice as much with half the resources of their White counterparts. Reformers of the era also increased principal credentialing requirements to a master's degree in a time where few females or people of color had access to graduate schools. Thus, Black students often arrived in hostile environments where White principals would inflict their racial and cultural biases through discipline, tracking, and a lack of respect for parents and the Black community. School–family relationships were fractured or broken. Many principals pushed minorities into low-tier academic programs, disproportionately punished them for misconduct, and sent into special education programs which maintained a lower set of expectations in separate and unequal classrooms (Harry & Klingner, 2014).

Principals who sought to promote social justice and civil rights often found few allies, as they were positioned between two or more groups with divergent interests. For example, principals in the South were ordered by federal courts to integrate, but local school boards and community councils threatened principals' jobs and livelihood if they complied. When R. Wiley Brownlee, a White principal of Willow Run High School in Ypsilanti, Michigan publicly supported desegregation and busing, he was kidnapped by the Ku Klux Klan at gunpoint, tarred, and feathered (*New York Times*, 1971). When Black and Latina/o activists gained community control of schools in New York and Chicago, principals reckoned with the demands of families from different racial backgrounds while balancing district loyalties and their legitimacy with majority White faculty. When teachers' unions challenged working conditions and went on strike, principals had to choose between maintaining legitimacy with staff and the loyalties of their district superiors. In 1946, Principal Helen Conway walked the picket line with teachers and offered them coffee and doughnuts on a cold day. Her superintendent reprimanded her for siding with teachers (Berggren, 2011).

Some principals thrived and emerged as progressive, culturally responsive, inclusive, and activist-oriented leaders. They valued families and found ways to undermine problematic and racist district agendas. Educational historian Vanessa Siddle Walker (1996) researched Black principals in the South before the *Brown* decision. She found Black principals covertly working to support the NAACP's efforts to build a case against segregation. Despite these outlier examples, many White principals could be described as conservative threats to alternative voices and lifestyles. During the "Red Scare," some principals, either for self-protection or based on their political beliefs, exposed teachers with leftist leanings to super-intendents, which in some cases led to dismissal. Others persecuted gay and lesbian teachers, which further reinforced the White, heterosexual, and con-servative norm of the principal (Tyack, 1974). Other principals warned teachers about their political behaviors, engaged in censorship activity, and utilized fear as a mechanism of control. Sometimes, principals enacted harsh discipline when concerned about student boycotts, student demands, sit-ins, and other forms of non-conforming behavior. At the behest of Congress and districts during the 1960s and 1970s, principals began collaborating with law enforcement agencies to monitor and suppress youth activism.[4]

The Accountability and Market-Based Reform Era (1980–Present)

Many of battles won during the Civil Rights Era were undone after the 1970s. Cities across the USA were heavily impacted by "White Flight" as well as a sharp post-war economic decline in the 1970s and early 1980s. Black and Latina/o middle-class families fled cities as they gained access to loans, mortgages, and middle-class professional jobs. Their departure left mostly the disenfranchised in racially and economically segregated urban communities. William Julius Wilson (2012) wrote about how discriminatory laws, policies, hiring practices, and hous-ing programs created "ghetto neighborhoods" heavily populated with a new underclass, "the most disadvantaged segments of the black [and Latino] com-munity" (p. 8). Inflation, unemployment, violence, and a suffering lower and middle class gave rise to a populist conservative movement known as the "New Right." This mixed group of evangelical Christians, advocates of free-market economics, disaffected White liberals, and anti-tax supporters elected Ronald Reagan president in 1980.

Reagan and the New Right attacked cities by pushing racialized narratives of the "Black welfare queen" while investing in a new War on Drugs that targeted Black and Latina/o communities (Jencks, 1993). In 1986, Reagan signed into law the Anti-Drug Abuse Act, which introduced harsher penalties, mandatory minimum sentences, and severe punishments for selling crack (a drug associ-ated with Blacks and derived from cocaine), but not for powder cocaine (a drug associated with Whites). Convictions skyrocketed amongst people of color in cities, and the U.S. penal population exploded from about 300,000 in 1980 to more than 2.1 million by 2015 (Bureau of Justice Statistics, 2016). The Reagan administration also adopted "supply-side economics," which included significant tax cuts, government spending cuts on social programs including education, and reduced government regulation and trade barriers. The New Right favored conservative, free-market economists like Milton Friedman who argued government bureaucracies were inefficient and slow to respond to changing needs of citizens and a modern society. The consequences were disastrous for low-opportunity communities of color and their schools.

An Attack on Public Schools

In 1983, Reagan's Department of Education released the controversial report *A Nation at Risk* (ANAR; National Commission on Excellence in Education, 1983), which warned that "the educational foundations of our society are presently being eroded by a rising tide of mediocrity that threatens our very future as a Nation and a people." ANAR claimed public schools "squandered" gains and achievements of the past and that public education "lost sight of the basic purposes of schooling, and of the high expectations and disciplined effort needed to attain them." ANAR also suggested teachers were poorly prepared, students were behind their international peers on standardized testing, and public schools were the cause of a declining economy.

ANAR was mostly anecdotal, and many contested its conclusions, but local, state, and federal policymakers were compelled to respond. ANAR recommended more significant attention to high school graduation requirements, teacher preparation and salaries, and academic standards. It ignored issues of racism, poverty, and segregation. ANAR did not explicitly argue for corporate and market-driven reforms, but "It laid the ideological and rhetorical groundwork for corporate-style reformers who three decades later maintained that our schools were declining and failing, that public education itself was 'broken' and obsolete, and that radical, free-market solutions were called for" (Ravitch, 2016, p. 31). A bipartisan consensus soon emerged around market-based reforms, testing and accountability, and, perhaps most importantly, that public education was broken, students were not learning, and teachers and principals were to blame.

The Carnegie Task Force on Teaching, which comprised the heads of both the American Teachers Union and the National Education Agency, presented the following statement: "Markets have proven to be very efficient instruments to allocate resources and motivate people in many sectors of American life. They can also make it possible for all public school students to gain access to equal school resources" (Carnegie Forum on Education and the Economy, 1986). The National Governors Association (NGA) (1987) adopted several primary educational tasks, including (a) creating a more professional teacher force; (b) strengthening school leadership; (c) promoting parent choice; and (d) helping at-risk students meet high academic standards. Other national organizations quietly became involved in supporting testing, parent choice, and improved educational standards (including the Council of Chief State School Officers (CCSSO)). Governors and state legislatures from both parties valued SAT and ACT score comparisons to assess the strength of their school systems (a problematic method given that SAT and ACT only measured college-bound students). Reform-oriented governors and state legislative bodies would eventually gain an appetite for state tests and state data systems to draw more meaningful comparisons.[5]

Two fellows at the Brookings Institute provided an important argument in support of market-based reforms. John Chubb and Terry Moe (1991), appropriating civil rights language focused on addressing educational inequalities, argued that superintendents, principals, and teachers were denied the discretion to exercise their professional expertise and judgment to improve their schools because of bureaucracies, unions, and democratically elected school boards. They contended that the democratic and bureaucratic nature of public school systems were too "politically sensitive" and favorable to the power of unions and union protections, which undermined principal authority to innovate, remove ineffective teachers, establish organizational conditions that support student achievement, and respond to the parent demands. Chubb and Moe's arguments set the stage for greater accountability in public education.

Setting the Stage for Accountability and Choice

When President George H. W. Bush took office in 1989, a national summit of governors set goals for the year 2000, including: (a) students would place first in the world in math and science; (b) at least 90% of students would graduate from high school; (c) all adults would be literate; and (d) all schools would be drug and violence-free. The Department of Education revised these goals emphasizing the need for a rigorous curriculum; teachers with subject area expertise; annual report cards for states, districts, and schools; a system of choice for parents; and requirements for school improvement plans for failing schools (Vinovskis, 1999). In 1993, President Bill Clinton supported an expanded federal role in public education, the development of national standards, and a voluntary system of national testing. In March 1994, Clinton signed The Goals 2000: Educate America Act into law, which provided federal dollars to help states increase student achievement, create safe schools, prepare students for the workforce, and promote partnerships and parent engagement.

In 1991, Minnesota passed the first charter school law. In 1995, the District of Columbia's City Council enacted a charter school law.[6] By 2014, 42 states passed charter school legislation. Charter school enrollment surged to about 2.5 million students. (Center for Education Reform, 2015). Since charters are often released from many bureaucratic policies of districts and state education agencies, charter school principals and teachers are arguably "freer" to innovate and create effective schools. After decades of research, charter schools on average are more segregated than public schools (Frankenberg, Siegel-Hawley, & Wang, 2010), while no evidence suggests that attending charters improves long-term student outcomes (Clark, Gleason, Tuttle, & Silverberg, 2015). Perhaps even more problematic, charters and voucher programs created thousands of unregulated schools that receive public funds but are unaccountable to school boards or local communities. This is particularly problematic in low-opportunity communities where parents may already feel disconnected to their public schools.

Goals 2000 remained in place until 2002, when President George W. Bush signed into law the No Child Left Behind Act (NCLB). For the first time, the Department of Education pressured states to enact reforms and held them accountable for performance. NCLB mandated every student be tested in mathematics and reading annually between grades 3 and 8 and at least once in high school. States, districts, and schools were required to disaggregate test score results by student race, income-status, disability, and English proficiency. The law required all students to pass all state tests by 2014. States and districts monitored all student groups and publicly reported adequate yearly progress (AYP). Schools that persistently failed were labeled "in need of improvement of status" and subject to sanctions, including having all staff fired, closing the school, or handing over the school's management to a charter school. There was almost no evidence to suggest charter schools could improve struggling schools at the time, highlighting to many critics that both Congressional Democrats and Republicans and a new group of reformers were acting on ideology rather than evidence.

The pressure to improve test scores disproportionately impacted schools in low-opportunity communities which were almost immediately found to be failing. Perverse consequences to NCLB in urban districts led to early testing beginning in kindergarten and narrowing curriculum (e.g., excluding the arts, music, foreign language, social studies). Ugly cheating scandals emerged in cities like Washington, DC, Atlanta, and El Paso, Texas (DeMatthews, 2014; Ravitch, 2016). Many districts and schools deprioritized public health issues, and social and emotional aspects of learning and development. Some districts and schools cut school counseling positions. Sadly, the racial achievement gap measured by the National Assessment of Educational Progress (NAEP) had barely narrowed between 2003 and 2017 (Center for Educational Policy Analysis, 2017).

Former U.S. Assistant Secretary of Education and educational historian Diane Ravitch (2016) argued that NCLB opened "the door to huge entrepreneurial opportunities" where tutoring and testing companies could make billions of dollars previously spent in public schools. When President Barack Obama assumed office, he widened the door for entrepreneurial opportunities with the Race to the Top (RTT) initiative. The RTT was a $4.35 billion federal grant that created a competition to spur state and district innovation around a set of reforms. States applying for RTT funds were awarded points for following practices: creating teacher and principal performance-based evaluations, adopting the Common Core State Standards (CCSS), developing charter school-friendly state policies, and developing systems for turning around low-performing schools and improving the collection and utilization of student data. Many states desperate for funds adopted the Obama administration's reform ideology and consulting firms emerged to provide schools, districts, and states with services and expertise to implement the CCSS, utilize school-level student data to target instruction, and manage and analyze large datasets to make policy decisions. According to the *Denver Post*, "vendors came out of the woodwork" to work with districts (Brown, 2012). Consultants in the state racked in as much as 35% of RTT funds awarded in Colorado.

In 2010 President Obama surprised educators across the country when he offered his support for the firing of an entire school faculty based on test scores in a low-opportunity community in Rhode Island. The President said, "If a school continues to fail its students year after year after year, if it doesn't show signs of improvement, then there's got to be a sense of accountability . . . And that's what happened in Rhode Island last week" (Greenhouse & Dillion, 2010). Finally, in 2011 the U.S. Department of Education began issuing waivers to states to get out from under NCLB accountability. By November 2014, 43 states received waivers (Klein, 2015). In December 2015, NCLB was finally reauthorized by Congress under a new name: Every Student Succeeds Act (ESSA). ESSA came into effect in the 2017–2018 school year. The law contains many of the same provisions of NCLB (e.g., testing students in grades 3–8 and once in high school, states publicly reporting performance and disaggregating data by school and different subgroups), but states have greater flexibility in selecting tests and standards as well as reforms for struggling schools.

Upon assuming office in 2017, President Donald Trump's nomination of Betsy DeVos (a wealthy pro-voucher philanthropist with no public education experience) as the Secretary of Education signaled that public charter schools, accountability measures, vouchers, and other pro-market reforms would remain. In some ways, the appointment of DeVos is not surprising as the Bush II and Obama administrations regularly coordinated and planned educational reform with major foundations like the Gates Foundation, conservative and moderate think-tanks, billionaires oriented toward market-based reforms, and newly emerging educational entrepreneurs.

Principals became more responsible for instruction and student achievement than ever before during this era and now had added duties of competing with charter schools for student enrollment. By 1996, national principal standards were created to solidify a new set of responsibilities. Private funding from the Wallace Foundation and support from the CCSSO and the NGA (both supporters engaged in the development of the CCSS) led to the development of the Interstate School Leadership Licensure Consortium (ISLLC) Standards. ISLLC contributed to changes in formal evaluations of principals as well as how professors of educational administration and leadership developed preparation programs. Principals are now held accountable for demonstrating standards-based leadership practices as well as raising student achievement.

Many urban districts now expect principals to be more li
a Master's in Business Administration and less like educators.
gests accountability policies force principals out of classrooms a1
communities (Abernathy, 2007). While some cities promoted lo
nity involvement in school governance (e.g., Chicago, New York),
principals are now more detached from communities and families giv ₋ ɩesting
priorities. Some feel they are leading in a "no-win situation," caught between
unjust policies, a lack of resources, a constant churn of top-down reform, and
the persistent challenges confronted by students in low-opportunity communities. While some urban principals thrive in this very difficult context, most
are burning out on the job, and others have engaged in a leading to the test
approach. In some instances, principals have participated in cheating schemes
and coaxed culturally and linguistically diverse students they viewed as testing
liabilities to drop out.

Takeaways for Principals

The history presented in this chapter highlights how education policy and school
reform has done little to narrow the racial achievement gap or improve other
educational outcomes, especially in low-opportunity communities. Corporate
elites and state and national political figures have heavily impacted school priorities and have largely ignored the physical, social, and emotional needs of students
and families that may be struggling with challenges within their community. The
voices of principals, teachers, families, and students have been largely ignored in
education policy and school reform discussions. Moreover, the past 100 years
of reforms have placed principals further away from teachers, classrooms, and
the needs of students and families. Many principals blindly lead in ways that are
authoritarian, hierarchal, and businesslike even though these approaches have
rarely yielded positive and long-term results. Principals who sincerely care about
low-income students of color must come to an understanding that no top-down
school reform as presently conceived at the federal or state level will meaningfully
narrow achievement gaps or help students in the long-term. However, schools
can make a difference, but it requires a different approach to school reform and
one that brings in the community as partners.

Notes

1 Clarendon County, South Carolina; Prince Edward County, Virginia; the District of
 Columbia; Wilmington, Delaware; and Topeka, Kansas.
2 In *Dred Scott v Sanford* (1857), Chief Justice Roger Taney handed down a decision
 describing Blacks as "so inferior that they had no rights which the white man was bound
 to respect". *Plessy v Ferguson* (1896) upheld racial segregation under the "separate but
 equal doctrine," and the majority opinion written by Justice Henry Brown included the
 following racist argument: "If one race be inferior to the other socially, the Constitution
 of the U.S. cannot put them upon the same plane."

3 A 1974 U.S. Supreme Court decision in the *Lau v. Nichols* (1974) case provided the necessary clarification and baseline for the act's implementation.

4 Supreme Court decisions in the 1960s and 1970s would eventually protect teachers and students against principal censorship activity (see *Tinker v Des Moines*, 1969).

5 During the Civil Rights Era, it would have been scandalous for progressive or moderate organizations to promote choice, standardized testing, or accountability, as activists of that period believed markets and testing maintained racial inequalities in public education. Arkansas Governor Bill Clinton was an active member of the NGA and co-chaired NGA school reform sessions.

6 Public charter schools are schools that are publicly funded but managed but with some degree of regulatory freedom and autonomy, although they are governed by an organization under a charter with a city, state government, or other group defined by state laws.

References

Abernathy, S. F. (2007). *No Child Left Behind and the public schools*. Ann Arbor: University of Michigan Press.

Bayor, R. H. (2000). *Race and the shaping of twentieth-century Atlanta*. Chapel Hill, NC: University of North Carolina Press.

Berggren, K. (2011, April 18). Historic St. Paul walkout. *Twin Cities Daily Planet*. Retrieved from https://www.tcdailyplanet.net/historic-st-paul-walkout/

Brown v. Board of Education, 347 U.S. 483 (1954).

Brown, J. (2012, May 1). Cost doesn't spell success for Colorado schools. *Denver Post*. Retrieved from http://www.denverpost.com/2012/02/18/cost-doesnt-spell-success-for-colorado-schools-using-consultants-to-improve-achievement/

Bureau of Justice Statistics. (2016). Correctional populations in the U.S., 2015. Washington, DC: Author. Retrieved from https://www.bjs.gov/content/pub/pdf/cpus15.pdf

Carnegie Forum on Education and the Economy. (1986). *A nation prepared: Teachers for the 21st century. The report of the Task Force on Teaching as a Profession*. New York: Author.

Center for Educational Policy Analysis. (2017). *Racial and ethnic achievement gaps*. Retrieved from http://cepa.stanford.edu/educational-opportunity-monitoring-project/achievement-gaps/race/#second

Center for Education Reform. (2015). *Choice and charter schools: Charter school law*. Retrieved from www.edreform.com/issues/choice-charter-schools/laws-legislation.

Chubb, J. E., & Moe, T. M. (1991). Politics, markets and America's schools. *British Journal of Sociology of Education, 12*(3), 381–396.

Clark, M. A., Gleason, P. M., Tuttle, C. C., & Silverberg, M. K. (2015). Do charter schools improve student achievement? *Educational Evaluation and Policy Analysis, 37*(4), 419–436.

Coleman, J. S., Campbell, E. Q., Hobson, C. J., McPartland, J., Mood, A. M., Weinfeld, F. D., & York, R. L. *Equality of educational opportunity*, 2 volumes. (OE-38001; Superintendent of Documents Catalog No. FS 5.238:38001). Washington, DC: U. S. Government Printing Office, 1966.

Cremin, L. A. (1957). *The republic and the school: Horace Mann on the education of free men*. New York: Teachers College Press.

Cubberley, E. P. (1909). *Changing conceptions of education*. Boston, MA: Houghton Mifflin.

DeMatthews, D. (2014). Looks like 10 miles of bad road: Cheating, gaming, mistrust, and an interim principal in an urban Texas high school. *Journal of Cases in Educational Leadership, 17*(4), 19–33.

Dittmer, J. (1994). *Local people: The struggle for civil rights in Mississippi*. Chicago, IL: University of Illinois Press.

Dred Scott v. Sandford. (1857). 60 U.S.393.

Frankenberg, E., Siegel-Hawley, G., Wang, J. (2010). *Choice without equity: Charter school segregation and the need for civil rights standards*. Los Angeles, CA: The Civil Rights Project.

Greenhouse, S., & Dillion, S. (2010, March 6). School shakeup is embraced by president. *New York Times*. Retrieved from http://www.nytimes.com/2010/03/07/education/07educ.html

Harry, B., & Klingner, J. (2014). *Why are so many minority students in special education?* New York: Teachers College Press.

Jencks, C. (1993). *Rethinking social policy: Race, poverty, and the underclass*. New York: HarperPerennial.

Katz, M. B. (1968). The emergency of bureaucracy in urban education: The Boston case, 1850–1884, part 1. *History of Education Quarterly, 8*, 157–160.

Klein, A. (April 14, 2015). State pitch changes as they seek NCLB waiver renewals. *Education Week*.

Labaree, D. F. (2012). *Someone has to fail*. Cambridge, MA: Harvard University Press.

Lau v. Nichols. (1974). 414 U.S. 563.

Mills v. Board of Education of District of Columbia, 348 F.Supp. 866 (D. D.C.1972).

National Commission on Excellence in Education (1983). *A Nation at Risk: The Imperative for Educational Reform*. Washington, DC: U.S. Department of Education.

NGA. (1987). *Results in education: 1987*. Washington, DC: National Governors' Association.

New York Times (1971, April 3). Michigan principal tarred, feathered. *New York Times*. Retrieved from http://www.nytimes.com/1971/04/03/archives/michigan-principal-tarred-feathered.html

Orr, M. (1999). *Black social capital: The politics of school reform in Baltimore, 1986–1998*. Lawrence, KS: University Press of Kansas

Patterson, J. T (2001). *Brown v. Board of Education: A civil rights milestone and its troubled legacy*. New York: Oxford University Press.

Plessy v. Ferguson, 163 U.S. 537 (1896).

Ravitch, D. (2016). *The death and life of the great American school system: How testing and choice are undermining education*. New York: Basic Books.

Reese, W. J. (2011). *America's public schools: From the common school to No Child Left Behind*. Baltimore, MD: Johns Hopkins University Press.

Rousmaniere, K. (2013). *The principal's office: A social history of the American school principal*. Albany, NY: SUNY Press.

Selden, S. (1999). *Inheriting shame: The story of eugenics and racism in America*. New York: Teachers College Press.

Tillman, L. C. (2004). (Un)intended consequences? The impact of the Brown v. Board of Education decision on the employment status of black educators. *Education and Urban Society, 36*(3), 280–303.

Tinker v. Des Moines School District, 393 U.S. 503 (1969).

Tyack, D. B. (1974). *The one best system: A history of American urban education*. Cambridge, MA: Harvard University Press.

Tyack, D. B., & Cuban, L. (1995). *Tinkering toward utopia*. Cambridge, MA: Harvard University Press.

Tyack, D. B., & Hansot, E. (1982). *Managers of virtue: Public school leadership in America, 1820–1980.* New York: Basic Books.

Vinovskis, M. A. (1999). *The road to Charlottesville: The 1989 education summit.* Alexandria, VA: National Education Goals Panel. Retrieved from: http://govinfo.library.unt.edu/negp/reports/negp30.pdf

Walker, V. S. (1996). *Their highest potential: An African American school community in the segregated South.* Chapel Hill, NC: University of North Carolina Press.

Wilson, W. J. (2012). *The truly disadvantaged: The inner city, the underclass, and public policy.* Chicago, IL: University of Chicago Press.

5

SCHOOLS AS SOCIAL INSTITUTIONS

I have argued that history has created low-opportunity communities and that mainstream school reform has been insufficient at providing meaningful life prospects to students of color in such communities. Top-down educational policy and school reform has fallen short of providing urban students of color with what they need to be successful partly because such reforms neglect the social nature of schooling. Schools are social institutions filled with people. Principals, teachers, custodians, counselors, crossing guards, psychologists, paraprofessionals, and other school personnel who work in schools, come from different backgrounds and neighborhoods. People enter schools with their cultural baggage. Rituals, routines, structures, and traditions within schools and districts influence their behavior, how they perceive students and families, how they prioritize different aspect of schooling, and how opportunities are distributed to students.

The primary task of this chapter is to lay the foundation for the idea that principals need to be conscious of the social aspects of their schools and rethink school reform in ways that value the diverse identities and assets of students and families. Such approaches to reform cannot be top-down or cookie-cutter approaches, but rather critical and locally relevant and responsive processes that build educator consciousness of the unequal power relations within schools, communities, and society. I begin with an introduction to sociology and some of the broad theoretical debates within the discipline that inform the ways sociologists view schools. Then I present more contemporary sociological work connected to education, inequality, and approaches to further understand the challenges confronting many urban schools and the potential avenues for transformation that validate and build upon the diverse assets of urban students of color and their families. Next, I examine social and cultural capital, critical pedagogy, and hidden curriculum. Finally, I conclude with recommendations for community engaged leadership and the creation of inclusive and socially just schools.

Schools as Social Institutions

Emile Durkheim, one of the academic founders of sociology, recognized that "social facts are things, that is, realities external to the individual" (Lemert, 2011, p. 6). Durkheim described sociology as the "science of institutions, their genesis and their functioning" (1895/2014 p. 45). Early sociologists argued that societies generate rituals and institutions to foster social cohesion and meaning. Schools have long been viewed as essential institutions for creating social cohesion, because they socialize children, teach values, and sort students based on ability. As the field of sociology matured, sociologists considered different ways of understanding societies and institutions. Functionalist, conflict, and interactionist theories emerged as three useful lenses for considering the role of schools in society and whether schools help reproduce or transform society. These theories have important implications for how principals might work to change schools in low-opportunity communities.

Functionalist Theory

Functionalism draws insights from the field of biology and embraces assumptions that the social world is objective and concrete. Just like in the human body, all organs have a function, all serve an interest, and all have an order. Functionalists study how different societal parts operate together to make society work or disintegrate. Each societal part has meaning only in relation to the whole and in performing specific functions in society. Shared values and consensus are assumed to be the normal state of society just as one might assume good health is the normal state of the body. Differences in income, status, and prestige (between individuals and across professions) are the fruits of labor and encouragement for talented people to work hard. These benefits are also society's way of guaranteeing specialized needs are met (Feinberg & Soltis, 2009).

From a functionalist perspective, schools are designed to promote: (a) role differentiation, to ensure different tasks will be performed in the future; (b) meritocracy, to create a narrative and incentive structure where differences in income and status are deserved and based on demand, personal sacrifice, innate ability, and achievement; and (c) democratic principles and shared values, to maintain social cohesion and a shared sense of purpose despite inequalities and emergent challenges within society. To perform these functions, schools teach social norms and skills, promote a favorable view of meritocracy, sort students into different tracks based on ability and effort, and provide knowledge and dispositions for life in a democracy. Universalism, or the uniform treatment of individuals as members of a specific group (e.g., a fourth-grade class, basketball team, incoming freshman), is fixed in students through their schooling and helps them accept that they should sacrifice their individuality in certain circumstances for the greater good of society.

Conflict Theory

Conflict theory rejects the notion that society is held together by consensus and shared values. Conflict theorists believe society consists of constant struggles between different groups for power and status. Consciously or not, dominant groups elevate their values and norms and assume their norms are universal. Non-dominant groups are misrepresented, disadvantaged, unrecognized, and trapped in lower social classes. Meritocracy is considered to be a myth to explain social and economic differences amongst groups within society. Differences are not a product of effort and ability, but rather the dominant groups' abilities and desires to impose their will on subordinate groups through force and manipulation.

The work of Karl Marx is foundational to conflict theories. According to Marxian theory, the way individuals think, feel, and live (their consciousness) are believed to be connected to their class and if they own capital (Marx & Engels, 1848/2002). Owners/employers exploit workers and narratives of a meritocracy disguise exploitation as fair and just. Arbitrary differences amongst workers (e.g., race/ethnicity, gender, sexual orientation, language, immigration status, religious beliefs) keep workers distracted and unable to recognize their common interests.

From this perspective, wealthy and powerful individuals operate and oversee public schools with the purpose of producing workers and smoothing over class tensions. Schools perpetuate existing social and economic relationships and help to integrate students into the workforce (Bowles & Gintis, 2011). Children are not trapped in poverty because of school quality, but rather the prevailing societal and economic inequalities do not allow for dramatic shifts in mobility. In part, schools reproduce the existing class order by reinforcing social norms. Schools reward poorer students for their docility and obedience and wealthier students for their initiative and assertiveness. Authority and control are organized hierarchically in schools. Principals oversee teachers and teachers supervise students who have limited control over what they learn or do. The power of principals and teachers produces docile and compliant students as well as misfits and rebels who are weeded out or placed in lower tracks. The influence of wealthy and powerful individuals over public schools does not necessarily suggest that dominant groups have firm control over schools or that there have not been times when marginalized groups have taken to the streets, protested, and forced issues of inequality into courts and legislatures (Bowles & Gintis, 2011).

Interactionist Theory

Interactionist theory is rooted in social psychology and examines how individuals are connected to and influenced by society. Many interactionists argue that functionalism and conflict theories are too focused on the "big picture" of society, and neglect the power of daily social interactions (Sadovnik, 2016). George Herbert Mead (1934/2015) influenced the development of symbolic interactionism, a sociological perspective where the self is socially constructed through ongoing interactions with individuals and different social forces and structures. Interactionist theories recognize not only the importance of structure and class but also human agency. Erving Goffman (1974) examined the micro-sociology of everyday life. He viewed speaking as a theatrical performance where a person attempts to control or guide impressions the other person will form. Goffman also contributed to labeling theory, which explains how self-identity and individual behavior is influenced by how it is described, classified, and associated by others. Labeling has implications on an individual's sense of self and contributes to the power of self-fulfilling prophecies and stereotypes.

Labeling theory calls attention to the formal and informal processes in which teacher expectations are driven not by facts or relevant information alone, but also by race, class, ethnicity, and gender. Teachers' pedagogical approaches and feelings of responsibility for student success are influenced by students' social class background, i.e., emphasizing compliance for low-income students of color (Anyon, 1980; Diamond, Randolph, & Spillane, 2004). When low-income students of color are labeled as problematic, unruly, or unintelligent, their definitions of self can be fundamentally changed with implications for their long-term academic success.

Functionalist, conflict, and interactionist theories provide useful models for considering the role of schools and whether they reproduce or help to transform society. Each highlight some of the inherent problems with public schools, especially when considering the overwhelming influence of business on education policy, school leadership, and reform. These sociological lenses suggest that low-income students of color may be marginalized and oppressed by routines, practices, and structures within schools as well as in the daily interactions with their teachers.

Sociological Insights into Urban School Reform

By the 1960s, sociological research and theory began to focus heavily on education and schools serving low-income students of color. Scholars identified many ways society influenced structures, practices, and individuals working in schools, which often translated into a schooling experience that did not value, meet the needs of, or empower urban, low-income students of color. While sociological research on education and urban schools underscores significant challenges, researchers have also found that public schools can improve student outcomes even in low-opportunity communities (Carlson & Cowen, 2015). I briefly review sociological research in education to highlight some of the challenges to urban schools and potential opportunities for improvement.

Educational Production Function

In the early 1960s, sociologists began investigating why schools in low-opportunity communities did not produce similar outcomes to majority White schools in suburban neighborhoods. Civil rights activists and parent groups pointed to funding inequalities and teacher quality. Sociologist James Coleman and a team of researchers were commissioned by the U.S. Department of Education to conduct a national investigation. Their 1966 report, *Equality of Educational Opportunity* (also known as the Coleman Report), was the first national, large-scale quantitative analysis to examine the importance of schools in student achievement and long-term outcomes. The report concluded: "It appears that variations in the facilities and curriculums of the schools account for relatively little variation in pupil achievement . . ." and that "a pupil's achievement is strongly related to the educational backgrounds and aspirations of the other students in the school" (Coleman et al., 1966, p. 22). One finding that significantly influenced policy was summarized in the report:

> One implication stands out above all: That schools bring little influence to bear on a child's achievement that is independent of his background and general social context; and that this very lack of independent effect means that the inequalities imposed on children by their home, neighborhood, and peer environment are carried along to become the inequalities with which they confront adult life at the end of school.
>
> *p. 325*

Some individuals and policymakers purposefully or accidentally misinterpreted the report's findings to support an argument that school funding did not matter. In 1986, Stanford economist Eric Hanushek claimed money did not matter when it came to improving outcomes. Hanushek (1986) concluded, "There appears to be no strong or systematic relationship between school expenditures and student performance" (p. 1162). His later work suggested:

- schools spend money inefficiently, and additional funding would not improve outcomes;
- how money is spent matters more than how much money is spent;
- schools with less money are positioned to make smarter spending decisions.

Hanushek's conclusions informed state and federal courts considering challenges to state school finance systems. As recent as 2017, Hanushek testified in a school finance case in New Mexico claiming research "gives us little reason to be confident that just putting money into the system will have any real impact . . . The notion that spending more money is going to bring about different results is ill-placed and ill-advised" (Nott, 2017).

Rigorous sociological investigations into Hanushek's work arrived at alternative conclusions. Teachers' overall wages affect the quality of those who enter the teaching profession and whether they stay on the job (Guarino, Santibanez, & Daley, 2006). In a study of 89 elementary schools in one urban school district, researchers found considerable funding disparities within the district based on patterns of racial and class stratification with clear consequences for student achievement (Condron & Roscigno, 2003). Money matters because reforms that positively impact achievement cost money, such as class size reductions and increased teacher compensation (Baker, 2016). Moreover, when urban schools lack the money to adapt the curriculum to the needs of students and provide high-quality professional development, students of color in low-opportunity communities continue to struggle and lack access to meaningful opportunities that can enable social mobility.

Organizational Context

Social structures within schools are important and relate to the willingness of educators to work together. Teacher-oriented and consistent professional development has been found to improve teacher practice and increase student achievement in urban schools (Johnson & Fargo, 2010). Relatedly, productive and positive relationships between teachers, principals, families, and other external stakeholders have been found to improve organizational processes that support student achievement (Leana & Pil, 2006). Urban schools that close achievement gaps and increase student achievement often develop:

- meaningful, tailored, and high-quality professional development with opportunities for teachers to build relationships, share knowledge and resources, and recognize and access the talents of other teachers (Newmann, King, & Youngs, 2000);
- a professional community and culture that promotes a willingness to engage in collective inquiry and reflection to address pressing, emerging, and evolving challenges (Louis & Marks, 1998; Vescio, Ross, & Adams, 2008);
- a professional environment where teachers receive continuous opportunities for coaching and additional time to implement new strategies previously acquired in professional development sessions (Blank, 2013; Kraft & Papay, 2014);
- professional development and planning opportunities where teachers discuss and plan schoolwide change and focus on achieving goals and continuous improvement (Gonzales & Lambert, 2014);
- interdisciplinary teams with a broad range of expertise and networks to develop structures, supports, and interventions for students with unique academic, mental, and physical health needs (Griffin & Farris, 2010)

Schools organized as communities have also been found to improve student achievement in schools by fostering the behaviors and conditions that promote shared goals, values, and meaningful and continuous social interactions amongst teachers (Bryk, Cambrun, & Louis, 1999; Dee, Henkin, & Singleton, 2006). Some urban schools are designed as "community schools" where shared goals, values, and school resources (including principals, teachers and staff) are used to address out-of-school factors that shape low-opportunity communities and influence student achievement and other educational outcomes (Green & Gooden, 2014). However, such efforts and organizational conditions require time, staff stability, and open-minded and well-trained teachers and principals. When schools have less experienced teachers and principals they may struggle to foster the behavior and conditions that promote student achievement. Rather than support students, organizational conditions associated with high rates of turnover can be harmful, especially when teachers resist change or cause change-oriented teachers to be moderates or disengaged with collaborative efforts.

Social Capital

Not all resources within schools are financial or human resources. Social capital is related to participation in networks that provide additional benefits. Coleman (1988) presented a theory of social capital suggesting individuals possess skills that are not wholly tangible, but rather a set of relationships and trust that connect them to other members of a group that has actual or potential resources. Pierre Bourdieu (1985) defined social capital as "the aggregate of the actual and potential resources which are linked to possession of a durable network of more or less institutionalized relationship of mutual acquaintance and recognition" (p. 248). Relationships and networks are converted into economic capital and passed on through generations. The volume of social capital possessed by an individual is related to the size of their network and how they mobilize it based on situational needs. Putnam (1993) similarly defined social capital as "features of social organization, such as networks, norms, and trust, that facilitate coordination and cooperation for mutual benefit" (p. 35). Putnam recognized two forms of social capital: bonding and bridging.

- Bonding social capital exists within homogeneous groups such as a neighborhood where immigrant families are from the same country and maintain a network tied to shared experiences.
- Bridging social capital exists across diverse groups such as parents and teachers who may have different backgrounds but are connected through norms of obligation and reciprocity related to a mutual interest in their children/students.

Schools can be viewed as "builders (or destroyers) of social capital" (Warner, 1999, p. 384) because they are linked to neighborhoods, families, and students.

However, schools do not always build trusting relationships with families and students or mutually beneficial networks. When parents and schools are meaningfully connected, students benefit via improved grade point averages (Gutman & Midgley, 2000), increased reading and mathematics achievement (Wilder, 2014), and lower truancy and dropout rates (Epstein & Sheldon, 2002; McNeal, 1999). These positive findings have been demonstrated in large urban districts and schools (Goddard, Tschannen-Moran, & Hoy, 2001; Monkman, Ronald, & Theramene, 2005). Unfortunately, Black and Latina/o families sometimes feel threatened by teachers and principals based on past experiences.

One should not forget how schools have been racially segregated and how a historically White teaching force has at times devalued Black and Latina/o students. Families might feel a sense of powerlessness based on their level of educational attainment or knowledge of school terminology that can be loaded with jargon (Allen & White-Smith, 2017; Clark, 2015; Noguera, 2001). Some of the pressing social issues in low-opportunity communities (e.g., public health issues, lack of housing, community violence) might also contribute to feelings of isolation and despair that solidify barriers to family–school relationships and trust. However, schools can (re)build relationships, validate families, and foster higher levels of student achievement by:

- collaborating with families to identify indigenous assets within the neighborhood;
- facilitating problem-posing and problem-solving activities to understand and address neighborhood problems that interfere with student success;
- providing a venue for parents to build relationships with each other and engage in educational decision-making;
- connecting families with resources and services within the neighborhood or beyond the neighborhood (DeMatthews, 2016, forthcoming 2018).

Cultural Capital

Cultural experiences in a child's home and neighborhood influence achievement. All children have access to cultural resources (knowledge, practices, and artifacts). However, schools are not neutral and prefer specific forms of cultural capital. Bourdieu (1986) suggested that middle- and upper-class families preserve their social privileges through formal education and the acquisition of cultural capital, which includes tastes in food, culture, literature, movies, makeup, and art. Since upper-class families have greater financial resources, their children are more likely to visit museums, attend cultural music performances, travel out-of-state and abroad, gain fluency in a foreign language, learn a musical instrument, and read well-regarded literature. Students with privileged cultural experiences can transform experiences into cultural capital that enable school success (Bourdieu, 1986).

Teachers and principals often act as "cultural gatekeepers" who use dominant linguistic and dress code as signals of student intellect (Carter, 2003). Consequently, schools can view the cultural capital of students from low-opportunity communities of color through a deficit lens. Students may take on these lower expectations and work to oppress themselves or give up (Bourdieu & Passeron, 1990). Race cannot be ignored in discussions about cultural capital. Race becomes an increasingly rigid identity construct as children learn about and experience historical, cultural, and ideological dimensions of race membership in society, in their neighborhoods, and in schools (Tatum, 2010).

Peer groups help to shape student identity, partly because they establish norms and sanctions for behavior while schools help to reinforce racial norms. Dominant culture, racial discrimination, and limited socioeconomic prospects further compel some students of color to lower their expectations and aspirations around schooling and achievement (Ogbu, 1974). In a study of a racially segregated low-income neighborhood in Washington, DC, Black students defined achievement-oriented behaviors as "acting White" and therefore were resistant to getting good grades (Fordham & Ogbu, 1986). Neighborhood "folk theories" also reinforced anti-achievement behaviors. Students of color may be exposed to folk theories which suggest hard work will never reap equal rewards with Whites. When students accept these theories as truth, they are more likely to participate in self-defeating behaviors (Ogbu, 1987).

While dominant cultural capital is essential to understanding educational inequalities, the individual agency and actions of principals, teachers, students, and families cannot be overshadowed. As Noguera (2016) noted:

> The choices made by an individual may be shaped by both the available opportunities and the norms present within the cultural milieu in which they are situated. However, culture is not static and individual responses to their environment cannot be easily predicted.
>
> *p. 365*

Urban students of color are powerful, intuitive, and resilient. They actively and passively resist social and cultural influences within their neighborhoods and schools. They challenge structural forces and inequality and frequently play a role in changing their schools and the world around them (Pazey & DeMatthews, 2016).

Non-dominant forms of cultural capital increase Black and Latina/o students' sense of self-worth in the face of racism. When they sense teachers view them through deficit lenses they can rely on their unique forms of cultural capital to persist and succeed (Carter, 2006). In a study focused on the schooling experiences of eight high-achieving Black girls, researchers found that some teachers stereotyped and scapegoated the girls (Archer-Banks & Behar-Horenstein, 2012). One Black girl described an incident, "One of our teachers told us toward the beginning of the semester that many of us would get pregnant before the semester was over . . . They don't talk to the White girls like that" (p. 209). Other students described other forms of prejudice toward Black girls, yet these girls survived and thrived, which is evidence of their strength and the valuable capital they possess. Thus, schools serving low-income students of color can play an important role in positively influencing and shaping the attitudes and behaviors of their students by:

- recognizing and valuing non-dominant student identity and culture;
- helping students understand the structural and cultural forces within schools, neighborhoods, and society;
- providing a curriculum that allows students to investigate, question, and critically examine how social and cultural forces shape their experiences and belief systems;
- changing school culture and teaching practices in ways that promote a positive self-image for Black and Latina/o students and counter potential folk theories they encounter;
- supporting students who are living and navigating an unequal and unjust society.

These approaches to school improvement differ from most mainstream reforms and shift emphasis away from testing and accountability, and toward empowering students and helping them develop a positive self-identity and understanding of the world.

Critical Theory

Critical theory is a philosophical approach that emerged from the Frankfurt School in Germany during the 1930s. The questions pursued by the School and its scholars (e.g., Theodore Adorno, Max Horkheimer, Herbert Marcuse) reflect the historical context of the time. Fascism, Nazism, and a new consumeristic society were emerging. New technologies and bureaucratic administration increasingly dominated life. Cultural institutions such as schools, workplaces, and mass media were changing the way people thought (Adorno & Horkheimer, 1972). Reasoning was becoming devalued, and people were directed by institutions to accept inequalities as part of progress and as a logical outcome of a meritocratic system. One of many areas of focus for the School was a critique of positivism (simply put, the idea that all authentic knowledge can be verified by the scientific method). Positivistic thought was viewed as a set of "mechanisms of ideological control that permeate the consciousness and practices of advanced capitalist societies" (Giroux, 1983, p. 13). From a positivist perspective, outcomes and facts are derived from the scientific method, quantifiable observations, and mathematical structures.

Adorno (2000) believed positivism ignored history and how history informs truth. Horkheimer (1975) claimed positivism fostered a worldview that did not allow for transformative possibilities. Positivism also separated important questions of ethics from inquiry. Scientific neutrality created a fetishism with facts that replaced reason, taking sides, and striving for a better world. In response to the flaws of positivism, Marcuse (1960) called for a connection between thought and action: "For to comprehend reality means to comprehend what things really are, and this in turn means rejecting their mere factuality" (p. xx). Thus, critical theories explore "the interconnections between the economic life of society, the psychic development of the individual, and transformations in the realm of culture" (Horkheimer, 1975, p. 43). Today, many critical theorists see high-stakes accountability and data-driven decision-making in schools as highly problematic, partly because it creates inaccurate labels that reinforce racial and class-based inequality. Many urban schools were deemed failing and hopeless based on test scores alone, which, in turn, rejected any recognition of the strengths and assets of low-performing schools and the students, principals, and educators within them.

The critical perspective takes the position that reality is shaped by social, economic, political, cultural, and ethnic considerations that have be developed over time and are now falsely believed to be real (Guba & Lincoln, 1994). Paulo Freire (1972/2007) was a Brazilian educator and philosopher whose book *Pedagogy of the Oppressed* provided a foundation for critical pedagogy, which sought to uncover, challenge, and address these hardened societal structures. Freire's work, which used Marxian language and critical theory, described how oppression is justified and reproduced through a mutual process between the oppressed and the oppressor. He rejected the notion of "banking" where teachers deposit static knowledge into the minds of students and instead argued for an "authentic" approach to teaching that fostered reflection and action. Freire's notion of "conscientização" underscored the need of the oppressed to learn about the social, political, and economic contradictions that affect their lives. He noted, "It is only when the oppressed find the oppressor out and become involved in the organized struggle for their liberation can they begin to believe in themselves" (p. 65). For Freire, literacy and critical pedagogy were not about preparing people for tests, careers, or political indoctrination. Instead, literacy and critical pedagogy helped foster a self-managed life where one could engage in critical reflection, become aware of the forces that rule and shape their lives and consciousness, and help rearrange the conditions for a better life and world. Care, love, and solidarity were core to Freire's work and beliefs about education.

Henry Giroux (1983), a contemporary of Freire, conceptualized critical pedagogy as the ways of engaging students with the social and political task of resistance, empowerment, and democratization. From this position, teachers and principals reject the idea that teaching is just a method, skill, or practice devoid of values, norms, and power. Memorizing facts and mastering meaningless skills for a test is "dead knowledge." Critical pedagogy raises important questions about the relationship between schooling and social change. Teaching is a moral and political act where teachers and students learn how to construct knowledge together. Students are allowed "to engage in a culture of questioning, to raise and address urgent, disturbing questions about the society in which they live, and to define in part the questions that can be asked and the disciplinary borders that can be crossed" (Giroux, 2013, p. 358).

Critical pedagogy "must address the specificities of the experiences, problems, languages, and histories that communities rely upon to construct a narrative of collective identity and possible transformation" (McLaren & Giroux, 1990, p. 263). It cannot ignore the importance of place and the linkages between environment, culture, and education (Gruenewald, 2003), as much of the mainstream school reform does. In low-opportunity communities, teaching must be linked to Black and Latina/o urban struggles. Schools should "establish the pedagogical conditions that enable blacks [and Latina/os] in the city to critically interpret how dominant definitions and uses of urban space regulate and control how they organize their identity around territory, and the consequences of this for black [and Latina/o] urban resistance" (Haymes, 1995, p. 114).

Critical race theory (CRT) arose as a critique of racism in the law and was initially developed through the legal scholarship (Bell, 1992; Crenshaw, 1991; Delgado, 1989). CRT provides a valuable framework to understand and uncover the ways racism operates in schools and through teaching and school leadership (DeMatthews, 2016; Ladson-Billings & Tate, 1995; Parker & McKinney, 2015; Yosso, 2005). A salient goal of CRT is to uncover racism and construct new modes of understanding that promote equity. The normality of racism allows principals and teachers to believe they are acting fairly and consistently, despite evidence that points to current and historic patterns of race-based inequality. Thus, CRT provides an opportunity to challenge claims of race neutrality, objectivity, and the ideas that camouflage self-interest, power, and privilege imbued in the master narratives of dominant groups (Solórzano & Yosso, 2002). Moreover, CRT provides a reason to challenge, critique, and evaluate the unquestioned faith in traditional educational policies, practices, and belief systems. Such efforts provide important opportunities for principals, teachers, and families to think through the challenges confronting students from diverse backgrounds and respond in ways that value student and family participation and the creation of safe, validating, and caring school spaces (Carey, Yee, & DeMatthews, 2018).

Critical theory, critical pedagogy, and CRT have important implications for principals working in low-opportunity communities of color. Through leadership, principals can prepare their schools to:

- Acknowledge that education is always political, whether they are critical pedagogues or narrowly adhere to state and national standards. In response, they should become "transformative intellectuals" (Giroux, 1988) and "cultural workers" (Freire, 1972/2007).

- Help students evaluate, reflect, and act on their own situations.
- Provide opportunities for students to connect with, inquire about, and love their neighborhoods and fellow neighbors so they can tell their own stories about their world (DeMatthews & Izquierdo, 2016).
- Build solidarity between students and neighborhoods for racial, economic, environmental, and cultural justice.
- Honor a student's developmental readiness to learn about critical issues within society and participate in social action.
- Collaborate with families and students to learn about the neighborhood, how their neighborhood has been disrupted and injured, and help families and students live in a place that has been disrupted and injured (Gruenewald, 2003).
- Include projects that embrace neighborhoods, such as developing community gardens and participating in community development and service work.

A Hidden Curriculum

Most of the sociological contributions described above are related to curriculum or how teachers interact with students and families. Almost 50 years ago, a "hidden curriculum" was described as "the norms and values that are implicitly, but effectively, taught in schools that are not usually talked about in teachers' statements or end goals" (Jackson, 1968 as cited in Apple, 2013, p. 27). The "hidden curriculum" includes "the inculcation of values, political socialization, training in obedience and docility, the perpetuation of class structure—functions that may be characterized generally as social control" (Vallance, 1973–1974, p. 5). Ideological messages are embedded within lessons driven by these standards, in mainstream reforms, and in the social relations between principals, teachers, and students. Almost 40 years ago, Jean Anyon (1980) illustrated differences in teacher–student interactions and curricula when she studied five classrooms in different communities (two working class, one middle class, one upper middle class, and one capitalist/elite class). In working class schools, teachers emphasized rote behavior, provided little opportunity for decision-making or choice, rarely explained why work was assigned, and rigidly forced students to adhere to rules. In affluent schools, rules were limited, and teachers emphasized individuality and the notion that not everyone's work should look the same. Students were asked to interpret and make sense of reality, teachers prompted students to think and reflect on their answers, and the principal wanted teachers to be creative.

Unfortunately, Anyon's study remains relevant in 2018. Teachers often utilize pre-scripted curriculum rather than planning themselves and relying on their judgments. Textbook companies and education businesses market curriculum and other related products for raising student test scores on state assessments, including those aligned to the Common Core State Standards (CCSS). Many of these schools who opt for such "products" struggle retaining principals and teachers, which translate into a lack of adequate support and professional development for teachers in desperate need. Some schools hire from alternative teacher education programs (e.g., Teach for America) because of high rates of teacher turnover. Consequently, teachers can have little connection or historical knowledge of their students and the neighborhoods in which they work. Many teachers have limited experience working with students from impoverished backgrounds (Darling-Hammond, 2010) or have their own biases and cultural baggage. The scripting of lessons and a focus on high-stakes testing robs students of color of the opportunity to develop their creativity or to be exposed to a sophisticated and complex curriculum (Milner, 2014). As students mature, they are at a disadvantage when the curriculum in middle school and high school becomes more complex. They become frustrated, as do their teachers. Crocco and Costigan (2007) summarized the way narrow curriculum and high-stakes accountability work against urban schools and students in New York City:

> Under the curricular and pedagogical impositions of scripted lessons and mandated curriculum, patterns associated nationwide with high-stakes test, the No Child Left Behind Act of 2001, and the phenomenon known as the "narrowing of curriculum," new teachers in New York City find their personal and professional identity thwarted, creativity and autonomy undermined, and ability to forge relationships with students diminished—all critical factors in their expressed job satisfaction.
>
> *p. 512*

The challenges within schools and society necessitate the preparation of racially competent principals and teachers with an "awareness of race, the possibility of their own racism and the racism of others, and the significance of these perceptions in the teaching and learning process" (Teel & Obidah, 2008, p. 4). Principals and teachers need class-consciousness, which means having "an understanding of how poverty does (and does not) impact students, a nuanced reading of how race and poverty overlap (and do not), and a keen eye to how stereotypes about poverty bias our interactions with poor children" (Ullucci & Howard, 2014, p. 174). Problematic myths also need to be rejected, such as the:

- Bootstraps Myth: any student can pull themselves out of poverty in this country and reach their economic goals.
- Individual Faults Myth: Those in poverty are lazy or made poor choices.
- Educability Myth: Students from low-income families and low-opportunity communities are not smart or school ready, partly because families don't care about their children.
- Culture of Poverty Myth: Students in low-income communities exhibit problematic behaviors and values that limit their ability to be successful (Ullucci & Howard, 2014).

Schools cannot ignore poverty and how it operates in the lives of students nor can they ignore race or accept color-blindness as a way of thinking. The hidden curriculum must be revealed, interrogated, challenged, and rejected. All schools should be locally and culturally relevant and explore how students' lives are impacted by racial and economic conditions within society. Schools must not engage in "othering" students in low-opportunity communities of color and reject the notion that these students live in a monolithic culture of poverty that is different from the rest of the world. When principals and teachers fail to think critically about poverty and race, they likely participate in maintaining the injustices present in schools and society. Recognizing that a hidden curriculum does exist requires all educators to continually be reflective about themselves, how they interact with students, and how they utilize curriculum to educate, empower, and care for students. Standards, high-stakes accountability, testing, and other top-down policies cannot be prioritized over the most important, empowering, transformative, affirming, relevant, and caring elements of curriculum and teaching.

Takeaways for Principals

The primary task of this chapter was to lay the foundation for the idea that principals and teachers need to be conscious of the social aspects of their schools and rethink school reform in ways that validate and enhance the self-identity of their students. I walked a tenuous line showing how schools can reinforce inequalities or work to address inequalities. No school is perfect, but schools can make a difference by learning from and with their students and families and not writing them off because of their backgrounds and relegating them to the weakest, narrowest, and most useless curriculum. Schools can make a difference when they recognize the significant power of race, class, poverty, and inequality in society and how these variables can manifest in daily social interactions, in curriculum, and school organizational processes.

To chart a new direction, principals need to lead courageously despite the weight of the status quo. A sociological lens enables principals to recognize that school reform cannot only be focused on improving teacher capacity to provide instruction aligned to standards and state-mandated assessments without also recognizing, rejecting, and replacing the hidden curriculum with a locally and culturally relevant one. The status-quo approach is insensitive and serves little purpose in students' lives. Each interaction between the student and the school is important and has implications for the future. With each interaction, an opportunity exists to build trust, affirm a student's identity, demonstrate care and kindness, and create an authentic desire to learn about the world to transform it.

References

Adorno, T. (2000). *Introduction to sociology*. Stanford, CA: Stanford University Press.
Adorno, T. W., & Horkheimer, M. (1972). *Dialectic of enlightenment*. New York: Seabury Press.

Allen, Q., & White-Smith, K. (2017). "That's why I say stay in school": Black mothers' parental involvement, cultural wealth, and exclusion in their son's schooling. *Urban Education*. Retrieved from https://doi.org/10.1177/0042085917714516

Anyon, J. (1980). Social class and the hidden curriculum of work. *Journal of Education, 162*(1), 67–92.

Apple, M. (2013). *Can education change society?* New York: Routledge.

Archer-Banks, D., & Behar-Horenstein, L. (2012). Ogbu revisited: Unpacking high-achievement African American girls' high school experiences. *Urban Education, 47*, 198–123.

Baker, B. D. (2016). *Does money matter in education?* Washington, DC: Albert Shanker Institute. Retrieved from http://www.shankerinstitute.org/sites/shanker/files/money matters_edition2.pdf

Bell, D. (1992). Racial realism. *Connecticut Law Review, 24*(2), 363–379.

Blank, R. K. (2013). What research tells us: Common characteristics of professional learning that leads to student achievement. *Journal of Staff Development, 34*(1), 50–53.

Bourdieu, P. (1986). The forms of capital. In J. G. Richardson (Ed.), *Handbook of theory and research for the sociology of education* (pp. 241–258). New York: Greenwood.

Bourdieu, P., & Passeron, J. C. (2000). *Reproduction in education, society, and culture.* London: Sage.

Bowles, S., & Gintis, H. (2011). *Schooling in capitalist America: Educational reform and the contradictions of economic life.* New York: Haymarket Books.

Bryk, A., Camburn, E., & Louis, K. S. (1999). Professional community in Chicago elementary schools: Facilitating factors and organizational consequences. *Educational Administration Quarterly, 35*(5), 751–781.

Carey, R. L., Yee, L. S., & DeMatthews, D. E. (2018). Power, penalty, and critical praxis: Employing intersectionality in educator practices to achieve school equity. *Educational Forum, 82*(1), 111–130.

Carlson, D., & Cowen, J. M. (2015). Student neighborhoods, schools, and test score growth: Evidence from Milwaukee, Wisconsin. *Sociology of Education, 88*(1), 38–55.

Carter, P. L. (2003). " Black" cultural capital, status positioning, and schooling conflicts for low-income African American youth. *Social Problems, 50*(1), 136–155.

Carter, P. L. (2006). Straddling boundaries: Identity, culture, and school. *Sociology of Education, 79*(4), 304–328.

Clark, R. M. (2015). *Family life and school achievement: Why poor black children succeed or fail.* Chicago, IL: University of Chicago Press.

Coleman, J. S. (1988). Social capital in the creation of human capital. *American Journal of Sociology, 94*, S95–S120.

Coleman, J.S., Campbell, E. Q., Hobson, C. F., McPartland, A. M., Mood, A. M., Weinfeld, F. D., & York, R. L. (1966). *Equality of educational opportunity.* Washington, DC: U.S. Office of Education.

Condron, D. J., & Roscigno, V. J. (2003). Disparities within: Unequal spending and achievement in an urban school district. *Sociology of Education, 76*(1), 18–36.

Crenshaw, K. (1991). Mapping the margins: Intersectionality, identity politics, and violence against women of color. *Stanford Law Review, 43*, 1241–1299.

Crocco, M. S., & Costigan, A. T. (2007). The narrowing of curriculum and pedagogy in the age of accountability: Urban educators speak out. *Urban Education, 42*, 512–535.

Darling-Hammond, L. (2010). *The flat world and education: How America's commitment to equity will determine our future.* New York: Teachers College Press.

Dee, J. R., Henkin, A. B., & Singleton, C. A. (2006). Organizational commitment of teachers in urban schools: Examining the effects of team structures. *Urban Education, 41*(6), 603–627.

Delgado, R. (1989). Storytelling for oppositionists and others: A plea for narrative. *Michigan Law Review, 87*(8), 2411–2441.

DeMatthews, D. E. (2016). Effective leadership is not enough: Critical approaches to closing the racial discipline gap. *The Clearing House: A Journal of Educational Strategies, Issues and Ideas, 89*(1), 7–13.

DeMatthews, D. E. (forthcoming 2018). School leadership, social capital, and community engagement: A case study of an elementary school in Ciudad Juarez, Mexico. *School Community Journal.*

DeMatthews, D. E., & Izquierdo, E. (2016). School leadership for Latina/o bilingual children: A social justice leadership approach. *Educational Forum, 80*(3), 278–293.

Diamond, J. B., Randolph, A., & Spillane, J. P. (2004). Teachers' expectations and sense of responsibility for student learning: The importance of race, class, and organizational habitus. *Anthropology & Education Quarterly, 35*(1), 75–98.

Durkheim, E. (1895/2014). *The rules of sociological method: And selected texts on sociology and its method.* New York: Simon and Schuster.

Epstein, J. L., & Sheldon, S. B. (2002). Present and accounted for: Improving student attendance through family and community involvement. *Journal of Educational Research, 95*(5), 308–318.

Feinberg, W., & Soltis, J. F. (2009). *School and society.* New York: Teachers College Press.

Freire, P. (1972/2007). *Pedagogy of the oppressed.* New York: Continuum.

Fordham, S., & Ogbu, J. U. (1986). Black students' school success: Coping with the "burden of 'acting white.'" *Urban Review, 18*(3), 176–206.

Giroux, H. A. (1983). *Theory and resistance in education: A pedagogy for the opposition.* South Hadley, MA: Bergin & Garvey.

Giroux, H. A. (1988). *Teachers as intellectuals: Toward a critical pedagogy of learning.* Westport, CT: Bergin & Garvey.

Goddard, R. D., Tschannen-Moran, M., & Hoy, W. K. (2001). A multilevel examination of the distribution and effects of teacher trust in students and parents in urban elementary schools. *The Elementary School Journal, 102*(1), 3–17.

Goffman, E. (1974). *Frame analysis: An essay on the organization of experience.* Cambridge, MA: Harvard University Press.

Gonzales, S., & Lambert, L. (2014). Teacher leadership in professional development schools: Emerging conceptions, identities, and practices. *Journal of School Leadership, 11*(1), 6–24.

Green, T. L., & Gooden, M. A. (2014). Transforming out-of-school challenges into opportunities: Community schools reform in the urban Midwest. *Urban Education, 49*(8), 930–954.

Griffin, D., & Farris, A. (2010). School counselors and collaboration: Finding resources through community asset mapping. *Professional School Counseling, 13*(5), 248–256.

Gruenewald, D. A. (2003). The best of both worlds: A critical pedagogy of place. *Educational Researcher, 32*(4), 3–12.

Guarino, C. M., Santibanez, L., & Daley, G. A. (2006). Teacher recruitment and retention: A review of the recent empirical literature. *Review of Educational Research, 76*(2), 173–208.

Guba, E., & Lincoln, Y. (1994). Competing paradigms in qualitative research. In N. Denzin & Y. Lincoln (Eds.), *Handbook of qualitative research* (pp. 105–117). Thousand Oaks, CA: Sage.

Gutman, L. M., & Midgley, C. (2000). The role of protective factors in supporting the academic achievement of poor African American students during the middle school transition. *Journal of Youth and Adolescence, 29*(2), 223–249.

Hanushek, E. A. (1986). The economics of schooling: Production and efficiency in public schools. *Journal of Economic Literature, 24*(3), 1141–1177.

Haymes, S. N. (1995). *Race, culture, and the city: A pedagogy for Black urban struggle.* Albany, NY: SUNY Press.

Horkheimer, M. (1975). *Critical theory: Selected essays.* New York, NY: Continuum Publishing.

Johnson, C. C., & Fargo, J. D. (2010). Urban school reform enabled by transformative professional development: Impact on teacher change and student learning of science. *Urban Education, 45*(1), 4–29.

Kraft, M. A., & Papay, J. P. (2014). Can professional environments in schools promote teacher development? Explaining heterogeneity in returns to teaching experience. *Educational Evaluation and Policy Analysis, 36*(4), 476–500.

Ladson-Billings, G., & Tate, W. F. (1995). Toward a critical race theory of education. *Teachers College Record, 97*(1), 47–68.

Leana, C. R., & Pil, F. K. (2006). Social capital and organizational performance: Evidence from urban public schools. *Organization Science, 17*(3), 353–366.

Lemert, C. (2011). *Social things: An introduction to the sociological life.* Lanham, MD: Rowman & Littlefield .

Louis, K. S., & Marks, H. M. (1998). Does professional community affect the classroom? Teachers' work and student experiences in restructuring schools. *American Journal of Education, 106*(4), 532–575.

Marcuse, H. (1960). *Reason and revolution.* Boston, MA: Beacon Press.

Marx, K., & Engels, F. (1848/2002). *The communist manifesto.* New York: Penguin

McLaren, P. L., & Giroux, H. A. (1990). Critical pedagogy and rural education: A challenge from Poland. *Peabody Journal of Education, 67*(4), 154–165.

McNeal Jr., R. B. (1999). Parental involvement as social capital: Differential effectiveness on science achievement, truancy, and dropping out. *Social Forces, 78*(1), 117–144.

Mead, G. H. (1934/2015). *Mind, self, and society.* Chicago, IL: University of Chicago Press.

Milner IV, H. R. (2014). Scripted and narrowed curriculum reform in urban schools. *Urban Education, 49*(7), 743–749.

Monkman, K., Ronald, M., & Théramène, F. D. (2005). Social and cultural capital in an urban Latino school community. *Urban Education, 40*(1), 4–33.

Newmann, F. M., King, M. B., & Youngs, P. (2000). Professional development that addresses school capacity: Lessons from urban elementary schools. *American Journal of Education, 108*(4), 259–299.

Noguera, P. A. (2001). Transforming urban schools through investments in the social capital of parents. *Psychology, 16,* 725–50.

Noguera, P. A. (2016). The trouble with black boys: The role and influence of environmental and cultural factors on the academic performance of African American males. In A. R. Sadovnik & R. W. Coughlan (Eds.), *Sociology of education: A critical reader* (3rd ed.) (pp. 3–22). New York: Routledge.

Nott, R. (2017, August 3). More money doesn't guarantee better education, expert testifies. *The New Mexican.* Retrieved from http://www.santafenewmexican.com/news/ education/more-money-doesn-t-guarantee-better-education-expert-testifies/article_ be841c28-1ee0-51c5-ac58-0afc61cde68d.html

Ogbu, J. U. (1974). *The next generation: An ethnography of education in an urban neighborhood.* New York: Academic Press.

Ogbu, J. U. (1987). Variability in minority school performance: A problem in search of an explanation. *Anthropology & Education Quarterly, 18*(4), 312–334.

Parker, L., & McKinney, A. E. (2015). Social justice leadership and critical race theory in the Mormon culture region. *Urban Education.* DOI: 0042085915618715.

Pazey, B., & DeMatthews, D. E. (2016). The quest for identity, stability, recognition and voice within a turnaround urban high school: An account of students with dis/Abilities seeking to break loose from accountability reform. *Urban Education.* DOI: 10.1177/0042085916666930

Putnam, R. D. (1993). The prosperous community. *The American Prospect, 4*(13), 35–42.

Sadovnik, A. R. (2016). Theory and research in the sociology of education. In A. R. Sadovnik & R. W. Coughlan (Eds.), *Sociology of education: A critical reader* (3rd ed.) (pp. 3–22). New York: Routledge.

Solórzano, D. G., & Yosso, T. J. (2002). Critical race methodology: Counter-storytelling as an analytical framework for education research. *Qualitative inquiry, 8*(1), 23–44.

Tatum, B. D. (2010). *Why are all the Black kids sitting together in the cafeteria? And other conversations about race.* New York: Basic Books.

Teel, K. M., & Obidah, J. E. (Eds.). (2008). *Building racial and cultural competence in the classroom: Strategies from urban educators.* New York: Teachers College Press.

Ullucci, K., & Howard, T. (2015). Pathologizing the poor: Implications for preparing teachers to work in high-poverty schools. *Urban Education, 50*(2), 170–193.

Vallance, E. (1973–1974). Hiding the hidden curriculum: An interpretation of the language of justification in nineteenth-century educational reform. *Curriculum Theory Network, 4*(1), 5–22.

Vescio, V., Ross, D., & Adams, A. (2008). A review of research on the impact of professional learning communities on teaching practice and student learning. *Teaching and Teacher Education, 24*(1), 80–91.

Warner, M. (1999). Social capital construction and the role of the local state. *Rural sociology, 64*(3), 373–393.

Wilder, S. (2014). Effects of parental involvement on academic achievement: A meta-synthesis. *Educational Review, 66*(3), 377–397.

Yosso, T. (2005). Whose culture has capital? A critical race theory discussion of community cultural wealth. *Race Ethnicity and Education, 8,* 69–91.

PART II

Toward a Critical and Community Engaged Leadership

6

THE SCIENCE OF EDUCATIONAL ADMINISTRATION

Given the challenges within many urban schools described thus far, it is hard to imagine any one set of administrative and leadership theories, perspectives, or practices could be sufficient to lead a school or fully prepare a principal. Unfortunately, in the field of educational administration and leadership, a set of dominant theories, perspectives, and practices have been privileged and, intentionally or not, reflect a hidden, vested interest in reinforcing the status quo in schools and society. I contend that even the most well-intended principals who have had a wealth of experiences with diverse cultures and groups can fall victim to a narrow set of principles if they are not conscious of how these ways of thinking can influence their behavior. Thus, as I have said in previous chapters, principals need an in-depth knowledge of history.

In this chapter, I examine the history of educational administration and leadership as a field of study. I present this history chronologically beginning with the rise of Taylorism and scientific management (1900–1935); the emergence of human relations perspectives (1935–1950); the development of a "new" and scientific perspective of administration emphasizing social science research and theory generation (1950–1980); and the current era where reform and accountability movements prompted the need for a knowledge base and professional standards (1980–present). While a chronological ordering is necessary to provide structure, the development of educational administration and leadership scholarship was, in reality, far less neat and tidy. During the first three eras, I primarily use the word "administration" and in the latter I use the work "leadership" to reflect a shift in the field's use of terminology beginning in the late 1970s and 1980s.

I focus on the dominant perspective in the field of educational administration and leadership because it has been central to the development of the role of the principal. It is essential to understand that most of the scholars who contributed to the field's dominant perspective had good intentions and made significant scholarly contributions. Furthermore, academic achievement, mastery of basic skills, and the general functioning of the school—i.e., the things that professors in the educational administration and leadership field focused on at various points in the past—are essential to creating quality urban schools that meet the needs of all students. The things focused on in the past, however, represent just the tip of the iceberg when it comes to leadership that responds to educational injustices and broader social problems in low-opportunity urban communities of color. These traditional foci can also serve as distractions from other pressing priorities. This chapter makes clear that a narrow approach to administration and leadership limits a principal's ability and wherewithal to identify and work with teachers and communities to address the underlying issues to poor student performance and depressed post-secondary outcomes.

Developments in Administration and Educational Administration

In 1887, Woodrow Wilson, a 31-year-old assistant professor who went on to be the 28th President of the United States, catalyzed thinking about public administration in his article entitled *The Study of Administration*. Wilson argued that the administration of public organizations required study to "discover, first, what government can properly and successfully do, and secondly, how it can do these proper things with the utmost possible efficiency and at the least possible cost either of money or energy" (p. 197). He added, "The field of administration is a field of business . . . The object of administrative study is to rescue executive methods from the confusion and costliness of empirical experiment and set them upon foundations laid deep in stable principle" (1887, pp. 209–210). Wilson catalyzed the replacement of administrative folklore and traditions with a new administrative and business-oriented science focused, primarily, on the public sphere.

At the time Wilson's article was published, American manufacturers were working vigorously to increase the productivity of their factories. Mass production emerged, and industrial pioneers like Henry Ford participated in a technological revolution that combined workers and machines on assembly lines engineered for maximum efficiency. These are the roots of administrative science and theory, a literature that overwhelmingly shapes how professors of educational administration created their field and made decisions about principal preparation and practice. Programs and instructors involved in preparing principals today are often informed by a belief that there is "one best way" of doing things and that principles of efficiency from business are necessary for improving schools.

One more point before proceeding: It is important to note that racism and sexism have also influenced society and have in turn influenced fields of administrative science and educational administration. Even as distinguished a figure as Woodrow Wilson engaged in practices that can only be characterized as *racist*. As president of Princeton University and as President of the United States, in fact, Woodrow Wilson set policies that segregated Blacks and removed them from management positions. Like some other founders of the administrative science field, Wilson left an ugly legacy and one of the ways this legacy reveals itself is in how White men have dominated the principalship and superintendency, even in communities of color.

The Era of Taylorism and Scientific Management: 1900–1935

Scientific Management

In the early 1900s, universities started following the pathway mapped out by Woodrow Wilson (1887) by studying problems within organizations, management, and administration. Many believed this scholarship could alleviate the social issues confronting cities. German sociologist Max Weber (1948/2009) saw hope in well-run bureaucracies. He envisioned a set of principles: (a) the division of labor based on expertise/specialization; (b) a hierarchy of authority; (c) a system of rules/expectations for employees; (d) clear procedures for dealing with work situations; and (e) the selection/promotion of employees based on competence and expertise. In theory, a well-run bureaucracy is politically neutral, recruits and promotes workers based on merit, prepares well-trained technical specialists to handle tasks free from emotions, and maintains a systematic salary structure that incentivizes performance and sanctions inefficiencies.

Weber also understood the dangers of bureaucracy. Bureaucracy can be dehumanizing and inflexible, and it can create boredom. Rules can become an end in themselves and devotion to rules can be blindly repeated despite evolving conditions. Managers compensated for rule enforcement can lose sight of the purpose of rules and broader organizational objectives. In doing so, worker creativity is, in effect suppressed, even at times when innovation is required. Lower-level employees can often feel detached and suffer from depressed morale. Managers can adhere to strict, top-down management approaches over-reliant on measurable outcomes, rule adherence, and narrowly developed objectives. Short-term progress might be made through such approaches, but perhaps at the expense of long-term objectives. While Weber considered the benefits and challenges associated with organizations and bureaucracies, others preached the gospel of efficiency with less attention to its drawbacks.

Near the start of the 20th century after Weber wrote about bureaucracy—and on another continent—Frederick Winslow Taylor (1911) published *The Principles of Scientific Management*. His main idea was to divide work into discrete tasks and then study each task to determine the quickest way to perform the function.

Like Woodrow Wilson, Taylor called administration a science, partly because he believed each element of every job should be thoroughly examined and assessed so that a "one best way" of doing a task could be identified. Taylor (1911) claimed an employer needed "a man equipped merely with a stop-watch and a properly ruled notebook" (p. 48). Step 1 would be to identify and observe a group of workers performing a work function. The observer would analyze each worker's actions and the tools used. Then, the observer would identify each incorrect, inefficient, or ineffective operation and ascertain the quickest, most efficient movements. Workers would be retrained and supervised for fidelity to the efficient procedures research had identified.

Taylor, like many men of his time, believed not all workers were suited for supervision: "The workman who is best suited to actually doing the work is incapable of fully understanding this science, without the guidance and help of those who are working with him or over him, either through lack of education or through insufficient mental capacity" (Taylor, 1911, p. 10). Thus, work needed to be divided between workers and supervisors able to identify the most efficient ways of doing work. Supervisors would also develop productivity goals and worker incentive systems and create training opportunities and tools to ensure goals were obtained. Workers and managers cooperate to ensure all work is completed consistent with scientific management techniques. The business community, always in search of higher profits, quickly accepted Taylor's system in the businesses they owned, and many used their wealth and influence to push public schools to adopt similar practices.

Scientific management provided the foundation for modern administrative theory, although it is now vilified for deskilling workers and creating harsh working environments filled with mundane, thoughtless tasks. Taylor, in fact, is often portrayed as an "oppressor" of workers, although he expressed support for labor unions (Witzel & Warner, 2015). Taylor (1911) saw the worker and employer or manager as mutually connected: "It would seem to be so self-evident that maximum prosperity for the employer, coupled with maximum prosperity for the employee, ought to be the two leading objects of management, that even to state this fact should be unnecessary" (p. 3). This was wishful thinking at best.

Henri Fayol's (1949) work was similar to Taylor's but focused on executives rather than managers and supervisors. He believed executives needed to be trained in schools that would provide technical expertise; after such schooling, they should continue to learn on the job. Fayol advanced a set of principles of administration which comprised planning, organizing, commanding, coordinating, and culturing. Whereas Taylor emphasized uniformity and the precise application of "scientifically" certified standard operating procedures, Fayol recognized the need for managers to be flexible based on situations. This difference undoubtedly had to do with the fact that Fayol focused on executives' work rather than the work of supervisors of workers on an assembly line.

Scientific Management in Educational Administration

Franklin Bobbitt, a professor of educational administration from the University of Chicago, adopted principles of scientific management soon after Taylor published his seminal text. Bobbitt (1913) believed in the idea that principals could identify one best way to administer schools:

> The new and revolutionary doctrine of scientific management states in no uncertain terms that management, the supervisory staff, has the largest share of the work in the determination of proper methods . . . The burden of finding the best methods is too large and too complicated to be laid on the shoulders of the teachers . . . The ultimate worker, the teacher in our case, must be a specialist in the performance of the labour that will produce the product.
>
> *pp. 52–53*

Bobbitt described the outcome of education as "the product" and concluded that it would be the principals' job to use tests to identify "weak" and "strong" teachers while also establishing teacher pay and privileges (Bobbitt, 1913).

Scientific management was applied to measuring educational program implementation, ensuring the efficient use of resources, and making policy choices to improve student outcomes (Bobbitt, 1918). Borrowing from principles of scientific management, professor of educational administration John Strayer of Teachers College used job analyses based on the work of principals to develop a set of preparation courses organized by administrative area or task (e.g., budgeting, law, curriculum, management). Ellwood Cubberley, dean of education at Stanford, called for administering schools and districts like businesses. He saw commonalities between "workers and teachers, products and students, administrators and managers" (Foster, 1987, p. 38). Cubberley (1916) believed scientific management would ultimately create an organizational environment where principals had direct oversight and an immediate ability to change and improve teacher practice:

> In time it will be possible for any school system to maintain a continuous survey of all the different phases of its work, through tests made by its corps of efficiency experts, and to detect weak points in its work almost as soon as they appear.
>
> *p. 325*

The emphasis on scientific management and a new professoriate studying educational administration emerged at a time when muckraking journalism was critical of public education administration. Journalists were quick to point out corruption and inefficiency in municipal government and schools (as noted in Chapter 3).

Professors like Cubberley, Strayer, and Bobbitt capitalized on this unique opportunity by transforming educational administration from storytelling and folklore
into a respected and profitable science. They published books, held seminars,
consulted with school districts, and gave keynote speeches at education-related
conventions across the country. They criticized school boards elected to represent particular sections of cities with different ethnic groups. They wanted
at-large election of school boards that invariably selected board members from
the mainstream culture and a corporate-like governance system that empowered
a few elite leaders, individuals who inevitably were White and male. Historian
David Tyack described the era:

> The new professors of educational administration gave the stamp of uni-
> versity approval to elitist assumptions about who constituted good school
> board members and to the corporate model of school organization. They
> tried to develop "scientific" ways of measuring inputs and outputs in
> school systems as a tool of management, and to elaborate ways in which
> the school might rationalize its structure and curriculum to fit new indus-
> trial and social conditions.
>
> *1974, p. 136*

The Human Relations Era: 1935–1945

Human Relations

Social scientists began to recognize that people and worker morale mattered to
organizational efficiency. Recognizing the human aspect of organizations was
not a rejection of scientific management altogether, but rather an addendum to
it. Between 1927 and 1933, Harvard researcher Elton Mayo and his colleagues
conducted research experiments at Western Electric's Hawthorne Plant with the
hopes of expanding Taylor's work and identifying ways to improve working conditions (Mayo, 1949/2014). Two research experiments were most notable. First,
researchers experimented with the lighting at the plant. The lighting was held
constant for one group of workers but decreased for another group. Changes in
the two groups' work productivity were analyzed. The researchers were surprised
to find that production increased for both groups. In a second experiment, nine
workers were paid on an incentive system. Their pay was increased as their productivity increased. Unexpectedly, the workers' performance did not improve to
any significant degree.

Over 20,000 employees were interviewed to better understand the initial
findings at the Hawthorne Plant. In the lighting experiment, the attention the
workers received from the researchers made them feel noticed and important.
The workers were motivated by a sense of increased morale and belongingness.
This became known as the "Hawthorne Effect." In the incentive pay experiment,

social relations between workers significantly impacted their productivity. The workers informally established their expectations for outputs, which was described as the "group norm." The group disciplined workers who did not meet the group norm. Group members who over-performed were labeled "rate-busters" and workers who underperformed were labeled "chiselers." Both outlier groups were subject to pressuring and threats from the rest of the group. The Hawthorne studies' primary conclusions about social and human relations challenged Taylorism and scientific management. The absurdity of a purely economic approach to management that overlooked human relations and needs was revealed.

Other scholars who were not directly focused on educational institutions such as schools also demonstrated the importance of focusing on human needs and interpersonal relations in the workplace. Kurt Lewin (1947) recognized the importance of group dynamics and how a group can shape the behavior of its members. He maintained that it was fruitless to focus on changing an individual's behaviors in isolation because group pressures constrain individual action. Thus, a focus on change must be at the group level and concentrate on group norms, roles, social interactions, and socialization processes. Lewin's research also emphasized the importance of reducing social conflict through democratic processes. For example, Lewin and his colleagues (Lewin, Lippitt, & White, 1939) investigated authoritarian, democratic, and laissez-fair work environments to understand which management approach increased productivity. They concluded that democratic approaches to administration were more useful for shaping group behavior than authoritarian environments because democratic approaches increased worker satisfaction and productivity.

The administrator's role, according to Lewin, was to assist workers with technical advice and options, and to help guide the decision-making process collaboratively (Lewin et al., 1939). It was essential for administrators to recognize that change can be a slow process, partly because it required all organizational members to learn and participate in change processes. As applied in practice, however, Lewin's work was not always emancipatory for workers, because managers sometimes utilized knowledge gained by ostensibly collaborating with workers to better control them, and artificially inflate morale and increase productivity in the process.

In the 1940s, the newly emerging field of administrative science attracted psychologists, sociologists, political scientists, and other behavioral scientists. The influential work of Bell Telephone president Chester Barnard initiated a weaving together of the economic thinking of Taylorism with the human relations perspective. In his book, *The Functions of the Executive*, Barnard (1938) provided a theory of cooperative behavior in organizations. His central thesis was that the work of the executive included the following: (a) establishing and maintaining a system of communication; (b) developing and sharing organizational purposes and objectives; and (c) managing people to ensure they complete their jobs aligned to organizational objectives. Barnard also clarified the differences between efficiency—using resources prudently—and effectiveness—realizing organizational goals. While Barnard emphasized the importance of efficiency, he did not ignore social relations, comradery, and recognition.

Executives needed to exercise cooperation, which Barnard described as "genuine restraint of self in many directions, it means actual service for no reward, it means courage to fight for principles rather than for things, it means genuine subjection of destructive personal interest to social interests" (in Scott, 1992, p. 119). Cooperation also required sincerity and integrity so workers could recognize the humanness and limitations of their leaders. Barnard viewed organizations as systems that could run smoothly if executives were attentive to the human and social needs of their workers. Barnard's work was not without critique despite its continued popularity into the present. Some critics argue Barnard neglected to portray or address conflicts, bargaining, and politics within organizations (Foster, 1986).

This blending of a focus on human relations matters for control and increasing productivity is arguably most clearly seen in the work of W. Edwards Deming. Deming was a statistician, professor, and management consultant who utilized a discourse about efficiency to describe how organizations should be administered. His management philosophy focused on limiting variability and enhancing control on worker actions, but he emphasized the importance of making management decisions in ways that engaged workers and, consequently, promoted worker morale. Deming focused intensely on how statistics can be used to investigate variance and organizational inefficiencies. For Deming, the central problem of management was to understand variation better so it can be tightly controlled. Beginning in the 1940s and 1950s, several Japanese manufacturers adopted methods inspired by Deming to develop quality products at lower prices. Years later, Deming (1993) published his book *The New Economics for Industry, Government, Education*, which laid out 14 management points emphasizing how to control variability and how to improve outcomes through evaluation. Followers of Deming's approach use statistical and analytic thinking to make organizational decisions, consider how decisions impact employee morale, manage employees through coaching, and utilize a systems-thinking approach that prioritized cooperation and organizational success rather than traditional hierarchies and silos (McNarry, 1999).

Human Relations in Educational Administration

By the 1930s, professors of educational administration were still concerned with scientific management. The field remained heavily focused on: "the spheres of finance, business management, physical equipment, and the more mechanical aspects of administration, organization, personnel management, and the like" (Newlon, 1934, p. 259). Much attention was given to "'technical and factual' dimensions of the profession and the mechanics of administration" (p. 99).

University of Illinois professor Oscar Weber (1930) proclaimed, "Organization is but a technical device to assure the attainment of the function of the thing or institution organized" (p. 109). He emphasized, "statesmanlike administration and businesslike management" (p. 136) as well as the standardization of facilities, routines, courses, and salaries. Much of this type of thinking remains visible in the educational administration discourse and the ongoing fascination with efficiency, cost reduction, Total Quality Management (TQM), management by objectives, merit pay, valued-added models, standardized curriculum, the identification of research-based teaching practices and interventions, and a seemingly unquestioned belief in statistical measurement.

The human and social dimensions of educational administration became more apparent during the Great Depression and economic and social upheaval of the 1930s. Some professors of educational administration wrote about the importance of "cooperation, participation, and democracy" (Parker, 2004, p. 45). A new school of thought challenged mainstream perspectives of the principal as a Taylorism devotee. For example, Newlon (1934) argued that principals should critically examine society and participate with community to discover social purposes of schooling and shift their schools' focus toward those purposes. Others believed principals should reject their traditional authority, align the school to the community, and cultivate leadership throughout the school (Koopman, Miel, & Misner, 1943; Koos, Hughes, Hutson, & Reavis, 1940).

The role of the principal evolved and expanded. Teaching became more professionalized with new requirements and standards. A principal who refused to value the human and social needs of teachers could find teachers fleeing to other schools with friendlier work environments. Some textbooks of the era described a shift from supervision as an expectation to collaborative work where teachers and principals worked together to improve instruction (Parker, 2004). Guba (1960) described a shift in which "the industrial engineer had to become a human engineer" (p. 117). As the 1950s approached, most professors of educational administration clung tightly to scientific management, but some acknowledged the human and social elements of administration.

"New" Administration and Scientific Era: 1945–1980

Administration in the Scientific Era

Herbert Simon, a Nobel laureate in economics, borrowed much from Barnard and Taylor in his famous book *Administrative Behavior* (1945/2013). The influential book's central task was to describe decision-making in complex organizations. Earlier writings on administration emphasized organizational efficiency, the division of work, and maintaining a hierarchy of authority and control. Simon claimed less attention was paid to determining how decisions were made by administrators even though the organization was a decision-making device. To reach a decision, Simon believed administrators deal with facts and human factors. He described an organizational hierarchy where administrators were tasked with making decisions to direct workers toward coordinated and efficient behavior. Therefore, administrative behavior involved the conscious or unconscious selection between choices, which could be a reflex action or a result of a complex set of planning activities.

Many choices could be selected for a decision and, by some process, an individual must narrow their options and make a "good" choice. A choice is considered rational or good in so far as it reflects a choice that appears to lead toward the achievement of previously selected goals. Simon emphasized that rational decisions maximized profit. He stated, "maximization is the aim of administrative activity" (1945/2013, p. 45). True rationality was impossible because it required complete knowledge and a recognition of all possible alternatives. Where the theoretical economic man maximizes, Simon argued that the administrator "satisfices" or "looks for a course of action that is satisfactory or 'good enough'" (p. 119). The administrator understands the world is confusing, can only take into account a limited number of factors, and can just deal with a few problems at one time. Thus, administrators simplify their decisions because there is no other real alternative.[1]

Educational Administration in the Scientific Period

During the scientific period, a "quest for a science of school administration was undertaken" (Murphy, 1998, p. 364). A newer generation of professors of educational administration was influenced by ideas of administrative scientists, which gave rise to a "theory movement" focused on creating a legitimate science based on universally accepted truths. Professors of educational administration increasingly saw their role as researchers who should test theories using quantitative methods that in turn can inform theory development and universal practices for principals and principal preparation. Schools were viewed as more complex organizations and influenced by larger social forces. Hall (1963) called on researchers in the field to continually and rigorously synthesize existing knowledge in the field while diligently cultivating a "sensitivity to trends in other segments of society, particularly those which affect administration directly" (p. 29).

Professors of educational administration believed that they must draw on social sciences to increase the development of knowledge in the field. Campbell (1963) noted that the professor of educational administration needed to "maintain an orientation with respect to the general field of education, the field of administration, and the social science disciplines," and "determine the relevance of social science concepts and findings and plan the adaption of these concepts and findings to school situations" (pp. 342–343). Campbell suggested that research in education might be divided into parts to understand the environment in which administration occurs, the organization in which administration functions, and the individual who works/functions within the organization. Twenty-eight years later, Campbell (1981) reiterated the importance dividing the study of administration and utilizing social science research:

> Psychology and social psychology have much to say about the nature of people and of groups of people. Sociology provides insights about organizations and group behavior. Political science provides useful concepts having to do with organizational relationships to the larger society. Economics deals, in part, with the allocation of resources, an obvious concern of educational administration. The law deals with equity and justice and other fundamental values in our society . . . An applied field such as educational administration depends not only on what is known in education and in management but on many of the basic disciplines as well.
>
> *p. 7*

Campbell added that professors of education administration were "charged with extending knowledge and improving practice" (p. 7), a difficult combination of expectations.

An important step to extending knowledge came with the creation of national and regional professional networks. In 1947, the National Conference of Professors of Educational Administration (NCPEA) was established. Soon after, the Kellog Foundation created a consortium of eight universities called the Cooperative Project in Educational Administration with the aim of improving preparation programs. The University Council of Educational Administration (UCEA) was established in 1956, which would have a significant influence on the development of research, scholarly writing, and a knowledge base. In 1957, UCEA and Andrew Halpin helped produce a "theory movement" with the following core ideas:

1. Statements about what administrators and organizations ought to do cannot be encompassed in science or theory.
2. Scientific theories treat phenomena as they are.
3. Effective research has its origins in theory and is guided by theory.
4. Hypothetico-deductive systems are the best exemplars of theory.
5. The use of the social sciences is essential in theory development and training.
6. Administration is best viewed as a generic concept applicable to all types of organizations (Culbertson, 1983, p. 15).

The theory movement and the focus on social science research prompted a change in the professoriate. In 1945, professors were often former superintendents who drew upon their professional experiences. Campbell (1963) suggested that professors of educational administration should be "men who are bright, who are young, who have strong liberal arts backgrounds, who have exhibited some independent creativity, and who have a commitment to education" (p. 344). Older candidates for the professoriate with more experience in school leadership were viewed as problematic because they may have family obligations and be narrowly focused on practical issues. By the late 1970s and early 1980s, most professors had little or no actual school leadership experience. They were primarily concerned with social science disciplines and making theoretical contributions to the development of the field. As Murphy (1998) noted:

> Consistent with the guiding vision of the scientific era, the predominant trend during the 40 year period was the infusion of content from the social sciences into preparation [principal] programmes. The infrastructure for this activity was the expansion of the conceptual and theoretical knowledge base of the profession by the development of a science of administration.
>
> *p. 365*

Mainstream administrative theory through this era remained tied to Taylorism and human relations approaches. Principal preparation programs became based on a belief in empiricism, predictability, and scientific validity. The content of preparation emphasized training for management functions that view schools as rational, mechanistic structures that operate like bureaucracies (Cambron-McCabe, Mulkeen, & Wright, 1991). Rules, regulations, incentives, and penalties are tied to an organizational structure that principals manage efficiently and effectively. Foster (1986) described the literature as dominated by quantitative, positivist research that assumed schools were organizations with "concrete entities populated by role players and that systematic study of these entities will yield reliable and predictable knowledge" (p. 59). He described empirical research of the era as "rife with studies of communication patterns, role structures, school climate, motivation patterns, and so on" (p. 59). Mainstream professors assumed research would eventually lead to a verified body of knowledge or at least a rationalized set of practices. In turn, this body of knowledge could inform practice and ensure principals acted rationally in response to school-based challenges (Hoy & Miskel, 1982).

The Knowledge Base and Standards Era: 1980–Present

While professors of educational administration continued to utilize social science research from other disciplines, the emergence of Effective Schools research became a significant emphasis within the field. Later, professors would build on this body of research to develop a knowledge base and professional standards. This section describes the Effective Schools research, the quest for a knowledge base, and the development of national principal preparation standards.

Effective Schools Research

By the 1980s, professors of educational administration began to focus more specifically on schools and the work of principals rather than abstract conceptions of administration and organization. Prompted by the Coleman Report and methodological improvements in quantitative research, researchers in the 1970s utilized large, quantitative data to identify "effective schools." An early example of Effective Schools research focused on four inner-city schools (two in New York City, one in Kansas City, and one in Los Angeles) where urban, low-income students of color were reading above their peers in similar schools (G. Weber, 1971). The principals in each school were described as instrumental to instruction because they made decisions about climate, instructional strategies, and resource distribution. Three years later, researchers set out to answer the question: Are there schools that are instructionally effective for poor children in Detroit (Lezotte, Edmonds, & Ratner, 1974)? Reading and math scores from the Stanford Achievement Test and Iowa Test of Basic Skills for 20 schools and 10,000 students were analyzed to identify effective schools. Statistical processes controlled for student family background and school resources, which resulted in the identification of two schools that were "most effective."

Ronald Edmonds, one of the primary contributors to Effective Schools research, believed schools serving low-income students of color could close reading and mathematics achievement gaps. His efforts to locate and describe effective schools were rooted in a sincere belief that effective organizational conditions could be replicated. He also believed desegregation policies (a primary recommendation of the Coleman Report) would confront significant, long-term resistance and may never achieve its goals. Decades later, his hypothesis was correct, as noted in Chapter 2. Edmonds and Fredericksen (1978) identified and analyzed urban schools serving low-income students of color that were instructionally effective. For Edmonds, this proved educators working in urban schools were not absolved of their responsibility to ensure all students receive an adequate education. Edmonds and Fredericksen even recommended that urban schools needed to be responsive to community context, describing how effective schools: "recognize the necessity of modifying curricular design, text selection, teaching strategy, etc., in response to differences in family background among pupils in the school" (p. 47).

Edmonds (1979) ultimately identified what he described as critical elements in effective schools. Strong administrative leadership was considered essential and without which other elements could not be brought together or maintained. The other elements included, a school climate with high expectations for all students, the prioritization of student acquisition of basic skills, an orderly and safe atmosphere that is not overly rigid or harsh, and a system where achievement is frequently and consistently monitored. Others emphasized the importance of principal "instructional management" (i.e., the managerial functions that improve student achievement) (Bossert, Dwyer, Rowan, & Lee, 1982).

An analysis of teacher perspectives in effective schools revealed that principals "contribute to the development of associative (cohesive), social (behavioral), and cultural (values, norms) patterns in schools" (Blasé, 1987, p. 594). They do so by increasing teacher confidence, making teachers feel valued as professionals, creating a sense of optimism and consistency, and problem-solving to minimize feelings of anger, frustration, and uncertainty. Principals were portrayed as visible, available, consistent with their decisions and enforcement of policies, clear and reasonable about expectations, and able to manage time. As it became clear that principals relied on their expertise and influence rather than just positional authority, the term instructional leadership replaced instructional management. The use of administration also became less utilized in the literature.

Instructional Leadership and the Knowledge Base

Effective Schools research generated broad agreement that principals have an impact on teachers, students, and schools. In fact, this research demonstrated that there was "no evidence of effective schools with weak leadership" (Sammons, Hillman, & Mortimore, 1995, p. 17). In 1982, Philip Hallinger developed what would become a widely-used framework and survey instrument for measuring instructional leadership: Principal Instructional Management Rating Scale (PIMRS) (Hallinger, 2011). The framework comprised dimensions (defining the school mission, managing the instructional program, and developing the school learning climate program). For the next 35 years, research on instructional leadership considered leader characteristics, styles, personal qualities, and professional knowledge. A list of behaviors and practices emerged. Principals were "experts in curricular development and teaching" and directive leaders focused on "school culture, academic press, and high expectations for student achievement" (Neumerski, 2013, pp. 318–319). PIMRS and research on instructional leadership influenced the 1996 development of the Interstate School Leadership Licensure Consortium (ISLLC) national standards for principals. A meta-analysis of studies from 1980 to 1995 found that principals can make a difference in student achievement, primarily when they focus on influencing internal processes (e.g., expectations, school mission and goals, student opportunities to learn, learning time allocated) (Hallinger & Heck, 1996).

After decades of research on educational administration and leadership, many in the field sought to develop a knowledge base. A knowledge base can be considered:

> core knowledge, or the canon, that every member of the profession should know. A knowledge base standardizes the profession in that all of its members are certified to have mastered this canon. It also standardizes the training necessary to become a member of the profession in such a way that it does not matter in which institution a person receives her or his training; she or he will receive basically the same training . . .
>
> *Scheurich, 1995, p. 18*

The quest for a knowledge base began in the 1980s. In 1987, the National Commission on Excellence in Educational Administration (NCEEA, 1987) released the publication *Leaders for America's Schools*. The report outlined sweeping recommendations for universities, districts, state education agencies, and private organizations that included, redefining educational leadership, modeling principal preparation after professional schools (e.g., business, law, medicine), and at least 300 of approximately 500 universities should stop preparing principals and superintendents. The National Policy Board on Educational Administration (NPBEA) was established based on these recommendations, which included representatives from multiple organizations to monitor the development of principals and superintendents as well as communicating key policy concerns with relevant stakeholders. NPBEA would soon after develop three core purposes, which included developing, disseminating, and implementing professional models for the preparation and in-service training of principals.

By 1992, UCEA created seven committees to study seven knowledge domains. These seven domains comprised the field: (a) societal and cultural influences on schooling; (b) teaching and learning processes; (c) organizational studies; (d) leadership and management processes; (e) policy and political studies; (f) legal and ethical dimensions of schooling; and (g) economic and financial dimensions of schooling (Bredeson, 1995).

Professional Standards

A half-century-long effort to develop a knowledge base culminated in the 1994 construction of the ISLLC and the 1996 creation of standards to reshape the profession of educational administration. ISLLC and the standards led to a concerted effort to define the role of the principal and other educational leaders as well as developing policy around licensure, professional development, program accreditation, and principal evaluation. Its founders emphasized the challenges, thoughtfulness, and limits to the standards:

> These indicators are examples of essential knowledge, practices, and beliefs, not a full map. No effort was made to include everything or to deal with the performances in the myriad of leadership contexts. Leadership is complex and context-dependent activity. To attempt to envelop the concept with a definitive list of indicators is a fool's errand.
>
> *Murphy, 2005, p. 174*

The standards were updated in 2005, but not significantly changed.

In 2015, the NPBEA (2015) published the Professional Standards in Educational Leadership (PSEL). The PSEL are described as "guideposts" that are "Grounded in current research and the real-life experiences of educational leaders" (NPBEA, 2015, p. 1). NPBEA suggested that PSEL was created to replace existing standards because students needed to be prepared for the emerging global economy, new jobs and workplaces, and the latest technologies. Authors of the standards noted that the knowledge base had expanded, but their revised description sounded familiar:

> educational leaders exert influence on student achievement by creating challenging but also caring and supportive conditions conducive to each student's learning. They relentlessly develop and support teachers, create positive working conditions, effectively allocate resources, construct appropriate organizational policies and systems, and engage in other deep and meaningful work outside of the classroom that has a powerful impact on what happens inside it.
>
> *p. 1*

The PSEL standards have clear differences from past standards. PSEL emphasizes equity, cultural responsiveness, and care with an emphasis on individuals (students, teachers, staff, families).

PSEL (NPBEA, 2015) consists of ten standards that apply to principals and assistant principals. The standards are made up of interdependent domains, qualities, and values associated with effective leadership. Each standard has a list of actions taken by "effective educational leaders." In what follows, I summarize each standard and some of the actions described.

- Standard 1 emphasizes the need for principals to develop a shared mission, vision, and set of core values. The standard suggests effective principals promote the well-being of each student, which is initiated through the development of a school vision and related to instructional and organizational practices.
- Standard 2 expects that effective principals act ethically and as stewards of resources. The standard underscores integrity, fairness, trust, transparency, and continuous improvement. A commitment to social justice, democracy, and diversity is also referenced.
- Standard 3 stresses the development of equitable and culturally responsive schools. An effective principal recognizes racial, cultural, and linguistic diversity as assets and then ensures policies are fair and implemented in an unbiased manner.

The first three standards emphasize human relations perspectives and the role of the principal in shaping the school's culture, belief systems, priorities, and commitments to students and families. Words like "advocate," "core values," "equity," "ethical," "understanding," and "context" are used throughout. Accordingly, effective principals are described as flexible, equity oriented, and knowledgeable of injustices that confront students within the school. They employ collaborative processes to root out injustices.

Standards 4 and 5 emphasize the technical aspects of increasing student achievement and organizational conditions that support student achievement.

- Standard 4 is focused on systems of curriculum, instruction, and assessment. Effective principals work collaboratively to promote a love for learning, value student assets, encourage technology usage, employ valid assessments, and analyze data to monitor progress and drive instructional improvement.
- Standard 5 stresses the relationship between academic success and an inclusive and caring school-community. Effective principals acknowledge the importance of attending to the social, emotional, and physical needs of students. They shape systems of support, learning environments, and school-community relations to promote academic achievement and student well-being.

Findings from the social sciences, the Effective Schools movement, and research on instructional leadership/management profoundly influenced both standards because principals are expected to focus on systems and organizational conditions. For example, Standard 4 suggests that "effective" principals, "Employ valid assessments that are consistent with knowledge of child learning and development and technical standards of measurement" (NPBEA, 2015, p. 12). To do so, principals must have technical knowledge of assessments and data analysis.

Standards 6, 7, and 8 suggest that effective principals increase teacher capacity, create working conditions that allow teachers to capitalize on their skills, and ensure families and communities are engaged in ways that benefit and support rather than hinder student academic success and well-being.

- Standard 6 emphasizes the principal's role in developing the professional capacity of school personnel through continuous improvement processes. Generic personnel management tasks are highlighted, i.e., recruitment and retention, coaching and providing actionable feedback, personnel evaluation, connecting personnel with learning opportunities, and reducing personnel burnout.
- Standard 7 is similar to Standard 6 because it focuses on workplace conditions. The standard emphasizes the importance of professional community where personnel is empowered, willing to take collective responsibility, and engage in continuous improvement processes while holding each other accountable.
- Standard 8 describes the actions effective principals take to engage families and communities. Effective principals are portrayed as visible, approachable, and welcoming. They establish two-way communication, recognize the community's unique forms of capital (e.g., cultural, social, intellectual, political), and advocate publicly for students and families.

These standards reflect findings from Effective Schools research and more recent work on instructional leadership. The language of business and efficiency are evident in phrases, such as "continuous improvement," "actionable feedback," "workplace conditions," "faculty-initiated improvement," and "productive partnerships." Effective principals develop workplace conditions and control external factors so teachers can focus on student academic success.

Standards 9 and 10 focus on administration and continuous improvement cycles that promote student academic success.

- Standard 9 concentrates narrowly on operations and management. Effective principals manage fiscal, physical, and other resources to support student learning in an ethical and transparent way. They buffer teachers from disruption, comply with laws, and monitor and respond to internal and external politics that might disrupt the school.
- Standard 10 stresses continuous school improvement for academic success. The standard incorporates aspects from previous standards, but essentially focuses on a systems-based approach to data collection and analysis, managing resources and uncertainty, and collaborating internally and externally to implement programs and professional development to increase school capacity.

These final standards resemble aspects of Taylorism, human relations perspectives, and administrative science theories. Effective principals "Institute, manage, and monitor operations and administrative systems" (NPBEA, 2015, p. 17). They "use methods of continuous improvement" and "Employ situationally-appropriate strategies" (p. 17).

Takeaways for Principals

In this chapter, I described the historical development of the field of educational administration and leadership, with a focus on dominant perspectives. Building on the work of social science researchers, early professors of educational administration provided new ideas and ways of thinking about the principalship. They engaged in research and scholarship that would extend beyond war stories and folklore to control schools in ways that produce the best possible results for children. For many of these professors, they engaged in this work in a sincere attempt to improve schools and the lives of children, teachers, and principals. Others sought to elevate the status of the profession, increase their potential earnings as faculty, and assuage business leaders with deep pockets that could provide funding for research and theory generation. Their efforts in seeking a knowledge base and grand theories as well as developing standards provided not only a foundation for what principals should know and do, but also an essential body of work that can be critiqued so that new avenues for principal practice can be theorized and identified.

The history of the field of educational administration and leadership should help principals recognize that any related set of theories, perspectives, or practices has underlying assumptions that can be problematic if they are invisible or unexamined. A principal has most likely been socially conditioned to dominant belief systems about how schools operate or can be improved if they believe in "the one best way" of doing things. Many principals rose through the ranks in public schools running under such conditions, attended universities and principal preparation programs that utilized professional standards, and then learned their craft through experience and mentoring from senior peers and supervisors who valued organizational hierarchy. Administrative science prompted an emphasis on efficiency and narrowly defined outcomes. Authentic community engagement was always an afterthought. While academic achievement, mastery of basic skills, and operating schools in an efficient manner is important, these foci have little to do with creating schools that can indeed shift the long-term outcomes of children living in low-opportunity communities. As the previous chapters noted, policies and approaches narrowly fixated on achievement, basic skills, and efficiency fail to serve marginalized groups of students. The naïve urban principal becomes a sprinter on a treadmill who eventually becomes tired and confused about why more progress has not been made. They may be running fast, with a purpose, and putting in maximum effort, but they are getting tired of the chase toward a finish line that never comes. In the next chapter, I consider alternative perspectives that might be more inclusive of the broad-based reforms needed to improve urban schools.

Note

1 English (1994) critiqued Simon's declaration as unethical and absurd. He provided an example of the Ford Motor Company's actions after discovering its Pinto exploded from rear-end collisions. The company calculated the cost of burn deaths and injuries, related expenses, and the likelihood of such accidents. It would be more expensive to fix gas tanks than cover costs for explosions. Thus, Ford refused to change the design. Ford's decision was clearly illogical but was potentially supported by Simon's emphasis on rational, maximizing decision-making.

References

Barnard, C. I. (1938). *The functions of the executive*. Cambridge, MA: Harvard University Press.

Blasé, J. J. (1987). Dimensions of effective school leadership: The teacher's perspective. *American Educational Research Journal, 24*(4), 589–610.

Bobbitt, J. F. (1913). The supervision of city schools: In S. C. Parker (Ed.), *The national society for the study of education: Twelfth yearbook, Part 1* (pp. 7–96). Chicago, IL: University of Chicago Press.

Bobbitt, J. F. (1918) *The curriculum*. New York, NY: Houghton Mifflin.

Bossert, S. T., Dwyer, D. C., Rowan, B., & Lee, G. V. (1982). The instructional management role of the principal. *Educational Administration Quarterly, 18*(3), 34–64.

Bredeson, P. V. (1995) Building a professional knowledge base in education administration: Opportunities and obstacles. In Donmoyer, R., Imber, M., & Scheurich, J. J. (Eds.), *The knowledge base of educational administration: Multiple perspectives* (pp. 47–61). Albany, NY: State University of New York Press.

Cambron-McCabe, N., Mulkeen, T. A., & Wright, G. K. (1991). *The Danforth program for professors of school administration: A new platform for preparing school administrators.* St. Louis, MI: Danforth Foundation.

Campbell, R. F. (1963). Training research professors of educational administration. In J. A. Culbertson J., & S. P. Hencley (Eds.). *Educational research: New perspectives* (pp. 341–344). Danville, IL: Interstate Printers & Publishers.

Campbell, R. F. (1981). The professorship in educational administration—A personal view. *Educational Administration Quarterly, 17*(1), 1–24.

Cubberley, E. (1916). *Public school administration.* Boston, MA: Houghton-Mifflin.

Culbertson, J. (1983). Theory in educational administration: Echoes from critical thinkers. *Educational Researcher, 12*(10), 15–22.

DeMatthews, D. E. (2015). Clearing a path for inclusion: Distributing leadership in a high performing elementary school. *Journal of School Leadership, 25*(6), 1000–1038.

Deming, W. E. (1993). *The new economics for industry, government, education.* Cambridge, MA: MIT Press.

Edmonds, R. R. (1979). Effective schools for the urban poor. *Educational Leadership, 37*(1), 15–24.

Edmonds, R. R., & Fredericksen, J. R. (1978). *Search for effective schools: The identification and analysis of city schools that are instructionally effective for poor children.* Cambridge, MA: Harvard University, Center for Urban Studies.

English, F. W. (1994). *Theory in educational administration.* New York: Harper Collins.

Fayol, H. (1949). *General industrial management.* Boston, MA: Pitman.

Foster, W. F. (1986). *Paradigms and promises: New approaches to educational administration.* Buffalo, NY: Prometheus Books.

Guba, E. G. (1960). *Research in internal administration—what do we know?* In R. F. Campbell & J. M. Lipham (Eds.), Administrative theory as a guide to action (pp. 113–141). Chicago, IL: University of Chicago.

Hall, R. M. (1963). Research priorities in school administration. In J. A. Culbertson & S. P. Hencley (Eds.), *Educational research: New perspectives* (pp. 19–30). Danville, IL: Interstate Printers & Publishers.

Hallinger, P. (2011). A review of three decades of doctoral studies using the principal instructional management rating scale: A lens on methodological progress in educational leadership. *Educational Administration Quarterly, 47*(2), 271–306.

Hallinger, P., & Heck, R. H. (1996). Reassessing the principal's role in school effectiveness: A review of empirical research, 1980–1995. *Educational Administration Quarterly, 32*(1), 5–44.

Hoy, W. K., & Miskel, C. G. (1982). *The school as a social system.* New York: NY. Random.

Koopman, G., Miel, A., & Misel, P. J. (1943). *Democracy in school administration.* New York: Appleton-Century-Crofts.

Koos, L. V., Hughes, J. M., Hutson, P. W., & Reavis, W. C. (1940). *Administering the secondary school.* New York: American Book Company.

Lewin, K. (1947). Group decisions and social change. In T. M. Newcomb, and E. L. Hartley (Eds.), *Readings in social psychology* (pp. 197–211). New York: Henry Holt.

Lewin, K., Lippitt, R., & White, R. K. (1939). Patterns of aggressive behavior in experimentally created "social climates." *The Journal of Social Psychology, 10*(2), 269–299.

Lezotte, L. W., Edmonds, R., & Ratner, G. (1974). *A final report: Remedy for school failure to equitably deliver basic school skills.* East Lansing, MI: Department of Urban and Metropolitan Studies, Michigan State University.

Mayo, E. (1949/2014). *The social problems of an industrial civilisation.* New York: Routledge.

Murphy, J. (1998). Preparation for the school principalship: The United States' story. *School Leadership & Management, 18*(3), 359–372.

Murphy, J. (2005). Unpacking the foundations of ISLLC standards and addressing concerns in the academic community. *Educational Administration Quarterly, 41*(1), 154–191.

NCEEA. (1987). *Leaders for America's schools.* Temple, AZ: University Council of Educational Administration.

NPBEA. (2015). *Professional standards for educational leaders 2015.* Reston, VA: Author.

Neumerski, C. M. (2013). Rethinking instructional leadership, a review: What do we know about principal, teacher, and coach instructional leadership, and where should we go from here? *Educational Administration Quarterly, 49*(2), 310–347.

Newlon, J. H. (1934). *Educational administration as a social policy.* New York: Scribner.

Parker, J. C. (2004). From conventional wisdom to concept: School-administration texts, 1934–1945. In T. E. Glass (Ed.), *The history of educational administration viewed through its textbooks* (pp. 45–74). Lanham, MD: Scarecrow.

Sammons, P., Hillman, J., & Mortimore, P. (1995). *Key characteristics of effective schools: A review of school effectiveness research.* London: University of London Institute of Education/Office for Standards in Education.

Scheurich, J. J. (1995). The knowledge base in educational administration: Postpositivist reflections. In R. Donmoyer, M. Imber, & J. J. Scheurich (Eds.), *The knowledge base in educational administration: Multiple perspectives.* (pp. 17–32). Albany, NY: SUNY.

Scott, W. G. (1992). *Chester Barnard and the guardians of the managerial state.* Lawrence, KS: University of Kansas Press.

Simon, H. A. (1945/2013). *Administrative behavior.* New York: Simon and Schuster.

Taylor, F. W. (1911). *The principles of scientific management.* New York: Harper and Brothers.

Tyack, D. B. (1974). *The one best system: A history of American urban education.* Cambridge, MA: Harvard University Press.

Weber, G. (1971). *Inner-city children can be taught to read: Four successful schools.* Washington, DC: Council for Basic Education.

Weber, M. (1948/2009). *From Max Weber: Essays in sociology.* New York: Routledge.

Weber, O. F. (1930). *Problems in public school administration.* New York: The Century Company.

Wilson, W. (1887). The study of administration. *Political Science Quarterly, 2*(2), 197–222.

Witzel, M., & Warner, M. (2015). Taylorism revisited: culture, management theory and paradigm-shift. *Journal of General Management, 40*(3), 55–70.

7

ALTERNATIVE WAYS OF KNOWING AND LEADING

Divisions and disagreements have always existed in the field of educational administration and leadership. For almost 100 years, some scholars and practitioners have argued that educational organizations should be run like businesses, but critics questioned businesslike management approaches. In the 1920s, Bode (1924) critiqued Bobbitt's popular scientific approach to curriculum management. Callahan (1964) outlined how business influenced public education in his seminal book *Education and the Cult of Efficiency*. He described how Taylor's gospel of efficiency forced principals to comply with the demands of business elites: "already under constant pressure to make education practical in order to serve a business society better, [principals] were brought under even stronger criticism and forced to demonstrate first, last, and always that they were operating the schools efficiently" (p. 18).

Another round of criticism surfaced in the 1990s when the field directed its interests toward developing a knowledge base and standards for principal practice. Some critics argued that the field was building walls that excluded important voices, perspectives, and approaches (Bredeson, 1995). Standards were called a false "regime of truth" that repressed new possibilities for the exercise of leadership in schools (English, 2000). Some questioned if standards were developed to "shore up" the legitimacy of the field of educational administration (Anderson, 2001). Standards were also criticized for reflecting a safe discourse that ignored injustices within schools and society. Even further, some contended that standards lowered the bar for principal preparation programs and opened a backdoor for privatization (English, 2006). In the context of high-stakes accountability, Ravitch (2016) suggested that principals and teachers who narrowly adhered to principles of Taylorism did so at the expense of "shaping character, developing sound minds in healthy bodies (*mens sana in corpore sano*), and forming citizens for our democracy" (p. 175).

In this chapter, I examine alternative perspectives in the field of educational administration and leadership and how they supply different ideas, practices, and values in relation to the principalship. I begin by tracing the development of major criticisms to dominant perspectives that provided a foundation for a focus on leadership for social justice. Much of this foundational work emerged in the 1970s as a small group of scholars questioned the efficacy of administrative science, logical positivism, and the idea that standardized theories and practices could be identified and applied in all schools. Next, I present alternative historical perspectives focused on the work of Black and Latina/o principals who, because of racist conditions, had little choice but to work with communities and lead for social justice. Finally, I conclude this chapter with a discussion of culturally responsive leadership and how Black and Latina/o professors of educational administration have critiqued dominant perspectives and instead offered alternatives that centered around community engagement, advocacy, and a form of instructional leadership that builds upon the unique assets of minoritized students and families. This chapter makes clear that while dominant approaches to principal leadership may provide some basic examples of actions that might improve school test scores, such approaches are wholly insufficient in low-opportunity communities. To get at the root of educational injustices, principals must shed the idea that school leadership is neutral, take a stance against social injustices within schools and in communities, and partner with families to transform their schools. I begin with a brief review of the work and key contributions of Thomas Greenfield, Richard Bates, William Foster, and Charol Shakeshaft, because their scholarship challenged traditional conceptions of the principalship and provoked the field to reconsider its direction.

Finding New Pathways in Educational Administration

Greenfield's Critique

In the 1970s, many scholars believed the field of educational administration was blinded by its assumptions about organizations and administrative science. Thomas Greenfield (1984) concluded that the field had inadvertently failed to recognize "all the contributions that individuals make to organizations as unique, independent, willful, erratic, and fallible human beings" (p. 17). He called for a more humane study of administration and schools:

> The difficult and divisive questions of purpose and morality, the questions arising from the necessary imposition of one person's will upon another, the questions that challenge the linking of ends and means—all these matters are set aside in a search for a pallid consensus and an illusory effectiveness. The great issues of the day in education are similarly set aside . . .
>
> *Greenfield & Ribbins, 1993, p. 164–165*

Educational administration required an emphasis on the individual and not on rational behavior or organizational structures.

Greenfield's (1984, 1986) definition of organizations differed from mainstream views because he believed organizations could not be separated from people. He defined organizations as, "subjective understandings that people choose to live by—thereby making them real only through their own will and effort" (Greenfield, 1984, p. 3). He also described organizations as: "definitions of social reality" and as "mechanisms for transforming our desires into social realities" (Greenfield & Ribbins, 1993, p. 16). These descriptions of organizations suggested that individuals and organizations are inextricably intertwined and cannot be understood independently of each other. Therefore, theory and research that tried to understand and solve organizational problems would always fall short. Using Greenfield's logic, researchers could not find the "one best way" or any universal laws of organizations and administration because the uniqueness of individuals interacting with each other in an organization makes reality too complicated for universals.

Greenfield (1984) apparently understood that organizations existed and provided structure for individuals to interact, negotiate priorities, discuss goals, and participate in bargaining and coalition building. However, he insisted on understanding schools on their own terms, rather than as abstract organizations. Schools are essential and different because they can transform the individual student. Relatedly, Greenfield argued that students did not learn from an environment, teacher demographic characteristics, or from having access to instructional resources. They learned from involvement and interaction with people and things around them (Greenfield & Ribbins, 1993). Thus, solving administrative problems and improving schools required not a change in structure per se, but in viewing schools historically and considering the varieties of experiences and conflicting views of people within and around schools (e.g., students, teachers, principals, parents, superintendents, school board members). In other words, research and theory in administration needed to begin with the individual and focus on understanding her or his interpretations of the world. Through these understandings, principals could improve the education students receive.

Critical Theory and Educational Administration

Critical theory and postmodernism influenced thinking about public education and educational inequality in the 1970s and 1980s. Richard Bates and William Foster's scholarship drew upon critical theory and postmodernism to reject positivistic thought and scientific neutrality. Their work emphasized understanding interconnections between economic life and schools as well as emancipatory and democratic avenues for change. Charol Shakeshaft's work was not necessarily rooted in critical or postmodern theory, but she still challenged the male-dominated field of educational administration and leadership and how social science research reinforced and perpetuated dominant social values. Today, theories and practices described as social justice leadership can be traced to the work of these scholars and a few others. This scholarship provided a foundation for reconsidering the role of the principal in low-income neighborhoods of color.

Richard Bates

Critical theory informed the scholarship of Richard Bates. Like Greenfield, Bates advocated for a phenomenological approach to studying educational administration that began with the individual. However, where Greenfield accentuated the role of the individual, Bates applied critical theory to understanding the power of culture and structures that maintain inequality. Bates (1981) stated:

> It is culture that gives meaning to life. The beliefs, languages, rituals, knowledge, conventions, courtesies and artifacts, in short, the cultural baggage of any group are the resources from which individual and social identity are constructed. They provide the framework upon which the individual creates his understandings of the world and of himself. Part of this baggage is factual. It is empirical, descriptive, objective. Another part of this cultural baggage, perhaps the greater part, is mythical. It is concerned not with facts but with meaning: that is, with the interpretative and prescriptive rules which provide the basis for understanding and action.
>
> *p. 37*

Before Bates and others who shared his critical-theory informed perspective, the cultural baggage people brought to schools, and how this baggage created conflict and educational inequalities had largely been ignored regarding the work of the principal.

In theorizing about schools and culture, Bates (1987) argued that divisions of race, class, and gender in society are also part of schools and influence social interactions between teachers and students and families. Bates was consistent with the work of Freire, Giroux, Bourdieu, Anyon, Apple, and other scholars (see Chapter 4) who critically considered how teachers brought cultural baggage into their classrooms in ways that marginalized and devalued low-income students of color. Giroux (1985) argued that schools were highly politicized and structured systems that reinforce dominant interests of economic elites while reproducing social inequalities. In response to the reproduction of social inequalities, Bates (1987) argued that principals could take a position and work with teachers to transform education and unequal power dynamics.

Bates advanced an educational administration theory in which community participation was prioritized. He believed that a participatory approach resolved conflicts that are part of the cultural politics of the school. The principal could catalyze such efforts by embracing their social and political roles within their communities. Educational administration would need to be context-specific and involve critical analysis, advocacy, "and the adoption of an active stance toward issues of social justice and democracy" (Bates, 1987, p. 110). A context-specific and critical approach could be understood as an "administrative praxis," which consisted of an ongoing analysis of school and community cultures. Central to administrative praxis was questioning school procedures, classroom relations, the organization and distribution of knowledge, and pedagogical tools and evaluation systems as well as how these different aspects of the school are reflective of students' cultures. Through this analysis, all stakeholders (e.g., teachers, students, staff, families) come to understand the power of culture and the vital role of the school as a source of producing new and transformative educational practices.

The application of critical theory helped reimagine the principalship from a neutral, apolitical actor to a caring individual attentive to context and cultural politics who takes stances against injustices within both schools and communities. Even so, the principal needed to think carefully about how they engaged in creating a more democratic and collaborative school because numerous threats, constraints, dilemmas, and uncertainties are part of challenging the status quo. For Bates, it was critical to view the principal within the system and not outside it. This view required pragmatic action and a varied and adaptive—not universal or standardized—approach. However, despite whatever the challenges and complexities, the priority of the principal was to always work "toward democracy, social justice, and a better world" (Bates, 1987, p. 112).

William Foster

Reconceptualizing schools as special places that can transform society and help eradicate social injustices was important to shifting the role of the principal. Foster's scholarship drew from Marxist and Frankfurt School theorists and was deeply concerned about the human beings schools educated and prepared for society. His scholarship reflected a concern for growing inequality, corporate control of schools, an increased emphasis on narrow standardized outcomes, and the loss of democracy (Anderson, 2004). Foster's (1986) seminal book *Paradigms and Promises: New Approaches to Educational Administration* powerfully defined educational administration with such concerns in mind:

> Administration is leadership. It is the communication of possibilities. In this sense, much of orthodox theory removes administration's ability to demand change, to revise the current way of doing things, to consider varied and different ways of approaching the same subject. Leadership, in our formulation, is not simply management: rather, it is a way of communicating a vision and an empowerment of others. Leadership lies not in the position *given*, but in the position *taken*.
>
> *p. 15*

Foster's scholarship suggested that principals could be "critical humanists" with "moral obligations" that worked to "develop, challenge, and liberate human souls" (p. 18). His words reflected an alternative view of administration as moral, critical, and empowering.

Educational administration also involved the resolution of various dilemmas, including two primary dilemmas: (a) dilemmas of control: related to how much teachers, parents, and students can participate in decisions about the school's orientation, curriculum, and adaptiveness to student and family culture; and (b) dilemmas on the relationship between school and society: related to the school's purpose as change agents, creating a more just society, or as socializers that help students adapt to the current social structure (Foster, 1986). Accordingly, principals need to recognize dilemmas, consider school context and the individual lives of teachers, students, parents, and citizens, and acknowledge that decisions should not just be made scientifically, but also through the application of moral values with a bias for social justice.

From Foster's perspective, leadership was educative and political because of its intention to empower people through demystifying unseen structures operating within and around schools, penetrating so-called normal conditions, working toward a participatory approach to decision-making, and communicating undistorted messages of hope for a better future. To be an educative and politically-oriented leader, Foster (1986) called for a viewing of "schools as texts" because:

> a text being written is in a continual process of transformation; it changes according to local characters, circumstances, and cultures. Like a novel, whose form is universal but whose content is individual, a school represents a given purpose accomplished through many narratives.
>
> *p. 200*

Foster used "texts" and "novels" as metaphors because they are understood, considered, and critiqued in their historical place in time. The work of principals requires similar efforts.

Foster has been called a "critical idealist" (Lindle, 2004). Relatedly, principals can be critical idealists who apply a synergistic vocabulary of critique and hope to work together to find ways to improve the lives of students and families. Despite high-sounding rhetoric, Foster (1989) acknowledged that principals confronted institutional constraints because they worked within public school districts. Principals are not leaders on the margins and they can be held publicly responsible by a bureaucracy or an elected body. Therefore, they must work democratically to transform schools in ways that better meet the needs of students, families, and the larger community.

Charol Shakeshaft

Sexism in schools and the principalship mostly went unexplored until the 1970s and 1980s. In her seminal text *Women in Educational Administration*, Shakeshaft

(1989) documented historical, political, and economic factors that advantaged men in gaining access to the principalship and considered the intersection of race, class, and gender in understanding the principal leadership. She traced how women educators were part of feminist social movements through the 20th century and documented the ways male hegemony placed women into low-visibility, dead-end jobs which "led to conditions that keep women from advancing into positions of power and prestige" (p. 83).

A content analysis of all ten volumes of *Educational Administration Quarterly* published in the 1970s highlighted some of the field's biases toward women (Shakeshaft & Hanson, 1986). The field generally ignored the fact that women existed in schools and administration. Methodological and conceptual foundations were narrowly conceived through male-only lenses that did not fully capture the social reality of schools. As she lifted the veil of male hegemony, Shakeshaft presented alternative viewpoints of administration including the viewpoints of women. While investigating women in the principalship, Shakeshaft found how women can transform their schools in ways that benefit students, teachers, and families. Often, women were leading schools in the value of student diversity and the broader social needs of families.

Shakeshaft's review of research found that women tended to spend more time interacting with teachers, students, and community members in comparison to men (Shakeshaft, 1989). Women also: (a) spent more time building relationships and caring about individual differences; (b) focused more attention on teaching and learning; (c) maintained greater knowledge of teaching methods and techniques; (d) built close-knit communities through democratic, participatory, and inclusive decision-making approaches; and (d) struggled with token status and sexist attitudes. These findings challenged conventional notions of principal leadership and underscored the importance of human relationships, listening and challenging the status quo.

Significant implications emerged from her research. Shakeshaft (1998) advocated for recruiting more women into leadership preparation programs, modifying programs to adapt to the needs of women, helping women develop essential support systems and professional networks, and raising consciousness about hiring and workplace biases that limit opportunities for women seeking leadership positions. She also recognized the structure and nature of society needed to change. She called upon the University Council of Educational Administration (UCEA) and other professional and academic organizations to prepare curriculum and programs that reflect the lives of women. She recommended that case studies of women in the principalship be conducted and used in coursework, that women be added to faculties in educational administration departments, and that research reflected the presence of women and female worlds.[1]

Social Justice Leadership in Black and Latina/o Neighborhoods and Communities

Critical scholars in the 1970s and 1980s redirected the field toward a focus on individuals within schools and social justice. In the 1980s and moving into the present, a more racially and culturally diverse field focused attention on issues of social justice in Black and Latina/o communities. While many of these scholars were influenced by Foster, Bates, and Shakeshaft, the growing presence of Black and Latino/a faculty allowed for a more vibrant, more culturally relevant, and critical discussion of the principals' roles in improving schools. Perhaps most importantly, those who studied Black and Latina/o leadership in schools found a rich history of leadership for civil rights and social justice that is highly relevant to the purpose of this book. In fact, what had been proposed by Foster, Bates, and others through the application of critical theory had already been well-established in practice by Black and Latina/o principals resisting racial oppression.

Historical Perspectives of Black and Latina/o Principals

Many Black and Latina/o principals innately understand critical theory and apply it in their daily practices not necessarily because they read the work of the Frankfurt School, but because of their lived experience with racial oppression, inequality, and need to resist the status quo. Oppression positioned Black and Latina/o principals to lead in ways that valued community and advocated for social change. Before the *Brown v Board of Education* decision in 1954, Black and Latina/o principals, especially in the South, oversaw racially segregated schools. Often, these principals worked in hostile conditions, battled for resources, and were instructional leaders that made the best of the resources they could muster. Their efforts focused on gaining resources to ensure student success, maneuvering around prejudicial district policies to ensure curricula built Black/Latina/o pride and resiliency, and using the school as a hub for the community (Dillard, 1995; L. Foster, 2005; Lomotey, 1993; McCray, Wright, & Beachum, 2007; Murtadha & Watts, 2005; Savage, 2001; Siddle-Walker & Byas, 2003; Tillman 2004).

Unfortunately, during the 1950s and 1960s, thousands of Black and Latina/o principals and teachers were demoted or removed from their positions after the *Brown* decision. Despite the loss, the historical record is insightful for reconsidering the principal in addressing various injustices within schools and society. For example, Tillman (2004) described what could be learned from Black principals in the pre- and post-*Brown* era:

> It was the Black principal who led the closed system of segregated schooling for Blacks . . . The Black principal represented the Black community; was regarded as the authority on educational, social, and

economic issues; and was responsible for establishing the all-Black school as the cultural symbol of the Black community . . . these individuals held a strong belief that while Blacks could be stripped of their money, civil rights, and property, the knowledge they acquired through education could not be taken away.

pp. 103–107

Black principals were forced to be more resourceful because of racism. They confronted obvious and hate-inspired obstacles each day which necessitated a need to be political and battle for civil and human rights. Resistance, disruption, and advocacy were essential civil rights tools. Principals became advocates who build a community support network to challenge racism at the district, state, and federal levels. As Murtadha and Watts (2005) noted, "educational leadership for African Americans meant fighting a larger, more complex battle with a moral imperative to overcome the social barriers of poverty and institutionalized racism's inequities within a democratic society" (p. 606). Principals had to reject neutrality and become radicals, agitators, provocateurs, and activists who at times publicly supported their district and the dominant power structure, while privately challenging White supremacy and advancing their community's interests.

Latina/o principals found themselves in similar situations. They could not count on districts or states for equal funding or curricular resources. It was never the case that curriculum valued their students' cultural and linguistic assets. Before the *Brown* decision, many Mexican-American children in the Southwestern U.S. attended segregated and underfunded schools. District and school policies often disciplined children for speaking Spanish, which could include corporal punishment (Valencia, 2010). Latina/o principals needed to have a strong understanding of their racial identity and needed to build a school-community that placed students' racial and linguistic identities and assets as priorities (Hernandez, Murakami, & Cerecer, 2014; López, Gonzalez, & Fierro, 2006). Latina/o principals were vital to building partnerships. Just by speaking Spanish as an agent of a school district, they signaled to families that change was possible and that the school could be on their side.

Below, I briefly discuss the leadership of four Black and Latina principals. What is evident about each of the principals is their rejection of a top-down approach to administration or a narrow focus on student achievement. Instead, each principal focused on developing safe, caring, and welcoming schools. They valued students' unique assets, inspired teachers, and engaged parents in decision-making processes. Each principal took a position and was political. Each school became a hub of its community.

Gertrude Elise McDougald Ayer[2]

A generation of women activists emerged in Harlem to challenge racial inequality in New York City between the 1930s and 1950s. Ayer was a Black woman born in New York City in 1885. In 1935, after years of challenging discriminatory hiring practices, she became the first Black principal in New York City appointed to P.S. 24 in Harlem. Ayer replaced a White principal and inherited a predominately White faculty despite 95 percent of the student body being Black. She relied on her activist skills to reshape the school's culture and help White teachers foster a more supportive learning environment for Black students. Historian Lauri Johnson (2004) described Ayer as "a caring administrator who gained the trust of parents, established a more relaxed atmosphere in the school, and provided additional relief services for unemployed families within weeks of her arrival as principal" (p. 229).

Ayer acted quickly by pioneering child-centered progressive reforms. Students engaged in experiential learning, self-directed projects, and curriculum that emphasized democratic living. Problem-solving and real-life experiences were essential to what Ayers believed would help her students thrive in life. The school also became a safe and nurturing environment. She changed student discipline to ensure her students were physically and emotionally cared for, because of a belief in "kindness and courtesy rather than force" (Johnson, 2004, p. 231).

Community partnerships were a significant part of P.S. 24. Students learned from local carpenters, butchers, grocers, and other experts in the community. During Ayer's tenure, the school produced many successful Harlemites, including the world-famous writer James Baldwin. In speaking about Ayer during an interview, Baldwin described Ayers' impact, "I guess she proved to me that I didn't have to be entirely defined by my circumstances . . . [E]very Negro child knows what his circumstances are . . . [Mrs. Ayer] was living proof that I was not necessarily what the country said I was" (Johnson, 2004, p. 231–232 from Clark (1963)). In her retirement, Ayer continued to advocate for principals and teachers to be engaged with the community. She also participated in activism that challenged racial inequality in public education.

Ulysses Byas[3]

Black principals in the segregated South needed to know more than how to manage a school's budget and oversee administrative processes. Ulysses Byas, a Black man born into poverty in Macon, Georgia in 1924, was a savvy and activist-oriented principal (Siddle-Walker & Byas, 2003). Byas had a graduate degree from Teachers College, Columbia and at age 33 became the principal of Fair Street High School (FSHS) in Gainesville, Georgia. He immediately focused on curriculum because he understood that most Black schools in Georgia were underfunded and lacked necessary curricular resources. (Siddle-Walker & Byas, 2003).

Byas was not surprised or discouraged when he found his White superintendent unwilling to provide his school with adequate resources. Black families still demanded excellence at FSHS regardless of district support and Byas saw opportunity in their demands. This tenuous situation caused Byas to be resourceful and capitalize on the engagement of Black families. He believed the Black community could be leveraged to obtain curricular resources for students, but Byas described a need to "leapfrog" the superintendent given his do-nothing approach. Leapfrogging required Byas to think multiple steps ahead. First, he needed to build relationships with the Black community and understand their concerns, which centered around dropout and truancy. Second, he framed the community's problem of dropping out as a curricular problem to gain the community's support. Third, Byas worked with teachers to study dropouts and graduates in the community and learned more about the interrelationship of dropouts and curriculum. Finally, a committee at the school delivered a 32-page typed report to the superintendent, which underscored needed resources. The superintendent was caught off-guard. He did not want to provide Byas with additional resources, but once the results made it to the local newspaper, the superintendent acquiesced.

Byas also emphasized the need to garner community support. While Black families had high expectations, many felt disconnected given their own negative experiences (or lack of experiences) with public schools. As an outsider with a graduate degree from an Ivy League institution, Byas recognized a need to build trust and connect with families. He did so partly by using a common vernacular. Nurturing, valuing, and supporting the Black community was also central to his efforts to build authentic relationships. He conducted home visits to build rapport and to show others he was down-to-earth and shared the community's values. He attended local churches and at times spoke during service.

Unfortunately, Byas felt forced to resign in 1968 because of integration and the superintendent deciding to name a younger, less experienced White principal to run the newly integrated high school. This was a significant loss to the Black community in Gainesville. Byas continued to serve as a leader and activist to improve issues related to the elderly, housing, and policing in his community.

Christina Sanchez[4]

Principals in Latina/o communities often confront similar challenges to principals in Black communities given the nature of racial oppression in U.S. society. Christina Sanchez was born in the 1960s to parents who emigrated from Mexico in search of work (Hernandez et al., 2014). Her father was a migrant worker who was committed to his family and Sanchez was lucky enough to grow up with her large extended family around her. Her family significantly impacted her development as a person and principal. Despite the powerful presence of family, Sanchez experienced racial discrimination while in school, including a time when her high school guidance counselor suggested that she would not fit in college and should consider a technical school instead. Such experiences helped her recognize the importance of affirming her racial identity in the wake of prejudice. She learned through her journey to the principalship that she could be a role model in her community.

Sanchez would eventually become principal of Mann Elementary School in an urban district in the Midwest. Mann was racially and economically diverse (91% students of color, 90% eligible for free and reduced meals, 55% English language learners (ELLs), primarily Spanish speakers). As principal, Sanchez described the importance of valuing family in each student's educational development. Central to her leadership approach was listening to others, carefully analyzing discourse to enhance her understanding of student and family perspectives. Sanchez also paid close attention to student–teacher relationships. She reflected on how certain barriers between her teachers and parents limited collaboration. A proactive approach was necessary and the school would need to be the catalyst for welcoming and engaging parents.

Part of her leadership revolved around helping teachers think about issues of race as well as helping them identify discriminatory practices within their classrooms. She described one of her central roles:

> I think my big role right here is to educate others about race and . . . in a school like this, we have to! We see ourselves as working with a variety of families; we see ourselves as working with diversity, and I've been able to help my staff understand the importance of race. I bring my perspective on the different situations based on cultural . . .
>
> *Hernandez et al., 2014, p. 585*

Sanchez clearly took a position and shared her perspective. She did not try to be neutral, but instead used her position and influence to help teachers think differently about their students.

Sanchez also recognized the unique assets of Latina/o families. She stated, "It's so important that we accept families from where they're at. We can't make assumptions or stereotypes about our children and whether they can be successful or not" (Hernandez et al., 2014, pp. 585–586). However, Sanchez also recognized that some families struggled to be engaged given different cultural, economic, and linguistic barriers. Sanchez adapted school protocols and practices, hired translators, and openly spoke Spanish to students, parents, and staff throughout each day. She became a model for valuing diversity. The school also became a place for cultural and social events that welcomed families and provided meaningful community outreach. Mann Elementary School became a place where families felt welcomed, shared stories about their lives, and developed networks of mutual support.

Kenneth Hinton[5]

A compassionate, caring, and family-centered approach was not exclusive to women in the principalship. Kenneth Hinton was a highly respected principal of an early childhood center in Peoria, Illinois (Lyman, 2000). The early childhood center was in a low-income and racially diverse area of the city. Under Hinton's leadership, the school was built from the ground up with local families, community organizations, and educators involved in each step. A task force divided into six working groups helped Hinton create school goals, develop partnerships, foster community engagement, and implement a rigorous process for teacher selection. As a principal and as a facilitator, Hinton demonstrated a caring, warm, and nurturing leadership approach as he worked with teachers and families to develop a family-centered school.

Hinton challenged district bureaucracy and worked closely with teachers and families to develop a curriculum that prioritized the social and emotional development of students. Such efforts reflect how Black principals serving underrepresented groups at times must work around districts and flawed policies or prosaic administrators. Challenging the status quo allowed the school to celebrate student individuality and design safe, supportive, and caring learning environments rather than rigidly implementing a standardized curriculum. Relatedly, Hinton empowered teachers and community members to continually review the school's instructional program to be as innovative and as adaptive to each student's needs as possible.

As a Black man who experienced discrimination, Hinton prioritized helping families overcome whatever obstacles they confronted. Like many other Black principals before him, Hinton envisioned the campus as a community hub. The school provided General Equivalency Diploma (GED) programs and parenting classes for adults and was the location for numerous social events. The school was also a place to stress the importance of family, instill spiritual values, and model compassion for all human beings. In describing his expectations for any educator, Hinton noted that "persons who work with children need to know they are loved, respected and cared for before they can really make an impact on the lives of children" (Lyman, 2000, p. 102). Hinton's leadership was informed by a belief that caring could break down barriers. He said, "Caring carries with it a loss of class, ethnicity, gender, and religion. If a teacher cares, then these things that separate us through ignorance and fear become unimportant. Status ceases to matter, and children are simply children" (Lyman, 2000, p. 116–117).

Staff members marveled at Hinton's patience in working with difficult parents. Hinton's secretary said, "He is so positive that you have to be, too. He has a positive spiritual demeanor and sees goodness in everyone. He always looks at the positive . . . It rubs off" (Lyman, 2000, p. 99). The secretary also noted:

> I have never heard him say "no" to a person who says, "Could I have a minute?" He always has time, no matter what he is doing, an appointment with the superintendent or any other important meeting. If the building were on fire and a kid said, "Mr. Hinton, I need to ask you a question," he'd sit down and talk.

Lyman, 2000, p. 89

Hinton's beliefs about caring for others had a transformative impact on his school. Rather than only focusing on systems, structures, and student achievement outcomes, Hinton's leadership style displayed a commitment to helping others through a caring and relationship-oriented approach.

Toward Culturally Responsiveness Schools

Each of the principals previously described emphasized the importance of valuing others and being responsive to students and families. Each principal represented a contribution to the long history of leadership for social justice in Black and Latina/o communities. Black and Latina/o faculty in the field of educational administration and leadership began to focus more attention on how principals address racial and social injustices. Many drew upon critical race theory (CRT) to expose how dominant hegemonic and racially neutral leadership approaches failed to challenge the social, political, economic, and educational problems that place students in low-income neighborhoods at high risk of academic failure. CRT is a valuable lens through which to analyze and interrogate how administrative and leadership practices reproduce, reify, and normalize racism (DeMatthews, Carey, Olivarez, & Moussavi Saeedi, 2017; López, 2003; Parker & Villalpando, 2007). CRT provides a starting point that racism is part of our everyday reality, and therefore allows for the interrogation and uncovering of patterns of exclusion and taken-for-granted principal leadership practices concerning race and privilege that marginalize students and families of color.

Different terms and frameworks have been advanced to address racism and related circumstances that marginalize low-income students of color, such as anti-racist leadership (Gooden & Dantley, 2012), multicultural leadership (Gardiner, Canfield-Davis, & Anderson, 2009), culturally proficient leadership (Gerhart, Harris, & Mixon, 2011), culturally relevant leadership (Horsford, Grosland, & Gunn, 2011), and color-conscious leadership (Mabokela & Madsen). Other frameworks challenge the dominance of positivism, the philosophy that suggests that all authentic knowledge can be verified by the scientific method, and instead aim to address multiple and intersecting issues of marginalization that have long been a part of U.S. history and society. These frameworks position race and culture with other interrelated identity, community, and social class issues, such as advocacy leadership (Anderson, 2009), Freirean leadership (Miller, Brown, & Hopson, 2011), community-oriented leadership (Khalifa, 2012), social justice leadership (DeMatthews, 2015, 2016; DeMatthews & Mawhinney, 2014; Theoharis, 2007), and transformative leadership (Shields, 2010). Each framework is helpful and, in many ways, can be traced back to pre-*Brown* Black and Latina/o principals, the work of Greenfield, Foster, and Bates, and other critical scholars like Giroux and Freire.

Given the history of Black and Latina/o principal leadership, it seems viable that a culturally responsive leadership approach can be used by all principals, not just those who are Black or Latina/o, to undo the broad range of injustices confronting low-income students of color in urban schools. I use the term "culturally responsive leadership" rather than "community engaged leadership" in this chapter partly because numerous scholars have used this term to describe the efforts of Black and Latina/o principals engaged in creating more socially just schools. While I will go into greater detail about community engaged leadership later in this book, understanding the foundations of culturally responsive leadership is important to the overall purposes of this book.

Like the principals described in this chapter, culturally responsive principals are not neutral because they are driven by explicit values, beliefs, and commitments to serving each student and family in their neighborhood (DeMatthews & Izquierdo, 2018; Khalifa, 2012; Khalifa, Gooden, & Davis, 2016). Culturally responsive principals are perceptive about how teacher expectations are influenced by their "cultural baggage" and how those expectations are mediators for teachers' sense of responsibility for student success (Diamond, Randolph, & Spillane, 2004). Central to this work is an awareness of how "niceness" and "decorum" can serve as barriers to meaningful and transformative dialogue. While principals should always be professional, caring, and welcoming to faculty, staff, families, and community, at times they must reject "niceness" when it serves to oblige the status quo or impede the development of broad-based coalitions that might advance a school's social justice mission (Alemán, 2009). Relatedly, Dantley and Green (2015) discussed how a principal's anger over injustice should not be repressed, but rather used purposefully. Principals should maintain:

> a deeply abiding anger over the educational conditions that many of our nation's underserved children and youth are currently experiencing. Anger must, in most cases, override privilege. Anger, not sympathy, must serve as a foundational motivation for the move toward self-reflection and self-disclosure that we believe must be integral parts of a social justice agenda in educational leadership.
>
> *p. 825*

Black and Latina/o principals fighting for justice like Ayers, Byas, Sanchez, and Hinton no doubt felt this anger. Anger coupled with critical reflection can be a powerful motivator for a focus on developing a school culture, curriculum, and pedagogy to respond to the unique needs of a school-community. To be clear, school improvement processes and instructional leadership practices are not merely viewed as mechanisms to close achievement gaps as measured by standardized tests or to meet top-down district mandates. Tests and mandates have their place, but they are not more important than social, culture, and political aspects of schooling. Of course, when tests and top-down mandates are not prioritized, principals can fear for their jobs and future career opportunities. Undoubtedly, principals like Byas were fearful of losing their jobs or even their lives, but they demonstrated courage in a far more difficult and openly racist society than we have today.

Takeaways for Principals

In this chapter, I described an alternative and social justice-oriented approach to school leadership. While professors like Bates, Foster, and Shakeshaft critically questioned dominant perspectives in the field and offered more humane and critical approaches, Black and Latina/o principals demonstrated an ant-racist and advocacy-oriented leadership centered around advocating for marginalized families, maneuvering to gain access to needed resources, and creating caring and culturally responsive schools. As more diverse professors entered the profession and theorized about the role of the principal, alternative leadership frameworks emerged to challenge the dominant perspectives. These scholars further questioned the efficacy of a politically neutral approach to leadership, especially in the context of high-stakes accountability. Whether professor or principal, this chapter demonstrated that alternative ways of leading schools can address a broader range of educational, social, and emotional needs and produce more meaningful outcomes for students and communities.

Alternative perspectives direct principals to be conscious of the social world, to recognize the innate value of each human being, and to reject neutrality. Both the professors and principals presented in this chapter realized that, while taking a political position is essential, one must do so cautiously and with great thought because principals work within the public school system. Therefore, principals cannot merely publicly challenge each policy they or their community takes issue with. Instead, principals must read the political landscape, be strategic when they seek to undermine harmful policies or structures that maintain inequality, and build a school-community where parents, teachers, and students have a meaningful voice. Leading in a complex political environment is challenging work because challenges evolve, people in organizations change, and sometimes circumstances require immediate action or a need to prioritize a multitude of problems. In the next chapter, I will unpack the meaning of social justice further, look at problems of practice that confront urban principals, and present a community engaged leadership framework that can guide principals in leading more equitable, inclusive, and community-oriented schools.

Notes

1 While I focused on the work of Charol Shakeshaft because of her early contributions to the field and the release of her seminal text, many other female professors of educational administration worked ardently to consider the role of women in the principalship and push the field toward a focus on social justice. Barbara Jackson, Catherine Marshall,

Margaret Grogan, Linda Tillman, Martha McCarthy, and many others made significant contributions during this time and well into the 21st century.

2 Historian Lauri Johnson (2006) provided a historical analysis of the life of Gertrude Elise MacDougald Ayer. Information presented in this section comes from Johnson's historical account of Ayer.

3 Historian Vanessa Siddle-Walker collaborated with Ulysses Byas to describe how Byas interacted with his superintendent, community, teachers, and students. Information presented in this section is from Siddle-Walker and Byas (2003).

4 Hernandez et al. (2014) conducted a phenomenological case study on the life and culturally relevant leadership practices of a Mexican-American principal. Both the school and principal names are pseudonyms. Information presented in this section comes from this study.

5 Linda Lyman (2000) conducted an in-depth case study of Hinton and his early childhood center. Information presented in this section mostly comes from Lyman's (2000) book *How Do They Know You Care? The Principal's Challenge*.

References

Alemán Jr., E. (2009). Through the prism of critical race theory: Niceness and Latina/o leadership in the politics of education. *Journal of Latinos and Education, 8*(4), 290–311.

Anderson, G. L. (2001). Disciplining leaders: A critical discourse analysis of the ISLLC national examination and performance standards in educational administration. *International Journal of Leadership in Education, 4*(3), 199–216.

Anderson, G. L. (2004). William Foster's legacy: Learning from the past and reconstructing the future. *Educational Administration Quarterly, 40*(2), 240–258.

Anderson, G. L. (2009). *Advocacy leadership: Toward a post-reform agenda in education*. New York: Routledge.

Bates, R. J. (1981). Management and the culture of the school. In R. Bates (Ed.), *Management of resources in schools* (pp. 37–45). Geelong, Australia: Deakin University Press.

Bates, R. J. (1987). Corporate culture, schooling, and educational administration. *Educational Administration Quarterly, 23*(4), 79–115.

Bode, B. H. (1924). Why educational objectives? *Journal of Educational Research, 10*(3), 175–186.

Bredeson, P. (1995). Building a professional knowledge base in educational administration: Opportunities and obstacles. In R. Donmoyer, M. Imber, & J. J. Scheurich (Eds.), *The knowledge base in educational administration: Multiple perspectives* (pp. 47–61). Albany, NY: SUNY.

Brown v. Board of Education of Topeka, 347 U.S. 483 (1954).

Callahan, R. E. (1964). *Education and the cult of efficiency*. Chicago, IL: University of Chicago Press.

Dantley, M. E., & Green, T. L. (2015). Problematizing notions of leadership for social justice. *Journal of School Leadership, 25*(5), 820–837.

DeMatthews, D. E. (2015). Making sense of social justice leadership. A case study of a principal's experiences to create a more inclusive school. *Leadership and Policy in Schools, 14*(2), 139–166.

DeMatthews, D. E. (2016). Competing priorities and challenges: Principal leadership for social justice along the US–Mexico border. *Teachers College Record, 118*(11), 1–38.

DeMatthews, D. E., Carey, R. L., Olivarez, A., & Moussavi Saeedi, K. (2017). Guilty as charged? Principals' perspectives on disciplinary practices and the racial discipline gap. *Educational Administration Quarterly, 53*(4), 519–555.

DeMatthews, D. E., & Izquierdo, E. (2018). Supporting Mexican-American immigrant students on the border. A case study of culturally responsive leadership in a dual language elementary school. *Urban Education.* DOI: 10.1177/0042085918756715.

DeMatthews, D. E., & Mawhinney, H. B. (2014). Social justice and inclusion: Exploring challenges in an urban district struggling to address inequities. *Educational Administration Quarterly, 50*(5), 844–881.

Diamond, J. B., Randolph, A., & Spillane, J. P. (2004). Teachers' expectations and sense of responsibility for student learning: The importance of race, class, and organizational habitus. *Anthropology & Education Quarterly, 35*(1), 75–98.

Dillard, C. B. (1995). Leading with her life: An African American feminist (re) interpretation of leadership for an urban high school principal. *Educational Administration Quarterly, 31*(4), 539–563.

English, F. W. (2000). Pssssst! What does one call a set of non-empirical beliefs required to be accepted on faith and enforced by authority? Answer: a religion, aka the ISLLC standards. *International Journal of Leadership in Education, 3*(2), 159–167.

English, F. W. (2006). The unintended consequences of a standardized knowledge base in advancing educational leadership preparation. *Educational Administration Quarterly, 42*(3), 461–472

Foster, L. (2005). The practice of educational leadership in African American communities of learning: Context, scope, and meaning. *Educational Administration Quarterly, 41*(4), 689–700.

Foster, W. (1986). *Paradigms and promises: New approaches to educational administration.* Buffalo, NY: Prometheus Books.

Foster, W. (1989). The administrator as a transformative intellectual. *Peabody Journal of Education, 66*(3), 5–18.

Gardiner, M. E., Canfield-Davis, K., & Anderson, K. L. (2009). Urban school principals and the "No child left behind" act. *The Urban Review, 41*(2), 141–160.

Gerhart, L. G., Harris, S., & Mixon, J. (2011). Beliefs and effective practices of successful principals in high schools with a Hispanic population of at least 30%. *NASSP Bulletin, 95*(4), 266–280.

Giroux, H. A. (1985). Critical pedagogy, cultural politics and the discourse of experience. *Journal of Education, 167*(2), 22–41.

Gooden, M. A., & Dantley, M. (2012). Centering race in a framework for leadership preparation. *Journal of Research on Leadership Education, 7*(2), 237–253.

Greenfield, T. (1984). Leaders and schools: Willfulness and non-natural order in organizations. In T. J. Sergiovanni & J. E. Corbally (Eds.), *Leadership and organizational culture: New perspectives on administration* (pp. 142–169). Urbana, IL: University of Illinois.

Greenfield, T. (1986). The decline and fall of science in educational administration. *Interchange, 17*(2), 57–80.

Greenfield, T., & Ribbins, P. (1993). *Greenfield on educational administration: Towards a human science.* New York: Routledge.

Hernandez, F., Murakami, E. T., & Cerecer, P. Q. (2014). A Latina principal leading for social justice. *Journal of School Leadership, 24*(1), 568–598.

Horsford, S., Grosland, T., & Gunn, K. M. (2011). Pedagogy of the personal and professional: Toward a framework for culturally relevant leadership. *Journal of School Leadership, 21*, 582–602.

Johnson, L. (2004). A generation of women activists: African American female educators in Harlem, 1930–1950. *The Journal of African American History, 89*(3), 223–240.

Khalifa, M. (2012). A re-new-ed paradigm in successful urban school leadership: Principal as community leader. *Educational Administration Quarterly, 48*(3), 424–467.

Khalifa, M. A., Gooden, M. A., & Davis, J. E. (2016). Culturally responsive school leadership: A synthesis of the literature. *Review of Educational Research, 86*(4), 1272–1311.

Lindle, J. C. (2004). William P. Foster's promises for educational leadership: Critical idealism in an applied field. *Educational Administration Quarterly, 40*(2), 167–175.

Lomotey, K. (1993). African-American principals: Bureaucrat/administrators and ethnohumanists. *Urban Education, 27*(4), 395–412.

López, G. (2003). The (racially neutral) politics of education: A critical race theory perspective. *Educational Administration Quarterly, 39*(1), 68–94.

López, G., Gonzalez, M., & Fierro, E. (2006). Educational leadership along the U.S.–Mexico border: Crossing border/embracing hybridity/building bridges. In C. Marshall & M. Oliva (Eds.), *Leadership for social justice: Making revolutions in education* (pp. 64–84). Boston, MA: Pearson.

Lyman, L. L. (2000). *How do they know you care? The principal's challenge.* New York: Teachers College Press.

Mabokela, R. O., & Madsen, J. A. (2005). "Color-blind" and "color-conscious" leadership: A case study of desegregated suburban schools in the USA. *International Journal of Leadership in Education, 8*(3), 187–206.

McCray, C. R., Wright, J. V., & Beachum, F. D. (2007). Beyond Brown: Examining the perplexing plight of African American principals. *Journal of Instructional Psychology, 34*(4), 247–256.

Miller, P. M., Brown, T., & Hopson, R. (2011). Centering love, hope, and trust in the community: Transformative urban leadership informed by Paulo Freire. *Urban Education, 46*(5), 1078–1099.

Murtadha, K., & Watts, D. M. (2005). Linking the struggle for education and social justice: Historical perspectives of African American leadership in schools. *Educational Administration Quarterly, 41*(4), 591–608.

Parker, L., & Villalpando, O. (2007). A race(cialized) perspective on education leadership: Critical race theory in educational administration. *Educational Administration Quarterly, 43*(5), 519–524.

Ravitch, D. (2016). *The death and life of the great American school system: How testing and choice are undermining education.* New York: Basic Books.

Savage, C. J. (2001). "Because we did more with less": The agency of African American teachers in Franklin, Tennessee: 1890–1967. *Peabody Journal of Education, 76*(2), 170–203.

Shakeshaft, C. (1989). *Women in educational administration.* Newbury Park, CA: Sage.

Shakeshaft, C. (1998). Wild patience and bad fit: Assessing the impact of affirmative action on women in school administration. *Educational Researcher, 27*(9), 10–12.

Shakeshaft, C., & Hanson, M. (1986). Androcentric bias in the educational administration quarterly. *Educational Administration Quarterly, 22*(1), 68–92.

Shields, C. M. (2010). Transformative leadership: Working for equity in diverse contexts. *Educational Administration Quarterly, 46*(4), 558–589.

Siddle-Walker, V., & Byas, U. (2003). The architects of black schooling in the segregated south: The case of one principal leader. *Journal of Curriculum & Supervision, 19*(1), 54–72.

Theoharis, G. (2007). Social justice educational leaders and resistance: Toward a theory of social justice leadership. *Educational Administration Quarterly, 43*(2), 221–258.

Tillman, L. C. (2004). African American principals and the legacy of Brown. *Review of Research in Education, 28*(1), 101–146.

Valencia, R. R. (2010). *Dismantling contemporary deficit thinking: Educational thought and practice.* New York: Routledge.

8

LEADING FOR SOCIAL JUSTICE

Principals in urban schools should not be narrowly focused on closing achievement gaps. We need leadership that addresses the needs of urban, low-income students of color who are marginalized and devalued in their schools and in society. We need leadership to repair damaged or broken relationships with families and communities. How can principals work within schools and communities to help remove or eliminate these barriers? To begin this work, principals need a clear conception of social justice. They need to understand that they can lead in non-traditional ways that make a significant difference in the lives of teachers, students, and families. They need to remove their blinders, summon the courage, and follow a long tradition of principals who have fought for civil and human rights within their urban schools and communities.

What is Social Justice?

Defining Social Justice

John Rawls was influential in theorizing about justice. He started with the understanding that society is a cooperative venture for mutual advantage, but is also marked by conflict. In *A Theory of Justice*, Rawls (1971/2005) related social justice to the basic structure of society and how major social institutions and the economic and social arrangements in society "distribute fundamental rights and duties and determine the division of advantages from social cooperation" (p. 7). Together, social institutions and societal structures make up a larger scheme that influences each person's life prospects, what they can do with their lives, and how well they can do it. Rawls understood that the effects of this basic structure provided differential starting positions for individuals which were not based on merit or deservedness, but chance. For Rawls, an unjust society had groups of people who were unfairly limited in their options and opportunities for a better life. A just society regulated the elements of an unjust economic and social system and redistributed advantages to make up for differential starting positions. Raj Chetty's (Chetty, Hendren, & Katz, 2016) recent analysis of the American Dream and how not all neighborhoods are "lands of opportunity" provided clear evidence of an unjust economic and social system that Rawls theorized about.

In *Responsibility for Justice*, Iris Marion Young (2011) agreed with Rawls that structural injustice existed and needed to be addressed, but she took issue with viewing injustice only as a structural issue. Young argued that structural injustice can appear to be "produced and reproduced by thousands or millions of persons usually acting within institutional rules and according to practices that most people regard as morally acceptable . . . but within these structural processes some people often do illegal or immoral things" (p. 95). For example, Young described the lack of affordable housing for Black and Latina/o families as not only a dynamic interplay of markets affected by "investment incentives, developers' imaginations, expertise, financial capacity, cultural assumptions concerning housing preferences, and local planning policies" (p. 95), but also corrupt individuals who refused to rent to Black and Latina/o families, bribed city officials for zoning variances, and engaged in other immoral or illegal acts that contributed to structural outcomes. When injustice is only viewed as a product of structure, there is no culprit to blame or to be liable for rectification. Young argued that existence of injustice implies both responsibility and action to rectify it.

Social justice is now viewed as plural in nature and broadly concerned with the equitable distribution of goods and resources coupled with the full recognition of all groups within society (Fraser, 1997; Young, 1990). To show how redistribution and recognition are intertwined, Fraser (2009) presented "folk paradigms" to justify how redistribution and recognition must be considered together rather than in isolation. She defined a folk paradigm as "sets of linked assumptions about the causes of and remedies for injustice" (p. 11). A folk paradigm for redistribution or distributive justice focuses on class politics and injustices that are socioeconomic and rooted in the economic structure of society, like Rawls' conception of social justice. The victims of injustice are Marxian classes defined by their relations to production (e.g., worker, owner). Differences between owners and workers are by-products of an unjust political economy and unequal starting points in life. Those concerned with social justice from this perspective are attentive to how workers are exploited, forced into undesirable and poorly paid work, and deprived from an adequate standard of living. Justice requires abolishing group differences and unequal starting points, which might include restructuring the economy or basic economic structures and redistributing income or wealth.

Recognition or cultural justice as a folk paradigm is commonly associated with identity politics and "with struggles over gender, sexuality, nationality, ethnicity, and 'race'" (Fraser, 2009, p. 11). Victims of injustice are status groups distinguished by less respect and esteem given to other groups. Racial and ethnic groups, women, and intersectional identities (e.g., Black girls, Gay Latina/o youth, low-income White families) are examples of often disrespected groups. In contrast to redistribution, the recognition folk paradigm targets cultural injustice rooted in social patterns, which include cultural domination (being exposed to hostile treatment for being associated with another culture), non-recognition (being made invisible in social interactions), and disrespect (being denigrated in social interactions and through stereotypical representations). Justice is brought about by cultural and symbolic change that involves revaluing disrespected identities and groups, valorizing cultural diversity, and "transforming wholesale societal patterns of representation, interpretation, and communication in ways that would change everyone's social identity" (Fraser, 2009, p. 13). The remedy for non-recognition and disrespect might include valuing group differences, rather than working to eliminate them.

Folk paradigms for redistribution and recognition reveal tensions in working toward a more just society. These tensions prompted Fraser (2009) to argue that redistribution and recognition should be understood together as a two-dimensional concept of social justice. For example, challenges confronting women in society are two-dimensional in nature. A class-like dimension and a status dimension are evident. As a class, women are often exploited, underpaid, assigned to "pink collar" service occupations, and deprived of important work-related opportunities. However, women also suffer from status subordination which is manifested through sexual and domestic violence, demeaning stereotypes, harassment, and other injustices that cannot be addressed through redistributive means alone. Similarly, racism is also two-dimensional because it is rooted in both the economic structure and in a status that privileges social patterns and traits associated with Whiteness. Racism cannot be uprooted without addressing both the economic structure and status order. As Fraser (2009) noted, "Overcoming the injustices of racism, in sum, requires both redistribution and recognition. Neither alone will suffice" (p. 23).

A constant consideration of both class- and status-based injustices is necessary given the two-dimensional nature of social justice. Ignoring one dimension may mean failing to address all the root causes of injustice, but may also mean those seeking justice through one dimension may find themselves working against natural allies. While integrating both dimensions into movements can come with increased organizing difficulty, such combinations are most likely to yield enhanced social justice outcomes. For example, the Black Lives Matter (BLM) movement not only has a mission focused on building local power to intervene against police violence in Black neighborhoods, but also in fostering an inclusive movement that affirms the lives of "Black queer and trans folks, disabled folks, undocumented folks, folks with records, women, and all Black lives along the gender spectrum" (BLM, 2017). BLM's mission and actions are aligned to working across multiple identities and class-based lines.

To create a more just society, Fraser (2009) underscored the importance of parity of participation, or a norm that "justice requires social arrangements that permit all (adult) members of society to interact with one another as peers" (p. 36). Power and Gewirtz (2001) described this as associational justice, or the absence of: "Patterns of association amongst individuals and groups which prevent some people from participating fully in decisions which affect the conditions within which they live and act" (p. 41). Parity of participation has two essential expectations:

- the distribution of material resources is sufficient to ensure each participant can independently exercise their voice;
- equal respect for all participants and equal opportunity for achieving social esteem is given (Fraser, 2009).

Accordingly, both conditions are necessary for participatory parity and neither are sufficient in isolation.

Participatory parity provides a justification for group action where decisions about injustices to address are determined dialogically through the "give-and-take of arguments in which conflicting judgments are sifted and rival interpretations are weighed" (Fraser, 2009, pp. 42–43). This is important because communities and groups often confront multiple injustices, creating a need to strategize or prioritize actions. The emphasis of participatory parity is on a democratic process of public debate and reflection. While this process is not without flaws or fallibility, each decision or priority is revisable and remains open to later challenges. Perhaps most importantly, social justice agendas are not externally imposed from above and will remain malleable through ongoing dialogue and critique.

Young (2011) presented a social connection model of responsibility that is helpful for formulating social justice agendas and making decisions about how to rectify injustices, especially when injustices are manifold and intersectional. Her model acknowledged that structural injustice is often the outcome of unintended and routine actions within institutions. People contribute to producing and reproducing structures that maintain injustice, but many do not know it given their privilege and vantage points. When it becomes clear to individuals that injustice exists, action must be taken and those within unjust structures have a responsibility to rectify injustices. This model suggests that "individuals bear responsibility for structural injustice because they contribute by their actions to the processes that produce unjust outcomes . . . All who dwell within these structures must take responsibility for remedying injustices they cause" (p. 105). Young (2011) identified several important features of the social connection model of responsibility that are central to bring about social justice:

- *Not isolating*: To focus narrowly on a few individuals for structural injustice caused by millions of people in institutions and practices is inadequate.
- *Judging background conditions*: Understanding the connection between individuals and structural injustice helps everyone who may feel powerless to change unjust structures become more conscious of their actions and identify ways that do not reproduce those structures.
- *Forward-looking*: All individuals and social institutions that produce structural injustice need to work together to transform or reduce injustice.
- *Shared responsibility*: Individuals need to recognize that they bear responsibility with others and therefore participate together in ongoing processes that reduce or eliminate injustices.
- *Discharged only through collective action*: Collective action is necessary to intervene and rectify injustice or produce more just processes, because individuals working in isolation are often constrained by rules, norms, and material effects of structural processes.

Fraser's parity of participation and Young's social connection model of responsibility share important features and are important considerations for community engaged leadership. Both approaches recognize the power of structural injustices, the responsibility of individuals and institutions at addressing these injustices, and the need to work collectively. Communication, dialogue, reflection, and ongoing action are also essential elements to both approaches. Context and attention to different perspectives, backgrounds, and identities are important features to identifying injustices and ways to rectify it.

Social Justice in Public Schools

The work of Rawls, Fraser, and Young clarified different forms of injustice in society and the critical and democratic processes that must be part of the rectification of injustice. The equitable distribution of goods and resources and the full recognition of all students and families remain a significant challenge within schools, particularly those in low-opportunity communities of color. Researchers have long documented how school resources, policies, and structures are not equitably distributed and exclude students with disabilities, English language learners (ELLs), racial/ethnic minorities and other marginalized groups from the most beneficial and meaningful learning opportunities and resources within a school (Blanchett, Klingner, & Harry, 2009). In many instances, structures and policies within schools and districts ensure marginalized student groups receive the least prepared and qualified teachers and the most inferior and narrowest curriculum (Gandara, Rumberger, Maxwell-Jolly, & Callahan, 2003). Other policies and practices funnel urban, low-income Black and Latina/o students into special education and school-to-prison-pipelines (Scott, Moses, Finnigan, Trujillo, & Jackson, 2017). Many of the same student groups and their families are devalued and their cultural and linguistic assets unrecognized by schools that privilege dominant forms of cultural capital (Valencia, 2010). Principals must recognize the two-dimensional nature of injustice and value the importance of school–family–community participation in rectifying these injustices.

Community Engaged Leadership for Social Justice: A Framework

Social justice leadership has been defined in many ways. Many scholars in the field agree that social justice leadership involves the recognition of unequal circumstances for marginalized groups and dedicated, collaborative, and democratic action aimed at eliminating and rectifying these inequalities (Bogotch, 2002; Dantley & Tillman, 2006; Furman, 2012; Murtadha & Watts, 2005). Below are several popular descriptions and actions of principals who lead for social justice. A social justice leader:

- Strives to "alter inequitable arrangements by actively engaging in reclaiming, appropriating, sustaining, and advancing inherent human rights of equity, equality, and fairness in social, economic, educational, and personal dimensions" (Goldfarb & Grinberg, 2001, p. 162).
- Is one who "interrogates the policies and procedures that shape schools and at the same time perpetuate social inequalities and marginalization due to race, class, gender, and other markers of otherness" (Dantley & Tillman, 2006, p. 19).
- "[M]akes issues of race, class, gender, disability, sexual orientation, and other historically and currently marginalizing conditions in the United States central to their advocacy, leadership practice, and vision" (Theoharis, 2007, p. 223).
- Identifies and works to undo "oppressive and unjust practices and replacing them with more equitable, culturally appropriate ones" (Furman, 2012, p. 194).

These descriptions emphasize the principal's critical orientation and an ability to recognize multiple injustices.

Research focused on principals who lead for social justice tends to focus narrowly on one or two injustices within the school, such as the racial achievement gap (Giles, Johnson, Brooks, & Jacobson, 2005), Eurocentric curriculum (Cooper, 2009), segregation of students with disabilities and ELLs (DeMatthews, 2015b; DeMatthews & Mawhinney, 2014; Theoharis & O'Toole, 2011), community disengagement (Goldfarb & Grinberg, 2001); and community marginalization and shared decision-making (Gerstl-Pepin & Aiken, 2009; Wasonga, 2009). Fewer studies and conceptions of social justice leadership have considered how principals take on a broad range of social justice issues within their schools and communities and how they work with others or prioritize their foci (Berkovich, 2014; DeMatthews, 2016a, 2016b; Santamaría, 2014).

I believe that several elements are vital to community engaged leadership for social justice. When each of these elements are reflected in the principal's values and leadership actions, principals can catalyze and meaningfully engage teachers, students, families, and communities in transformational change. Below, I describe each of these elements and their relationships to each other.

Personal Experiences and Commitments

Personal and professional experiences shape each principal's worldviews, historical position within society, and how they make sense of prevailing power relations. When principals lead for social justice with community, they often do so because their experiences enable them to recognize injustice, empathize, and act courageously. Many principals feel committed and called to this work. Such callings are often initiated by experiencing or witnessing educational and social injustices. Some principals have powerful memories from their own childhood experiences. Others recall witnessing the painful effects of marginalization of their students prior to becoming principals.

Examples of experiences are frequently detailed in case study research. For example, one principal recalled how her mother went to Tijuana, Mexico to volunteer in a literacy program on a regular basis (Merchant & Shoho, 2006). In turn, her mother's example instilled a commitment to helping and empowering others through education. A female principal in Ciudad Juarez, Mexico founded a school after 20 years of community service work (DeMatthews, Edwards, & Rincones, 2016). Her service work exposed her to how some adults could not read, write, or complete basic mathematical calculations. She could not envision students being successful without parents being literate so she committed to helping adults. In South Africa, some White principals reflected on the pain and injustice from apartheid and advocated for racially inclusive schools (Jansen, 2005). Their efforts confronted significant community unrest and they felt threatened, but proceeded with their work. A principal in the USA who was born in Vietnam but fled with his family amid the Vietnam War became an advocate for racial justice (Theoharis, 2008). His family lost everything when immigrating to the USA. This principal watched his parents struggle to survive and he was raised to believe education can be transformative. This principal's early experiences with immigrating to the USA and struggling with poverty and racism fostered a deep and personal commitment to addressing racial injustice in schools.

Principals like Gertrude Ayer and Ulysses Byas experienced racism throughout childhood and their professional careers. They understood that the educational system was set up to deny students of color with meaningful learning opportunities. Their experiences feed their courage and allowed them to transform their schools in the face of danger and uncertainty. More recently, Khalifa (2012) studied a Black principal with 33 years of experience working in a majority Black urban school-community. The principal taught some of the parents and grandparents of his current students. He drew upon his deep and sustained relationships to act courageously. Rather than dictate the school's objectives and missions, this principal empowered families, engaged in dialogue, and aligned community-related goals with school-related goals. His commitment to leadership that empowered others was based on his experiences within the community, his knowledge of how families can feel isolated from schools, and his appreciation for how larger neighborhood and social issues can constrain the school's ability to serve its students.

Women continue to experience oppression and are often viewed by many as less suitable for the principalship. Many women in the principalship report confronting various forms of sexism, but they persist and often lead for social justice because of their awareness of how various forms of oppression operate within schools, districts and communities (Blackmore, 2006; Normore & Jean-Marie, 2008; Theoharis, 2008). Women of color are often doubly-impacted by racial and gender biases. While sexism and racism are unfortunate and problematic elements of our society, they often provide women with a source of strength and commitment to creating more socially just schools and communities (Alston, 2005).

Situational Awareness

Personal experiences and commitments to social justice can lead to a heightened sense of awareness and sensitivity to oppression, exclusion, and marginalization. For some principals, personal experiences foster a commitment to "choosing to remove blinders and recognize the multiple needs of children and families" (Lopez et al., 2010, p. 69). However, recognizing injustice is only half the fight. Research on the micropolitics of schools have revealed how various actors within and around schools "seek to promote and protect their vested material and ideological interests" (Malen, 2006, p. 87). More recently, Berkovich (2014), drawing on the work of Bronfenbrenner (1979) and socioecological theory, suggested the social justice efforts must be constructed and synchronized with complementary actions and groups working in the broader social context of neighborhoods, communities, and other political realms. In other words, principals need an awareness of other forms of community activism and social movements to work in conjunction with these groups. Relatedly, principals need a deep understanding of their position within the hierarchy of a district and within an evolving school community context where history, unequal power dynamics, political struggles, and competing priorities and interest groups shape, constrain, or create avenues for transformation. Situational awareness requires both an accurate reading of the school context as well as the external forces that may be beyond the principal's control.

Situational awareness can be understood as the principal's "awareness of the details and undercurrents of running a school" which "involves knowing the positive and negative dynamics that occur between individuals in the school, and using this information to forecast and head off potential problems" (Marzano, Waters, & McNulty, 2005, p. 103). Ryan (2016) suggested, principals must "come to know, or know about, the people who work in the system . . . know the values and priorities of teachers, parents . . . 'what makes them tick'" (p. 92). Principals also need to be aware of emerging crises, grasp the significance of underlying events, and predict how these events might impact the school. Situational awareness is an active part of leadership and requires the principal to engage in multiple roles. Deal and Peterson (2013) identified the roles of historian, anthropological sleuth, actor, and healer as central to improving schools. The historian and anthropological sleuth invest in learning about their school's history and pay close attention to school norms, values, underlying beliefs, and language that make up school culture. Principals engage in conversations and listen for clues to understand how teachers, students, and families feel about the school and barriers to success. The actor and healer capitalize on critical incidents (successes, failures, losses) to reaffirm or redirect the cultural values and beliefs within the school-community. They also use critical incidents as opportunities to recognize and validate the struggles of teachers, students, and families because creating more inclusive and equitable schools is hard work and requires motivation.

Principals who lead for social justice have been described as trying to understand what people are going through and the circumstances that give rise to their expressions, beliefs, and taken for granted practices (Ryan, 2016). Thus, situational awareness also requires a recognition of the social and political issues that exist beyond the principal's locus of control, but can still positively or negatively influence or effect social justice agendas within the school. Some scholars have described administrators working within public agencies who challenge the status quo as "tempered radicals." Tempered radicals are individuals who:

> identify with and are committed to their organizations and institutions, yet who also consider themselves part of, or allied with, some group, cause or ideology that is fundamentally different from (and possibly at odds with) the dominant culture of their organizations.
>
> *Zanetti, 2004, p. 146*

As tempered radicals, principals do not have to take sides or always agree with families or their districts. Instead, they can utilize school resources and their positional authority to provide spaces for diverse groups and people to speak and help draw out meaning. They can create, encourage, and raise up counter-narratives. Principals can slow the rush to resolve problems and dilemmas and instead help facilitate a process that allows a collaborative and just resolution to emerge (Zanetti, 2004).

Principals need to be aware of competing demands from parents, how district mandates may be poorly aligned to social justice agendas within the school, and how powerful constituents and district administrators can disrupt or squeeze efforts to create schools that meet the needs of low-opportunity communities. While principals cannot control how external actors think, feel, or act, an awareness and an ability to predict resistance and challenges can inform strategies and courses of action. Consider the case of Ulysses Byas, the principal discussed in the prior chapter who worked in a segregated Black school in the Jim Crow south (Walker & Byas, 2003). Byas could "leapfrog" his White superintendent because he understood the political landscape and predicted his superintendent resistance to change. He then strategized a plan to force the superintendent to support his cause.

Situational awareness can be understood as a perpetual investigation into school and external dynamics. Surely, all principals need to be curious and inquisitive. Saul Alinsky (2010), a community organizer and activist, described situational awareness as "a constant hunt for patterns, universalities, and meanings" and noted the importance of leaders "constantly moving in on the happenings of others, identifying with them and extracting their happenings into his [or her] own mental digestive system" (p. 70). The effort of developing situational awareness allows principals to be politically astute, which can provide them access to deeper in-roads into the social and political issues within and around their schools. This means recognizing: (a) who are friends, enemies, and those individuals who can span multiple groups of friends; (b) the individuals who hold power and influence over others; and (c) historical hot button issues that might disrupt social justice agendas (Buchanan & Badham, 1999). Principals also need political acumen to accurately interpret their colleagues' words, actions, and gestures as well as monitor their own actions and how they are interpreted by other people (Bolman & Deal, 2008; McGinn, 2005; Ryan, 2010). Situational awareness and political acumen are essential because both provide the foundation for principals to "understand the situations in which they find themselves and then decide on the best courses of action" (Ryan, 2010, p. 361).

Advocacy

Advocacy is one way of acting in response to situational awareness. Anderson (2009) described what advocacy might mean for a principal or superintendent and is worth quoting at length:

> Advocacy leaders are skilled at getting beneath high-sounding rhetoric to the devil in the details. They are skeptical by nature. They know the difference between the trappings of democracy and the real thing. They refuse to collude in so-called collaborative teams or distributed leadership endeavors that are inauthentic . . . They know the hard ball politics of influential parents and the ways to work the system to get privileges for their children at the expense of others. They are not seduced by business models yet they

don't close off any avenue of new ideas . . . They find time to read widely, and have a well-developed social analysis, but do not agree on all issues, and do not follow a "party line." They are learners much like their students, and they are constantly pushing their comfort zone . . .

p. 14–15

Anderson also noted that advocacy leaders operate on multiple levels, see themselves as advocates for children and families who are treated unfairly, and work to address the systemic problems in the classroom, school, district, and community. Principals who engage in such work must do so with courage, a willingness to take risks, and with a bias toward democratic engagement. Thus, advocacy necessitates a political stance and not a neutral or impartial approach to leadership.

Power dynamics and local context are important to how principals pursue social justice agendas (Ryan, 2016). When principals confront significant challenges to their social justice agendas, they must find ways to lead in more low-profile ways and be very calculating about how they advocate for students and families. Principals must be careful about how their actions may upset powerful people and elicit additional resistance. Principals can also engage in caring actions that connect schools to families which in turn build important networks for social change. Communicating a profound sense of care to families through small acts, kind words, and thoughtful gestures has been described as "implicit activism," or "small-scale, personal, quotidian and proceeding with little fanfare" (Horton & Kraftl, 2009, p. 14). Implicit activism has the power of uniting schools and families in powerful ways. Principals can also engage in advocacy around social justice agendas by provoking the emotions of students, teachers, and families. They can show care through modest daily actions, that include standing up for marginalized groups within communities, which can promote broad-based support around other social justice causes in the future.

Advocacy is also demonstrated through a commitment to ongoing dialogue with a broad range of stakeholders. Advocacy can be enacted simply by collaborating with community-based organizations or community organizing groups. Such partnerships and joint efforts can fuse the priorities of schools and external groups together and stimulate collective action on a diverse range of issues within multiple policy arenas (Ishimaru, 2013; Mediratta, Shah, & McAlister, 2009). However, principals need to be willing to share leadership not only with teachers, but with families. This requires that principals are actively fostering caring, trusting relationships with families. Principals can initiate this work through fundraising and literacy nights, but through such ongoing activities the formation of bonding and bridging social capital can bring families and schools together and create a powerful network for joint work, advocacy against prosaic district policies, toward larger social justice issues impacting the school-community (Ishimaru, 2013). Moreover, these networks allow principals to "fly under the radar" when challenging district policies and instead rely upon a new alliance of teachers, students, families, and community groups.

Advocacy can build broad-based support and networks and provide a sense of cohesion and solidarity between principals, educators, students, and families. These conditions are conducive for principals who seek to publicly engage in ongoing and truthful dialogue about social justice issues within their schools. Anderson (2009) called such approach a "politicized notion of leadership . . . that acknowledges that schools are sites of struggle over material and cultural resources and ideological commitments" (p. 13). Underlying the politics of change is the principal's moral and political responsibility to educate and attend to both students, teachers, and families. By engaging in these educative processes, principals do not need to solve problems alone, but rather engage others in conversations about "what constitutes an appropriate course of action or an appropriate distribution of utilization of time, attention, talent, money, and other individual or organizational resources" (Malen, 2006, p. 84).

In sum, advocacy is purposeful communication. "Framing" has been described in the social movement literature as "action-oriented sets of beliefs and meaning that inspire and legitimate the activities and campaigns of a social movement organization" (Benford & Snow, 2000, p. 614). Principals can frame issues in ways that propel communities or their district to act on behalf of the school and its students and families. They may also frame issues to resist harmful or unjust district policies or the preferences of powerful families and constituents seeking to take advantage of unequal power dynamics. Framing allows principals to talk with diverse audiences, but in ways that unite all around a common purpose or cause. Framing can appear as "problem-posing," where principals shape public opinion by highlighting injustices and asking "why" questions. Finally, principals might frame issues in ways that make people uncomfortable and that disrupt the status quo. For example, principals seeking to address racism may reject "niceness" and "decorum" that comes with efforts to build broad-based coalitions, and instead choose to re-frame coalition building around the interests of marginalized groups (Alemán, 2009). Advocacy is situational, adaptive, and encompasses a broad set of skills that include framing, reclaiming problem-solving processes, and engaging in community organizing processes.

Critical Reflection and Praxis

Critical reflection and praxis are terms commonly associated with social justice and have been applied by scholars in educational leadership for more than 30 years (Black & Murtadha, 2007; Brown, 2004; Carey, Yee, & DeMatthews, 2018; Foster, 1986; Furman, 2012). Most uses of critical reflection and praxis refer to what Freire (2007) called, "conscientização," which is the process of "learning to perceive social, political, and economic contradictions, and to take action against the oppressive elements of reality" (p. 35). Relatedly, Freire was committed to challenging false consciousness that might lead people in and around schools to be swayed by racist, sexist, and classist ways of knowing. As Taylor (1998) observed:

> Freire sees critical reflection as central to transformation in context to problem-posing and dialogue with other learners. However, in contrast, Freire sees its purpose based on a rediscovery of power such that the more critically aware learners become the more they are able to transform society and subsequently their own reality.
>
> *p. 17*

Applying Freire to the work of educational leaders, Foster (1986) argued that principals need to see their responsibility to engage in continuous dialogue with their staff so that the inherent dilemmas of leading a school are critically considered, reviewed, challenged, and ultimately addressed or transformed.

Foster also recognized a need for critical reflection to be not only the work of a heroic leader, but a community endeavor. Foster (1989) argued:

> Leadership, in the final analysis, is the ability of humans to relate deeply to each other in the search for a more perfect union. Leadership is a consensual task, a sharing of ideas and a sharing of responsibilities, where a 'leader' is a leader for the moment only, where the leadership exerted must be validated by the consent of followers, and where leadership lies in the struggles of a community to find meaning for itself.
>
> *p. 61*

From Foster's perspective, principals need to work together in a shared enterprise with students, teachers, and families to understand the undesirable and unjust features of schools and society. Only through this shared work and ongoing critical reflection can meaningful transformation occur.

Others have argued for more introspective and multifaceted processes of critical reflection and praxis. Dantley (2004) argued that central to a principal's practice is a continuous process of exposing one's predispositions and attitudes to inspection and reflection. Dantley (2004) stated:

> These are examined through critical theoretical lens that compels the person reflecting to consider the hegemonic ways schools and their leadership perpetuate undemocratic procedures and practices and marginalize those who are external to any accepted positionality, be it race, class, gender, or exceptionality.
>
> *p. 45*

Critical reflection and praxis are both an individual process for each member of a school-community and an iterative and collective process that allows for everyone to expose their own predispositions and attitudes and build a new, critical, and collective consciousness within schools and communities that can be transformative.

Praxis, rather than practice, is not simply about wrestling with the daily realities and complexities of the principalship (e.g., shifting policies and reforms, technological changes, growing/shrinking budgets, new curricula, testing, and evaluation criteria) or the physical and emotional toll of the principalship which can challenge and constrain a principal's ongoing ability to lead. Praxis is beyond practice because there is an emphasis on learning through reflection, being hopeful, and acknowledging and working toward the new possibilities that lay ahead. From a leadership perspective, praxis can be understood as an understanding how previous structures and practices worked and failed, the necessity of adapting new socially just school goals and practices by experimenting with new processes, practices, and systems, and retaining those that work (Bolman & Deal, 2008). Praxis, therefore, is connected to critical reflection and inherently dialogical, because generating new ideas, processes, systems, and opportunities is most useful and innovative when drawing from a diversity of experiences and expertise.

In sum, principals need to engaged in continuous learning with others. Freire's notion of "unfinishedness" encapsulates how principals engage in critical reflection and praxis. According to Freire (1998), each person passes through this world and her or his life is not predetermined or pre-established. Destiny is constructed through daily actions. Human beings are involved in making history with others. The future for each of us, for principals, and for the creation of more socially just schools is inextricably linked to a future that is constructed through trial and error and not locked into accepting or rejecting any set of practices, systems, structures, values, or belief systems.

Technical Expertise and Standards-Based Practices

Critical reflection and praxis call for a locally relevant approach to school leadership that is built together with teachers, students, families, and other community members. Principals have a valuable contribution to these collaborative efforts. Their prior training and formal job requirements include an important set of technical knowledge and skills associated with educational administration and leadership that can be adapted for social justice agendas. Technical expertise includes an applied knowledge of:

- federal, state, and district policy and law;
- school-based budgeting;
- curriculum, instruction, assessment, classroom management and student discipline practices;
- teacher and staff evaluation processes;
- school-level systems of support (e.g., positive behavioral supports, restorative justice, response to intervention, professional learning communities) (DeMatthews, 2015a).

Such expertise cannot be overlooked or deemphasized. Consider how many schools segregate students with disabilities and ELLs, maintain high levels of suspension or racial discipline gaps, and produce racial and class-based achievement gaps. Even if principals are conscious of how such practices and structures marginalize students, if they do not have the knowledge and expertise to navigate law and policy, more efficiently utilize school resources allocated in the budget, or redevelop a master schedule to allow for increased co-planning, co-teaching, and professional development activities, the school will continue to be unjust.

Relatedly, principals need to apply and adapt standards-based practices to fit the unique aspects of their school and community. These practices generally include developing a school mission that encourages high expectations, providing high-quality professional development, creating professional learning communities and a culture of inquiry, engaging in shared leadership and empowering teacher leaders, and efficiently and equitably allocating district resources (Leithwood, Harris, & Hopkins, 2008; Leithwood & Jantzi, 2005). While such practices are generalizable, they need to be locally and culturally responsive. For example, Standard 1 in the Professional Standards for Educational Leaders (National Policy Board for

TABLE 8.1 From Standards-Based School Leadership Practices toward Critical Questioning

Standards-Based School Leadership Practices	Critical Questions
Developing a school mission that encourages high academic expectations for all students	How can we highlight existing inequalities in ways that inspire and bring together our school-community so that we can better serve all students?
Providing high-quality professional development	How can we better prepare our school-community to teach a diverse student group while at the same time ensuring each individual teacher has his or her specific learning needs met?
Ensuring teachers and professional learning communities utilize data to inform instructional and other related decisions	How can we use data to understand inequality and then make ethical and social justice oriented decisions to better support all learners?
Engaging in shared leadership by incorporating teachers into meaningful leadership activities and roles	How can we draw upon the unique backgrounds and experiences of our school-community to reimagine our school and improve our decision-making processes?
Efficiently and flexibly managing the school's resources for an effective learning environment	In what ways can we alter our school's resource allocations to better support high-quality inclusive instruction and the equitable distribution of social, emotional, and academic learning opportunities?

Source: Adapted from DeMatthews (2015b)

Educational Administration (NPBEA), 2015) emphasizes the role of the principal in developing, advocating, and enacting "a shared mission, vision and core values of high-quality education and academic success and well-being for each student" (p. 9). A school in Washington, DC serving a high-proportion of Black students with a majority White faculty and a curriculum that is Eurocentric and non-responsive to students requires a school vision focused on high-quality education and academic success, but also curriculum and instruction meaningfully adapted to their lived experiences and cultural identities of students. Moreover, teachers must be supported and prepared to accept, value, and effectively educate students from a different racial background than their own. Similarly, schools in El Paso that serve high proportions of Mexican-American students and ELLs require a shared mission of inclusive and bilingual education that recognizes and values Latina/o students' assets. Thus, standard practices are relevant, but must be locally and culturally responsive.

In sum, technical expertise and standards-based practices provide principals with knowledge and skills that teachers, students, families, and community groups may lack. Sharing their knowledge and skills to co-construct a new school is essential to creating the schools that are needed in low-opportunity communities. Table 8.1 summarizes empirically supported standards-based leadership practices and then offers critical questions for how each practice might be adapted to create more equitable schools.

Takeaways for Principals

It may be true that mainstream reform and turnaround policies will remain driven by student achievement measured by standardized tests, but principals who lead for social justice can still find ways to build broad-based community support around social justice agendas. It may also be true that community engaged leadership aimed at addressing social injustices is an uphill battle that may take extensive time and energy, especially in low-opportunity communities and schools that have long failed to provide meaningful educational or social mobility options to families and children. The challenges that are ahead should not be viewed as barriers, but rather as important learning opportunities. The challenges and subsequent learning opportunities of practicing community engaged leadership for social justice, which could enable principals to transform their schools and the lives of urban students, are the subject of the next chapter.

References

Alemán Jr., E. (2009). Through the prism of critical race theory: Niceness and Latina/o leadership in the politics of education. *Journal of Latinos and Education, 8*(4), 290–311.
Alinsky, S. (2010). Rules for radicals: A practical primer for realistic radicals. New York: Vintage.

Alston, J. A. (2005). Tempered radicals and servant leaders: Black females persevering in the superintendency. *Educational Administration Quarterly*, *41*(4), 675–688.

Anderson, G. L. (2009). Advocacy leadership: Toward a post-reform agenda in education. New York: Routledge.

Benford, R. D., & Snow, D. A. (2000). Framing processes and social movements: An overview and assessment. *Annual Review of Sociology*, *26*(1), 611–639.

Berkovich, I. (2014). A socio-ecological framework of social justice leadership in education. *Journal of Educational Administration*, *52*(3), 282–309.

Black, W. R., & Murtadha, K. (2007). Toward a signature pedagogy in educational leadership preparation and program assessment. *Journal of Research on Leadership Education*, *2*(1), 1–29.

Blackmore, J. (2006). Social justice and the study and practice of leadership in education: A feminist history. *Journal of Educational Administration and History*, *38*(2), 185–200.

Blanchett, W. J., Klingner, J. K., & Harry, B. (2009). The intersection of race, culture, language, and disability: Implications for urban education. *Urban Education*, *44*(4), 389–409.

BLM. (2017). *About Black Lives Matter*. Retrieved 3 November 2017, from https://black livesmatter.com/

Bogotch, I. E. (2002). Educational leadership and social justice: Practice into theory. *Journal of School Leadership*, *12*, 138–156.

Bolman, L. G., & Deal, T. E. (2008). *Reframing organizations*. San Francisco: Jossey-Bass.

Bronfenbrenner, U. (1979). *The ecology of human development: Experiments by nature and design*. Cambridge, MA: Harvard University Press.

Buchanan, D., & Badham, R. (1999). Politics and organizational change: The lived experience. *Human Relations*, *52*(5), 609–629.

Carey, R. L., Yee, L. S., & DeMatthews, D. E. (2018). Power, penalty, and critical praxis: Employing intersectionality in educator practices to achieve school equity. *Educational Forum*, *82*(1), 111–130.

Chetty, R., Hendren, N., & Katz, L. F. (2016). The effects of exposure to better neighborhoods on children: New evidence from the Moving to Opportunity experiment. *American Economic Review*, *106*(4), 855–902.

Cooper, C. W. (2009). Performing cultural work in demographically changing schools: Implications for expanding transformative leadership frameworks. *Educational Administration Quarterly*, *45*(5), 694–724.

Dantley, M. (2004). Moral leadership: Shifting the management paradigm. In F. English (Ed.), *Handbook of educational leadership* (pp. 34–46). Thousand Oaks, CA: Sage.

Dantley, M., & Tillman, L. (2006). Social justice and moral transformative leadership. In C. Marshall & M. Oliva (Eds.), *Leadership for social justice: Making revolutions happen* (pp. 16–29). Boston, MA: Pearson.

Deal, T. E., & Peterson, K. D. (2013). Eight roles of symbolic leaders. In M. Grogan & M. Fullan (Eds.), *The Jossey-Bass reader on educational leadership* (pp. 274–286). San Francisco, CA: Jossey-Bass.

DeMatthews, D. E. (2015a). Clearing a path for inclusion: Distributing leadership in a high performing elementary school. *Journal of School Leadership*, *25*(6), 139–166.

DeMatthews, D. E. (2015b). Making sense of social justice leadership: A case study of a principal's experiences to create a more inclusive school. *Leadership and Policy in schools*, *14*(2), 139–166.

DeMatthews, D. E. (2016a). Competing priorities and challenges: Principal leadership for social justice along the US–Mexico Border. *Teachers College Record, 118*(8), 1–38.

DeMatthews, D. E. (2016b). Social justice dilemmas: Evidence on the successes and short-comings of three principals trying to make a difference. *International Journal of Leadership in Education*. Retrieved from https://doi.org/10.1080/13603124.2016.1206972

DeMatthews, D. E., Edwards Jr, D. B., & Rincones, R. (2016). Social justice leadership and family engagement: A successful case from Ciudad Juárez, Mexico. *Educational Administration Quarterly, 52*(5), 754–792.

DeMatthews, D., & Mawhinney, H. (2014). Social justice leadership and inclusion: Exploring challenges in an urban district struggling to address inequities. *Educational Administration Quarterly, 50*(5), 844–881.

Foster, W. (1986). Paradigms and promises: New approaches to educational administration. New York: Prometheus books.

Foster, W. (1989). Toward a critical practice of leadership. In J. Smyth (Ed.), *Critical perspectives on educational leadership* (pp. 39–62). New York: Falmer Press.

Fraser, N. (1997). Justice interruptus: Critical reflections on the "postsocialist" condition. New York: Routledge.

Fraser, N. (2003). Social justice in the age of identity politics: Redistribution, recognition, and participation. In N. Fraser & A. Honneth (Eds.), *Redistribution or recognition? A political–philosophical exchange* (pp. 7–109). New York: Verso.

Freire, P. (1998). Pedagogy of freedom: Ethics, democracy, and civic courage. Lanham, MD: Rowan and Littlefield.

Freire, P. (2007). *Pedagogy of the oppressed*. New York: Continuum.

Furman, G. (2012). Social justice leadership as praxis: Developing capacities through preparation programs. *Educational Administration Quarterly, 48*(2), 191–229.

Gandara, P., Rumberger, R., Maxwell-Jolly, J., & Callahan, R. (2003). English Learners in California Schools: Unequal resources, unequal outcomes. *Education Policy Analysis Archives, 11*(36), 1–54.

Gerstl-Pepin, C., & Aiken, J. A. (2009). Democratic school leaders: Defining ethical leadership in a standardized context. *Journal of School Leadership, 19*, 406–444.

Giles, C., Johnson, L., Brooks, S., & Jacobson, S. L. (2005). Building bridges, building community: Transformational leadership in a challenging urban context. *Journal of School Leadership, 15*(5), 519.

Goldfarb, K. P., & Grinberg, J. (2001). Leadership for social justice: Authentic participation in the case of a community center in Caracas, Venezuela. *Journal of School Leadership, 12*, 157–73.

Horton, J., & Kraftl, P. (2009). Small acts, kind words and "not too much fuss": Implicit activisms. *Emotion, Space and Society, 2*(1), 14–23.

Ishimaru, A. (2013). From heroes to organizers: Principals and education organizing in urban school reform. *Educational Administration Quarterly, 49*(1), 3–51.

Jansen, D. J. (2006). Leading against the grain: The politics and emotions of leading for social justice in South Africa. *Leadership and Policy in Schools, 5*(1), 37–51.

Khalifa, M. (2012). A re-new-ed paradigm in successful urban school leadership: Principal as community leader. *Educational Administration Quarterly, 48*(3), 424–467.

Leithwood, K., Harris, A., & Hopkins, D. (2008). Seven strong claims about successful school leadership. *School Leadership and Management, 28*(1), 27–42.

Leithwood, K., & Jantzi, D. (2005). A review of transformational school leadership research 1996–2005. *Leadership and Policy in Schools, 4*(3), 177–199.

López, G. R., González, M. L., & Fierro, E. (2010). Educational leadership along the U.S.–México border: Crossing borders/embracing hybridity/building bridges. In C. Marshall & M. Oliva (Eds.), *Leadership for social justice* (2nd ed.) (pp. 100–119). Boston, MA: Allyn & Bacon.

Malen, B. (2006). Revisiting policy implementation as a political phenomenon: The case of reconstitution policies. In M. I. Honig (Ed.), *New directions in education policy and implementation: Confronting complexity* (pp. 83–104). Albany, NY: SUNY Press.

Marzano, R. J., Waters, T., & McNulty, B. A. (2005). *School leadership that works: From research to results.* Alexandria, VA: ASCD.

McGinn, A. (2005). The story of 10 principals whose exercise of social and political acumen contributes to their success. *International Electronic Journal for Leadership in Learning, 9*(5), 1–11. Retrieved from http://files.eric.ed.gov/fulltext/EJ985389.pdf

Mediratta, K., Shah, S., & McAlister, S. (2009). *Community organizing for stronger schools: Strategies and successes.* Cambridge, MA: Harvard Education Press.

Merchant, B. M., & Shoho, A. R. (2006). Bridge people: Civic and educational leaders for social justice. In C. Marshall & M. Oliva (Eds.), *Leadership for social justice: Making revolutions in education* (pp. 279–306). Boston, MA: Pearson.

Murtadha, K., & Watts, D. M. (2005). Linking the struggle for education and social justice: Historical perspectives of African American leadership in schools. *Educational Administration Quarterly, 41*(4), 591–608.

NPBEA. (2015). *Professional standards for educational leaders 2015.* Reston, VA: Author.

Normore, A. H., & Jean-Marie, G. (2008). Female secondary school leaders: At the helm of social justice, democratic schooling and equity. *Leadership & Organization Development Journal, 29*(2), 182–205.

Power, S., & Gewirtz, S. (2001). Reading education action zones. *Journal of Education Policy, 16*(1), 39–51.

Rawls, J. (1971/2005). *A theory of justice.* Cambridge, MA: Harvard University Press.

Ryan, J. (2010). Promoting social justice in schools: Principals' political strategies. *International Journal of Leadership in Education, 13*(4), 357–376.

Ryan, J. (2016). Strategic activism, educational leadership and social justice. *International Journal of Leadership in Education, 19*(1), 87–100.

Santamaría, L. J. (2014). Critical change for the greater good: Multicultural perceptions in educational leadership toward social justice and equity. *Educational Administration Quarterly, 50*(3), 347–391.

Scott, J., Moses, M.S., Finnigan, K.S., Trujillo, T., & Jackson, D.D. (2017). *Law and order in school and society: How discipline and policing policies harm students of color, and what we can do about it.* Boulder, CO: National Education Policy Center. Retrieved 11/2/2017 from http://nepc.colorado.edu/publication/law-and-order

Taylor, E. W. (1998). *The theory and practice of transformative learning: A critical review.* Columbus, OH: ERIC Clearinghouse on Adult, Career, and Vocational Education.

Theoharis, G. (2007). Social justice educational leaders and resistance: Toward a theory of social justice leadership. *Educational administration quarterly, 43*(2), 221–258.

Theoharis, G. (2008). Woven in deeply: Identity and leadership of urban social justice principals. *Education and Urban Society, 41*(1), 3–25.

Theoharis, G., & O'Toole, J. (2011). Leading inclusive ELL: Social justice leadership for English language learners. *Educational Administration Quarterly, 47*(4), 646–688.

Valencia, R. R. (2010). *Dismantling contemporary deficit thinking: Educational thought and practice.* New York: Routledge.

Walker, V. S., & Byas, U. (2003). The architects of black schooling in the segregated south: The case of one principal leader. *Journal of Curriculum & Supervision*, *19*(1), 54–72.

Wasonga, T. A. (2009). Leadership practices for social justice, democratic community, and learning: School principals' perspectives. *Journal of School Leadership*, *19*, 200–224.

Young, I. M. (1990). *Justice and the politics of difference*. Princeton, NJ: Princeton Press.

Young, I. M. (2011). *Responsibility for justice*. Oxford, UK: Oxford University Press.

Zanetti, L. A. (2004). Repositioning the ethical imperative: Critical theory, Recht, and tempered radicals in public service. *American Review of Public Administration*, *34*(2), 134–150.

9

CRITICAL CASES OF LEADERSHIP IN LOW-OPPORTUNITY COMMUNITIES

Urban principals can and should be at the center of creating school conditions that meet the needs of students and families in low-opportunity communities, not because they have all the answers or authority (they do not), but because they are in a conspicuous position to catalyze an authentic locally responsive learning process that can bring new possibilities and opportunities. A principal's personal commitments, situational awareness, advocacy, critical reflection, and technical expertise can enable them to rethink and collaboratively reconstruct schools in ways that bring about social transformation. They can catalyze change by being sympathetic, compassionate, reflective, and hopeful individuals. They can serve as "tempered radicals" that learn with communities, and they certainly cannot wait any longer for a magic bullet reform or be afraid to make mistakes. To accentuate why I believe principals should be at the center of creating schools that can change the lives of their students, this chapter supplements previous chapters focused on alternative and social justice leadership approaches with cases that required principals to work with teachers, families, and communities to learn, reflect, and transform their schools. Each principal recognized the power of the status quo in their district, sought to improve the lives of students and families, succeeded in many areas, and struggled in others.

Case Studies

Over the past seven years, I have studied principals engaged in social justice efforts in the mid-Atlantic region of the USA and along the USA–Mexico border in El Paso and Ciudad Juarez, Mexico. In this chapter, I review four case studies of urban principals with a focus on their priorities, actions, successes, and shortcomings. In each case, I highlight the principal's commitment to community, families, students, and teachers. I also identify key contextual challenges and reveal their shortcomings as leaders working under challenging conditions. In each case, I underscore the principal's incompleteness and their personal critical reflections on their practices. The purpose of these cases is to illustrate the personal commitments, situational awareness, advocacy, critical reflection, and technical expertise of principals in low-opportunity communities trying to make a difference.

Case 1: Competing Priorities on the Border

Saenz Elementary School

Saenz Elementary School (ES) is in El Paso, Texas, a city directly adjacent to Ciudad Juarez, Mexico (DeMatthews, 2016). The school is walking distance to the border fence and in proximity to areas regularly patrolled by U.S. Border Patrol agents. Many nearby families and students are fearful of loved ones being deported. Many residents struggled financially, but the surrounding neighborhoods are known to be close-knit. Saenz ES serves a predominately Latina/o (99%) student body, with many students (90%) receiving free and reduced meals and almost half the school (45%) identified as English language learners (ELLs). Some Saenz students cross an international bridge from Mexico each day to attend school while others are El Paso residents. Saenz ES historically outperformed other schools in the district and region with similar demographics.

The Principal

Ms. Uribe is the principal at Saenz ES and her supervisor and other principals in her district describe her as a "strong leader" and one who cares about each student and family. She is a Mexican-American woman in her 40s and was in her fourth year as principal. She was driven to improve her school. She was passionate about bilingual education and literacy and believed public education can contribute to a more just society. Mrs. Uribe was conscious of the multiple and intersecting educational and social injustices confronting her students and their families. Her consciousness stemmed from her own experiences as a child growing up on the border and as an ELL. She remembered feeling isolated in a class where nobody would speak to her in Spanish, even though she knew very little English. She was excluded from activities, sat in the back of the classroom, and placed in what she called, "a sink or swim environment." She said she felt "called" to work at Saenz, stating: "When I'm here, I'm home. I'm serving my community. This is where I'm supposed to be."

Ms. Uribe's childhood experiences of being excluded hurt her self-confidence, but her family was a powerful motivating force. She stated, "My mother was my motivation. She gave me courage to better myself and eventually I learned English and was successful." Her mother's motivation inspired her as a principal to think about how important families are to student success. Relatedly, she believed her students need to be proud of where they come from and of their Mexican and Mexican-American heritage. She stated:

> We live in a very oppressed community, some of our students come from indigenous families, some are from slums in Juarez, many of whom have lost their connection to Mexican culture and identity. As Mexicans and Mexican Americans, we have a rich culture and, unfortunately, that culture is sometimes lost due to poor schools, poverty, and other circumstances . . . The more our students know who they are, their ancestors, their traditions, the more they can believe in themselves and overcome the obstacles they face.

Ms. Uribe communicated a keen awareness of how Mexican and Mexican-American students are marginalized due to limited school resources, a culturally irrelevant curriculum, and deficit views of ELLs.

Priorities and Action

Ms. Uribe understood that being a principal in Texas meant being accountable for test scores. She said, "A new principal needs to know that scores are important . . . because if you are doing well, you have more freedom to innovate . . . There isn't anyone looking over your shoulder, you have more trust with your district." For Ms. Uribe, "scores needed to be taken care of first." In other words, she prioritized student achievement on standardized tests not as an end goal, but as a buffer to allow her to innovate on her campus. She also believed raising student achievement required the school to be responsive to students and families. Many students were ELLs and teachers often viewed such students as a testing liability. Ms. Uribe felt differently. She framed students from Spanish-speaking families as having important assets. However, she noted that her teachers needed to "recognize and exploit" that asset. She also believed students not identified as ELLs on her campus "most likely still had some deficits in language development that are holding them back [academically]." Her beliefs were based on years of experience working in similar communities and her analysis of student achievement data.

In Ms. Uribe's first year as principal, she called her assistant principal and a group of teachers together to develop a plan to improve the quality of instruction. The group met over the summer and weekly for a few months until they agreed on three priorities. First, the school needed to utilize student data better to improve instruction and identify professional development needs. Second, the school needed to become more inclusive, particularly for ELLs. Third, stronger relationships needed to be built with families. Ms. Uribe viewed these goals as interwoven:

The way I see it is this, you need your data to see what's going on at a general level. You can use student data to help facilitate conversations. What I mean is, to get the conversation started about what's going on in the classroom . . . These conversations can help us know what we need to do next. Of course, all teachers need professional development. If I can have more insight into what they need, then we all can be more effective . . . So, the more effective we all are, the more students we can serve in a regular classroom, less students will need to be removed . . . Finally, and this is big, we need parents involved. They are the key to everything. I know and you know, kids will be successful if the parents are involved.

Ms. Uribe and her teachers developed two data analysis tools: Individual Student Portfolio (ISP) and the Class Roster Analysis (CRA). All teachers continuously refined the tools. The CRA is focused on raising student achievement on state assessments. Every 3–4 weeks all teachers proctored interim assessments aligned to the standards and then recorded in the CRA how each student performed on each standard, identified areas of weakness, and analyzed student responses to test questions. Later, teachers met in groups and with an administrator to identify ways to reteach materials as well as potential areas of professional development.

The ISP is a student work portfolio where teachers tracked each student's progress on state assessments, curriculum-based assessments, writing assignments, and classroom projects. The ISP also had a journal. The journal consisted of teacher observations and interactions as well as meeting notes. Teachers met with either Ms. Uribe or the assistant principal on a regular basis to discuss each student's progress. At the end of each year, teachers passed the ISPs and CRAs to the next group of teachers assigned to students. Ms. Uribe compared the ISP to an Individualized Educational Program (IEP), which is a document required by law for all students receiving special education. She felt all students deserved a specialized learning plan. To Ms. Uribe, the ISP reflected the importance of "taking time and thinking about the unique needs of each student."

The tools created a data-driven school ritual where teachers spent significant time assessing students and analyzing results. One teacher felt the CRA and ISP gave her a head start in preparing, "Each year, I get all this great information on all my students." Another teacher said, "I never knew how much you can learn from studying a child's work . . . It's opened up so many new ideas for me." Ms. Uribe viewed the tools also as a way of advocating for students. She said, "A lot of times teachers vent or complain about their struggling students and they make excuses rather than take responsibility for their learning." The tools provided data and opportunities for teachers to talk amongst each other to improve instruction and what type of professional development was necessary for continued improvement. Ms. Uribe said, "Right off the bat, some teachers who used to blame students have become really empowered . . . It's like they are new teachers." For other teachers, she noted, "It takes seeing how well a child did in another teacher's class, seeing the work samples and the teacher's journal . . . It causes them to reflect."

Creating a more inclusive, bilingual, and family-engaged school was also central to Ms. Uribe's priorities. She advocated for dual language education and presented her idea about inclusive, bilingual classrooms to parents. The feedback she received took her by surprise. Some Mexican-American families did not want their children mixed with immigrant students from Mexico or worried that immigrant students would slow down the pace of instruction in English. One parent concluded that the curriculum would be "watered down" if ELLs were included. Another group of parents shared their past experiences of "being included," which meant sitting in the back of a classroom unable to speak English and not receiving any help from the teacher. These parents, who mostly spoke Spanish, feared the same fate for their children and instead wanted to keep the separate classrooms for ELLs. Ms. Uribe asked herself, "Why did I even ask?" She forced her agenda through without full parent support because she felt she knew what was best for her students. She also felt that educational decisions could not be made based on parents' deficit views of other students or based on fear. She said, "Parent input is important, but not as important when parents are wrong about how to help their own children." Ms. Uribe was not mad at parents because she felt their beliefs were rooted in the past oppressive acts of educators in the region and she hoped parents would see the benefits of her decision.

Saenz teachers and staff also worked hard to develop family relationships and engage parents. The school became more of a community hub as Ms. Uribe and teachers brought adult education classes into the school. Social workers and nonprofit community-based organizations provided parent workshops and shared resources and job opportunities that were available in the surrounding area. Numerous social events were held to help parents feel welcome in the school. The school hosted a Latina/o literature night on a regular basis where families and students came in and read stories together. Sometimes, the literacy night was hosted off campus at a recreational center that was more convenient and accessible for families.

Outcomes and Principal Reflections

During Ms. Uribe's 4-year tenure, approximately 90% of all students scored proficient or advanced on state reading and mathematics assessments. The school district and the Texas Education Agency (TEA) distinguished Saenz ES for progress in closing achievement gaps. Saenz ES also won distinctions from the state and educational organizations for academic success. Teachers viewed Ms. Uribe as the catalyst for their school's improvements and for increased rates of student achievement.

Ms. Uribe reflected on her leadership priorities and practices and felt like she had fallen short in many other areas. First, she concluded that her school had not significantly adapted a culturally relevant or responsive curriculum that taught students about their culture and helped build a positive self-identity. While the school shifted toward a dual language model that valued Spanish language, students learned very little about Mexican-American culture and history, especially relevant to the border. Second, she recognized that parent engagement had mostly been "one-directional" and focused on building buy-in for school initiatives, like dual language. She did not regret deciding to adopt dual language, but she recognized that by forcing the change through without meaningful parent buy-in, she contributed to the marginalization of families. She understood a better approach might have been to take more time educating families about the benefits of dual language education.

In sum, Ms. Uribe's commitments to her school helped her collaborate with teachers and families to increase student achievement and narrow racial and linguistic achievement gaps. Her instructional leadership skills were evident in how she led a team to create data analysis tools used to improve instruction and identify professional development needs. Parent literacy nights emphasized the importance of literacy with parents, which was a strategic investment of school resources. Her recognition of how vital test scores were to her district reflected a degree of situational awareness, although, as she admitted, she had not taken advantage of her school's high test scores in ways that truly and deeply contributed to more meaningful and culturally responsive curriculum. Families were more engaged and welcomed at the school, which was an important success, although Ms. Uribe admitted to minimizing parent perspectives when they were not aligned to her agendas. Her reflection and awareness of her shortcomings reflected a leadership praxis that is not perfect, but that is bent toward learning, generating new ideas, and finding new ways to make good on past decisions that reproduced injustices within schools.

Case 2: Valuing Community Cultural and Linguistic Assets

Villa Elementary School

Villa ES is also in the El Paso area and located within walking distance to the border and an international bridge. Villa ES students are mostly Latina/o (97%) and a large proportion of students receive free and reduced meals (97%) and are identified as ELLs (86%). Approximately 95% of the people in the U.S. census tract where Villa is situated identified as Mexican and Mexican-American and many residents were recent immigrants. The community has long been a destination for families immigrating to the USA and is filled with murals and art installations that symbolize the community's American, Mexican, and Aztec ancestry. Housing projects and multiple shelters are near the school and house many Villa students. The community was described by parents and teachers as tight-knit, but as one that struggled with issues associated with drug abuse, gang activity, and the negative effects of deportation on families.

Mrs. Leon

Mrs. Leon had been principal of Villa ES for 2.5 years and worked hard to create a more culturally responsive and community engaged school (DeMatthews & Izquierdo, 2018). She was a Mexican-American woman from the El Paso region with extensive experience in bilingual education. She felt called to lead at Villa and its students and families. She described her calling as follows:

> I was prepared to do this. I'm an English language learner myself. I've taught ELLs along the border. I have a special master's degree where we learned about linguistics, research-based instructional practices, and how to create an inclusive school. I'm where I'm supposed to be.

Mrs. Leon was also deeply committed to dual language education. Her commitment came from her past experiences as well as her awareness of research on dual language. She said, "Way back, we [Mexican-American] were included and you know what that meant? We sat in the back, it was sink or swim . . . That's not inclusive." When Mrs. Leon spoke about dual language she always spoke with passion and referencing the work of researchers like Virginia Collier and Wayne Thomas (2004). A deputy superintendent described her as "a new breed" of principal who was not complacent and was an expert in serving Mexican and Mexican-American communities. Her teachers described her as "fiery," "relentless," "dedicated," and "direct."

Priorities and Actions

Mrs. Leon was hired by the district to transition the school from a less effective language acquisition model (transitional bilingual education) into a "50:50" dual language school where all students received instruction in English and Spanish for half the day. Mrs. Leon had experience in developing a dual language school as an assistant principal and bilingual education teacher. She understood that implementing dual language was complicated because it required a cultural shift in the school, a revamped curriculum, and a new set of instructional practices. However, she believed the work was well worth it. She stated, "Dual language is all about social justice. It values students and families . . . It validates what students learn at home from their families . . . [and] research finds that it increases student achievement." For Mrs. Leon, dual language was not about improving test scores but about building on student and family assets.

The first year of dual language implementation began with the pre-k and kindergarten teachers. Each year one additional grade would be added until the entire school was fully implementing dual language. In year 1, pre-k and kindergarten teachers described dual language as confusing and frustrating. Mrs. Leon predicted and understood that teachers who were new to dual language often struggled because they never co-planned, developed learning materials in English and Spanish, or followed a classroom structure aligned to a dual language education model. She assumed that some resistance was likely. In response, she was proactive, maintained an open-door policy with teachers, and participated in professional development with her faculty. She provided teachers and grade-level teams with professional development sessions on biliteracy, co-planning, and effective teaching strategies. She co-planned and modeled instruction with teachers and was a constant support for teachers to vent frustrations and ask questions. When teachers struggled in year 1, she described her role as principal:

> I think they will see when it works, it's all worth it . . . I'm counting on the ah-ha moment to come at some point. So, I am a cheerleader, and if cheerleading keeps them on track, then that's what I will do.

Mrs. Leon also paid close attention to morale and the school culture. She understood her district historically placed a lot of pressure on teachers to improve student achievement. She also understood that teachers sometimes viewed ELLs as testing liabilities. She said, "This is a sad part of the district's past, and, as principal, I need to acknowledge that it exists and reject it." Some teachers were concerned that dual language was implemented too quickly or that dual language would negatively impact test scores. Mrs. Leon always took efforts to validate teacher concerns. For example, Mrs. Leon agreed with her teachers that the district pushed dual language implementation at a rapid pace, but also advocated for change by underscoring the prevailing history of educational injustice, "How much longer should we hold off change? We should have been doing this for decades." Occasionally teachers blamed themselves or students for shortcomings in the classroom. Mrs. Leon was there to reframe failures as learning through trial and error. She motivated teachers, frequently stating, "Tomorrow is a new day."

In year 2 of dual language implementation, pre-k and kindergarten teachers were more enthusiastic and strong grade-level bonds emerged between teachers from consistent co-planning and co-teaching. Teachers also felt better about their second year of dual language. Mrs. Leon was strategic in having her most experienced pre-k and kindergarten dual language teachers share the benefits of dual language to the rest of the faculty. Mrs. Leon said, "In year 1, I was selling it . . . and I know people are saying, you're selling it because you have to." Now, experienced teachers advocated for dual language to their peers. Mrs. Leon also solicited feedback and advice from her experienced teachers to help plan for future years where new teachers would be implementing dual language for the first time.

Dual language was a central component to creating a more inclusive and high-performing school, but parent engagement continued to lag. Less than 15% of families attended parent–teacher conferences and many teachers did not have working phone numbers for parents. While public schools cannot ask about a parent's immigration status, Mrs. Leon understood that some parents were fearful of interacting with the school. The district's history of providing a poor-quality education to Mexican-American students was another barrier to engagement. Some parents had bad experiences in public schools when they were children. Some recalled being scolded or hit by teachers for speaking Spanish. Mrs. Leon recognized the school and community were not always on the same page but tried to work with teachers and families as much as possible.

The school worked to engage with community-based organizations to provide adult education classes, supports and legal services to help with immigration and deportation problems, and access to social workers and government agencies that help families secure housing and meet other basic needs. The resources brought into the school helped position the school as a centerpiece of the community. The school also hosted several monthly events to attract families into the school and had a program that provided families in need with groceries on a regular basis. Mrs. Leon also worked on behalf of several families to help resolve immigration, housing, and other related issues. Relatedly, Mrs. Leon heard from teachers that a small subset of students struggled because of home and community issues associated with poverty, housing insecurity, and immigration status of family members. Some students who commuted to school from Mexico were tardy and others missed extended periods of time or had loved ones lost to violence in neighboring Ciudad Juarez.

Sometimes teachers expressed concern for students that lacked family support and other times they conveyed deficit perspectives of students and families. One teacher described a subset of students she felt should not be in dual language education, "They are just too far behind, and we do and try everything, but I have a whole class to handle. There is only so much personal attention I can give." Another teacher added, "I think this shows that dual is maybe for everyone, but not everyone right away." Mrs. Leon challenged teachers to improve the quality of their instruction, to adapt curriculum to student needs, and to stay focused on what they can control, but she also recognized some of the severe challenges confronting a handful of students. She stated:

> This place is like no other. I mean, the bridge is right here. That comes with a lot. Some of our students come to us with little academic Spanish and no English. I'm talking about a third grader who cannot read or a fourth grader who can read but not understand anything he reads . . . So does dual work? Of course, but the results are going to take much longer. When they cannot rely on either language as a base, that's a problem.

The effort to help some of the school's most vulnerable students took a physical and emotional toll on Mrs. Leon and some of her teachers.

While Mrs. Leon gave teachers opportunities to vent frustrations and discuss struggling students, she did not accept teachers who labeled students as deficient.

Mrs. Leon reported that some of her teachers had made blatant remarks about students not being "smart enough," being "too dumb to get the material," or "just not capable." She also disliked how teachers used terms like "lows" and "bubble kids" to describe students as testing liabilities or close to passing state assessments. In response, Mrs. Leon was demanding and assertive. She advocated to her teachers that it was their job to call out any other teacher who looked down on students or families. She said to her teachers, "This is your school, if you hear something negative it's your job to challenge it." Mrs. Leon also dealt with the teachers who maintained deficit beliefs. She assumed a few teachers were "unsalvageable" and refused to change their practices or beliefs. She said, "For these people, my job is to get you out. I need good teachers, passionate teachers, not people who aren't willing to work and try to give our kids, who deserve so much, a chance."

Outcomes and Principal Reflections

Villa ES showed little improvement on standardized test scores after two years, but Mrs. Leon was not worried nor did she care about test scores. She discussed how her superintendent was upset with stagnant test scores. She told him change takes time and that the school was improving teacher quality and building relationships with families. She privately questioned his priorities stating that she could not understand how a superintendent in a high-poverty, majority Mexican-American school district along the border could be so narrowly focused on test scores and so obtuse with regards to students social and emotional well-being. In year three, Villa ES made significant gains on state assessments and was one of the highest performing schools in the region when compared with schools with similar student demographics. It took three years to demonstrate results. Her superintendent and district celebrated the success. Admittedly, Mrs. Leon was personally relieved and validated. While dual language implementation and test scores improved, Villa ES still struggled to engage all families. On a one-on-one basis, the school helped several families with complex social issues, but school-wide family engagement was far less successful. Mrs. Leon and some of her teachers acted to develop important family and community partnerships, but nothing seemed to consistently work. There were no real meaningful shared leadership or governance activities. The same parents participated in the Parent–Teacher Association and on the School Improvement Team. Shared-governance was an area the school would need to focus on continually.

Mrs. Leon was always reflective and was a harsh critic of herself. She admitted that, on occasion, she viewed some individuals as "bad teachers" and "bad parents." She recalled times when she looked herself in the mirror and had to recommit herself to being positive. She described part of her reflection process:

> A lot of times I leave the office close to tears . . . I think about the day and some of the things I hear teachers say, or I think about a student who is struggling and I get mad . . . I blame others and think to myself, why can't people just do the right thing? I want to scream, like yell at them. I do the right thing, why can't they? I know in these moments, that's not right . . . I know most teachers and most parents really want what's best and my job is to make their jobs easier. Not to blame them for falling short or not being able to deal with all the pressure and challenges they are dealing with.

Her reflective process and honesty revealed the emotional toll of the principalship and how even a dedicated principal can participate in deficit-thinking during times of weakness and fatigue.

Despite some frustrations and shortcomings, Mrs. Leon advocated for her students, for dual language, and for the school to serve as a community resource to students and families. While she was passionate about the technical aspects of dual language, she did not rank implementation fidelity over the needs of her teachers and students. She said, "We need to be more flexible here, because we can't just ignore the social and emotional, we can't just focus on dual and forget everything else." She understood that her district placed pressure on teachers and principals to perform. As a leader, she felt compelled to challenge that structure and to buffer her teachers from those pressures. Mrs. Leon brought tremendous expertise around dual language into her school. She advocated for dual language and for teachers to attend to student needs and not test scores. She worked hard to help families struggling with broader social issues and admitted that she was not perfect and needed to recommit herself on occasion. She was intolerant of teachers who viewed students through deficit lenses and was not afraid to lead in ways she thought would benefit her students.

Case 3: Creating an Inclusive School in a Segregated District

Hall Elementary School

Center City Public Schools (CCPS) is a medium-sized urban district in the mid-Atlantic USA. The district had a long history of failing to educate students with disabilities which is evidenced by three long-standing federal class action lawsuits (DeMatthews & Mawhinney, 2013). At one point in time, the district had approximately 2,400 of its 8,500 students with disabilities in non-public or residential facilities and operated six special education schools designated for students with disabilities. Numerous self-contained programs were also administered in schools across the district. Students with disabilities were bused to these programs and segregated from their peers for all or most of the day.

Hall ES was in a rapidly gentrifying neighborhood. While 95% of the students were Black and over 90% received free and reduced meals, million dollar apartments and renovated homes were for sale within walking distance to the school. Hall ES enrolled about 250 students of which about 35 students received special education. Most students were not passing state-mandated assessments in reading and math when Mrs. Jackson arrived as principal, but fewer students in special education passed these same assessments. Historically, Hall ES housed two segregated classrooms for students with emotional and behavioral disabilities. Most students in these classrooms were bused in from other areas of the city. Of the 16 students in the two classrooms, 14 were Black boys. Each class had one special education teacher, one paraprofessional, and did not have any classes or interactions with the rest of the school. Hall ES teachers were primarily veterans who had spent most of their careers at the school, but most teachers struggled with building relationships with families.

Mrs. Jackson

Mrs. Jackson was the principal of Hall ES and in her second year at the time of the study (DeMatthews & Mawhinney, 2014). She was a Black woman in her mid-40s who dedicated her career to working with students with disabilities. Fellow principals and teachers knew her to be fair, stern, and plainspoken. Before serving as principal, Mrs. Jackson was an ES special education teacher, a high school special education teacher in a state prison for teenagers, and a certified speech and language pathologist. She also had experience working in the district's Office of Special Education in a key leadership role. She asked to be principal of Hall ES because she knew the school segregated almost all students with disabilities. Having worked in prison, she was also well-aware of the school-to-prison pipeline. She said, "There is a special ed-to-prison pipeline. When I was working in the jail, let me tell you, many of my students had IEPs." When Mrs. Jackson took over as principal, her superintendent directed her to raise test scores by 8 percentage points per year, increase student enrollment, and try to build positive relationships with the upper-middle-class families who were gentrifying the community. She wanted to improve test scores and enrollment, but she was more concerned with the long-term outcomes of her students, including those in segregated classrooms.

Mrs. Jackson prioritized inclusion and high-quality instruction. She was admittedly less focused on culturally relevant and responsive curriculum, especially considering many students were not even included in the general education classroom to benefit from any school-wide curricular improvements. Her experiences as a teacher and central office administrator fostered in her a belief that most students in self-contained programs were being under-taught and not provided with meaningful access to the general education curriculum. She believed principals need to address segregation by advocating for inclusion. Mrs. Jackson said:

placing all students in their least restrictive environment . . . [and] almost every student should be included in the general education class . . . for some kids, at a particular point in their life, the general education class isn't what's best . . . Our job is to make sure we get each kid to a place where they can thrive and be successful in inclusion.

While Mrs. Jackson prioritized inclusion, she was not blind to the realities of her school or district. She realized many teachers were unprepared to work in inclusive classrooms, especially since Hall ES had a long history of segregating students with disabilities. For inclusion to take root, she understood she must act as a facilitator, motivator, expert, and connector.

Priorities and Actions

Mrs. Jackson immediately began to build support for inclusion, especially with veteran teachers who needed additional training on how to differentiate instruction, utilize research-based instructional approaches for teaching students with disabilities, and develop more proactive and positive classroom management techniques. Mrs. Jackson started by changing the school's schedule to allow teacher teams to co-plan and work together on a regular basis. By changing the schedule, special education teachers had time to plan with general education teachers and make co-teaching more effective. Mrs. Jackson always attended these sessions, gave feedback on lessons and unit plans, helped stimulate dialogue about new instructional practices, distributed readings and articles to encourage ideas, and tried to make teachers feel comfortable sharing their challenges and their good ideas. She said her main priority as a leader was to: "create a collaborative environment where teachers feel comfortable sharing and giving feedback."

Mrs. Jackson also relied on her administrative knowledge and expertise to facilitate inclusion. She scrutinized the school budget to look for ways to use money more efficiently. She sought out grant opportunities to pay for half- and full-day professional development sessions each month to help teachers develop their co-planning and co-teaching skills. She repurposed professional development away from a focus on test-taking strategies and toward inclusive practices. Professional development specialists were hired to help teachers plan, share ideas, and provide actionable feedback following lesson observations. Teachers identified areas for professional development with Mrs. Jackson and the specialists. Since Mrs. Jackson once worked in the central office, she used her professional network to gain access to additional district resources. She knew district staff who were former principals or special education teachers and she solicited them to help improve her school.

Hall ES teachers became more prepared to co-teach and more comfortable talking about instruction. Mrs. Jackson formed a team of general and special education teachers to collaboratively review data on students with disabilities that were segregated for all or most of the school day. The group identified students with disabilities who were incorrectly placed in segregated settings. She explained, "we prioritized certain kids for inclusion . . . if we could find a few students who are successful relatively quickly, we help fight the negative views teachers have against these kids and begin to change the way they think." Her comments reflect her awareness of being proactive toward teacher resistance. By showing teachers that inclusion could work for students with disabilities, more teachers would be willing to adopt inclusive practices and work with students with disabilities.

Mrs. Jackson welcomed parents. She tried to predict and assuage their concerns with inclusion while at the same time soliciting valuable information parents knew about their child. One of Mrs. Jackson's former jobs was handling school–family disputes in special education. She understood some parents could be confrontational to change because they felt the district was trying to take away special education services they had to fight for in the first place. Mrs. Jackson attended each IEP meeting, helped facilitate conversations about student areas of strength and needs, and ensured teachers and parents were comfortable with inclusion. She was always reassuring and promised that the school would be in close contact.

Mrs. Jackson and teachers began to turn their attention to dismantling the self-contained programs for students with emotional and behavioral disabilities. Many students had never been in the general education classroom. Some experienced serious trauma in their personal lives. Three students were initially targeted for inclusion based on classroom observations and academic performance. Mrs. Jackson mandated that all students in the self-contained program would participate in recess, lunch, and physical education with the rest of the school. The mandate was not just about including students, but also about reducing stigmas and deficit views of teachers in the rest of the school. Mrs. Jackson said:

> These kids [from the self-contained programs] are stigmatized in the school. Regular teachers here think they are bad or criminals or something because they are bused in and not allowed to interact with other students . . . I needed to debunk the myth that these kids were no good or out of control.

Behavioral incidents occurred from time to time, but more general education teachers saw that students with emotional and behavioral disabilities could be successful in inclusive settings. Some outright questioned why there was a need for the self-contained programs, which Mrs. Jackson viewed as a positive sign in creating an inclusive school culture.

For the three students who were moved into an inclusive setting, Mrs. Jackson was a significant support structure for teachers and families. She wanted to see these boys and their teachers be successful so she was highly visible, provided ongoing feedback, checked-in with teachers regularly, and held joint parent–teacher conferences to build rapport. She also hired a classroom management specialist who provided ongoing support and feedback to teachers. When two of the three students were successful, the school began to target more students for inclusion.

Outcomes and Principal Reflections

Inclusion as a school-wide reform was a tremendous success at Hall ES. In one year, the number of students with disabilities who were in the general education classroom for less than 39% of the day dropped from 16 to 5. Test scores also went up in the school for both students with disabilities and their non-disabled peers. Mrs. Jackson reflected on what she viewed as a more balanced and student-centered school:

> Kids are happier and more kids are learning. Some of our kids are so low [performing on reading and mathematics assessments] that even a year and a half's worth of growth would not yield growth on the test after a year, but the test scores will come if we stay focused.

Mrs. Jackson was correct and student achievement continued to improve year after year. Teachers attributed the improvement in test scores to the professional development they received and the opportunities to co-plan, try new strategies, and build new skills. Mrs. Jackson believed that test scores improved because teachers accepted the challenge of teaching a more diverse set of students and in doing so expanded their skills.

While inclusion was successful, a few students struggled significantly. Mrs. Jackson was reflective of how difficult inclusion could be under certain conditions and for certain students. She described a dilemma that emerged:

> One the one hand, a student who has been stuck in a classroom with behavior problems his whole life may never learn how to behave appropriately in a regular class. Behavior is learned, so he needs access to other students. On the other hand, if we give him access he will build new skills but may be too disruptive to the rest of the class. The issue is, how do you find a balance? Can you find a balance? Where do you draw the line? There's not always a clear answer for what's right. You also have to respect your teachers. It's not fair to put them in a position to fail . . .

It was in these instances, where students and teachers struggled with inclusion, that Mrs. Jackson's values and commitments to inclusion were tested.

Daquan was a student with an emotional disability who stood out for Mrs. Jackson. She described Daquan as a "real sweetheart" who was "very smart" and had mostly A and B grades. He rarely had any trouble in his small, self-contained classroom and was a perfect candidate to be in a more inclusive classroom.

However, once he was in the inclusive class, he began to have behavioral problems. He occasionally bullied students and was also a victim of bullying. Mrs. Jackson, general and special education teachers, and Daquan's family frequently met to try and adapt his IEP and try new practices in the general education classroom. They looked at data and conducted observations together. However, as the year progressed, Daquan's behavior became more problematic, and his grades dropped. Eventually, Daquan told his parent and teachers that he was unhappy and wanted to return to his old class. He was self-advocating, as teachers and his parents wanted. Mrs. Jackson, Daquan's family, and the team ultimately decided to return Daquan to the self-contained program, but did so reluctantly.

Mrs. Jackson admitted to feeling upset and angry with the pace of change and with setbacks. She felt Daquan was a victim of a system that labeled Black boys as criminals, segregated them, and destroyed their self-esteem. She believed inclusion was best for Daquan, but that his long-term experiences in a self-contained program created significant challenges that Daquan himself could not overcome in the short-term. Daquan represented a dilemma of inclusion to Mrs. Jackson because he thrived in his self-contained classroom and struggled in the inclusive setting. Mrs. Jackson was angry that her district created structures like self-contained programs, mislabeled many Black boys as "Emotionally Disturbed," and funneled them into classrooms far away from their peers. At times, she felt like her district did not care and was not interested in serving its students or communities. She admitted to asking herself, "What am I doing working in this place?" She acknowledged that there were days the district made her want to give up. However, she never allowed such feelings to overcome her. She explained how she felt as principal and offered advice to future principals:

> There are some rough days as a principal, because the buck stops with you, but, still, there are things that you can't control. Think about that, you are responsible, everyone is looking to you, but you're not in complete control. That's stressful, especially when you are talking about the lives of teachers. You are going to have bad days and sometimes you are going to feel like a complete failure. Good principals, they get back up. They are fighters. I'm not the best principal or the smartest, but I believe in what we are doing and I don't feel like anyone or anything can stop us. Until they fire me, I'm going to be here working for a better school.

Case 4: Connecting Schools to Social Movements or Missing Opportunities

Baltimore Schools

On April 12, 2015, Baltimore Police arrested a 25-year old Black man named Freddie Gray. During the arrest and transportation to the city jail, Gray sustained injuries to his spine and died on April 19. Spontaneous and planned protests occurred after Gray's funeral and led to the arrest of more than 250 people. About 100 students from Frederick Douglas High School walked out during the school day. Some students became involved in a chaotic standoff with the police. Buildings, civilian vehicles, and police cars were destroyed. Many Baltimore youth played an active role in protesting, civil unrest, and vandalism. The governor deployed the Maryland National Guard, the mayor enacted a state of emergency and citywide curfew, and the district canceled schools the following day.

Some members of the national media were shocked to see Baltimore's decrepit conditions where thousands of boarded-up and vacant rowhomes, known as "shells," dominated the city's landscape. A journalist described Baltimore as: "a place in which private capital has left enormous sections of the city to rot, where a chasm separates the life chances of black and white residents – and where cops brutally patrol a population deemed disposable" (Gude, 2015). In Freddie Gray's neighborhood, almost 52% of people were unemployed, 33% of homes were vacant, and nearly 8% of children had elevated blood-lead levels (Covert, 2015).

Mr. Monroe and Ms. Janice

Mr. Monroe is a Black man in his early 40s who worked in Baltimore as an educator for more than ten years. Ms. Janice is a Black woman in her mid-40s who grew up in Baltimore and worked in the city for more than 15 years (DeMatthews & Tarlau, forthcoming). Both worked as principals at schools near the Baltimore riots and many of their students grew up in the same neighborhood as Freddie Gray. Mr. Monroe and Ms. Janice spoke eloquently and passionately about their students and social justice issues. They loved being educators in Baltimore and were motivated given what they knew about the community injustices many of their students confronted. Mr. Monroe believed that public schools were "not just about getting kids to pass the test, but to prepare them for life." He expanded on what he meant by life: "I mean prepare them to be a Black man or woman in America, in Baltimore." Ms. Janice felt similar, stating that "In the Black community, schools can be like churches. A safe place, a place to come together, to discuss our issues, and to act."

Leading During Social Upheaval

Both principals recognized the important presence of the Black Lives Matter (BLM) social movement and were supportive of candid conversations about race, class, discrimination, and police brutality, primarily as it related to Baltimore's most marginalized and racially segregated neighborhoods. Ms. Janice felt her students were marginalized not only because of their race but because where they lived. She said, "The way police treat me, as an educated Black woman in a nice car, it's not the same as how they treat our kids. These kids aren't only Black, but they are from this place that has such a negative stigma." She added that many of the city's police officers are White and perceive young Black boys as threats. Mr. Monroe also supported BLM and was concerned with the incarceration of Black men, youth, and the school-to-prison pipeline. He stated:

> I don't know the stats offhand, but it's horrible here. These boys are treated by the police as if they are dangerous, they get a criminal record by eighth grade, we fail them in schools, their community fails them. They are set up to fail, you know?

Both principals' comments reflected a connection between BLM and the everyday life and struggle of their students.

Mr. Monroe and Ms. Janice believed issues of racial justice were important topics for public schools to cover. Moreover, they believed that helping students explore such issues is vital for their social and emotional development. Each principal spoke at length about how teachers in their school developed different curricular experiences for students and many of the schools' athletic coaches and afterschool program mentors engaged students in dialogue about community issues, racism, and police violence. Mr. Monroe's students engaged in letter writing campaigns to challenge harmful district policies or provoke the city government to address a community issue, frequently visited the city's African American museums to learn about various topics related to racial justice in Baltimore and the USA, and engaged teachers in critical conversations about the effects of racism, poverty, housing insecurity, and community violence.

Each principal also acknowledged that the city and their school had a piecemeal approach to providing a culturally relevant and responsive curriculum and failed at adopting a formal curriculum that enabled all students to critically analyze contemporary society. Neither of their schools took full advantage of current and potential partnerships with nearby grassroots community organizations or advocacy groups, such as Baltimore United for Change (BUC), the American Civil Liberties Union of Maryland, or local universities.

While both principals recognized that formal curriculum and partnerships were lacking at their schools, they pointed to informal and impromptu ways in which they educated and empowered students. Mr. Monroe gave one example:

> When you see a young man and he is getting in trouble and making poor choices, you need to engage him in a dialogue. Like, help him understand the path he's on. You hope you can help him in a way that makes him change courses.

Ms. Janice made similar remarks concerning mentoring boys but also emphasized the importance of mentoring girls around issues of domestic violence, teenage pregnancy, and gang membership.

Outcomes and Principal Reflections

The lack of formal curriculum and structure was problematic, and both principals understood this needed to be addressed. However, Ms. Janice noted that principals were given limited time and resources while being stressed by their district to raise student achievement and keep students safe with a constantly shrinking budget. She said, "We aren't given much resources and there isn't much time in the day to do all the things you'd like to do." Mr. Monroe and Ms. Janice spoke at length about how significant portions of their day could be wasted trying to access basic resources or repairs for their schools, on replacing faculty and staff who quit during the year, and ensuring each of the school's testing days (which is more than 10 days per year) ran smoothly.

Immediately after the riots when school returned, both principals encouraged teachers and students to discuss the riots and police brutality, but also expected teachers to emphasize that students act responsibly and stay away from situations that could turn violent, such as protests. Mr. Monroe said, "It's our job to help them understand the laws, to tell them to stay in, and that they need to stay safe." Ms. Janice said, "Our job, first and foremost, is to make sure everyone is safe . . . Unfortunately, if you are a principal here you know far too many students that have been killed . . . So it's our job, as much as possible, to protect students." Both principals felt conflicted about the protests and their students being involved. They understood civic engagement was important, but feared violence could claim the lives of their students or that students could be antagonized by police or their peers and make decisions that could negatively impact the rest of their lives.

Mr. Monroe and Ms. Janice were reflective of their shortcomings in engaging students in issues related to racism, police brutality, and the Baltimore riots. They both felt constrained in their actions as well. Mr. Monroe said:

> Activism, especially for teachers and students is not out of the question. However, as a principal, I work for the district. I need to be more careful . . . My mentor told me, as a principal, you need to pick your battles . . . So, in this case, with Freddie Gray, this is a battle I want to fight, but I know that I need to make sure all my students are safe first. It wasn't safe. So, I couldn't just say what I wanted to say. I had to be the voice of reason. I had to exercise control . . . Now, if you ask me what I would do if I was a teacher, or if I was in college, or a teenager, you'd get a different answer.

Ms. Janice had similar remarks. She underscored the importance of "the daily work of principals working to improve the lives of Baltimore's students" as well as how principals do this within the system and over the long-term:

Principals are activists, but sometimes you have to do these things more quietly. You need to find partners . . . but more importantly, I think it's not about what you do the day after the riots. It's about what you do every day. I'm proud of what I do and I'm so proud of all of our teachers. It isn't easy working here . . . We fight every day for our kids . . . When Cooper Anderson [CNN News Anchor] leaves, I will be here. You know? This isn't something I just got into because I was in college and had free time . . . This is my life. I'm committed to this place. So, if you ask me do I think principals are activists, they are in Baltimore . . . The good ones at least are.

Takeaways for Principals

Each principal took responsibility for addressing some of the pressing challenges they believed were impacting their school, students, and communities. They demonstrated a commitment to social justice rooted in their personal and professional experiences. These experiences prompted them to collaborate with others and, to varying degrees, reject top-down, authoritarian approaches. Their priorities and actions were not simply driven by test scores, but nuanced and reflective of the on-the-ground reality they confronted as principals working in complex and evolving environments. In some ways, they worked with communities and transformed the structures and culture within their schools. They also made important connections between their school and the needs of students, families, and communities. Each principal navigated and maneuvered in ways that revealed a situational awareness of competing priorities, and demonstrated political astuteness in their work. Despite their commitments, skills, and consciousness of the injustices confronting schools and communities, each principal recognized that their practice was imperfect, that at times they contributed to injustices inadvertently, and that creating more just schools and communities took time and long-term commitments. Much of what they learned through critical reflection helped them adapt their practices. Finally, each case revealed that more work was to be done.

References

Collier, V. P., & Thomas, W. P. (2004). The astounding effectiveness of dual language education for all. *NABE Journal of Research and Practice, 2*(1), 1–20.

Covert, B. (2015, April 28). The economic devastation fueling the anger in Baltimore. *Think Progress.* Retrieved from https://thinkprogress.org/the-economic-devastation-fueling-the-anger-in-baltimore-8511b97c0630/

DeMatthews, D. E. (2016). Competing priorities and challenges: Principal leadership for social justice along the US–Mexico border. *Teachers College Record, 118*(11), 1–38.

DeMatthews, D. E., & Izquierdo, E. (2018). Supporting Mexican American immigrant students on the border. A case study of culturally responsive leadership in a dual language elementary school. *Urban Education*. DOI: 10.1177/0042085918756715

DeMatthews, D. E., & Mawhinney, H. B. (2013). Addressing the inclusion imperative: An urban school district's responses. *Education Policy Analysis Archives, 21*(61), 1–30. Retrieved from http://epaa.asu.edu/ojs/article/view/1283

DeMatthews, D.E., & Mawhinney, H.B. (2014). Social justice and inclusion: Exploring challenges in an urban district struggling to address inequities. *Educational Administration Quarterly, 50*(5), 844–881.

DeMatthews, D. E. & Tarlau, R. (forthcoming). Activist principals: Leading for social justice in Ciudad Juarez, Baltimore, and Brazil. *Teachers College Record*.

Gude, S. (2015, April 28). Why Baltimore rebelled. *Jacobin*. Retrieved from https://www.jacobinmag.com/2015/04/baltimore-freddie-gray-unrest-protests/

CONCLUSION

New Knowledge Requires New Commitments

In this book, I have shown some of the limits to traditional approaches to principal leadership in urban schools. I began by describing both the positive assets and harsh social and economic realities within many of low-opportunity communities. I also highlighted how the conditions of today's urban schools and communities is not a function of poor choices by families or lazy principals and teachers, but rather part of a long and ugly history of racially explicit government policies that have segregated cities and fostered the development of unequal public schools. I used Baltimore, Maryland and El Paso, Texas as reference cities to highlight how racism and segregation denied urban families and students of color from access to healthy food and healthcare, safe communities, employment opportunities, and quality schools. I took further effort to detail more than 200 years of urban school reform, which included how the principal's role evolved, to demonstrate that top-down school reforms and traditional leadership approaches have rarely provided urban students of color with meaningful opportunities for social mobility. I narrowed in on the social processes and interactions within schools to further demonstrate how traditional approaches failed to meet the needs of students and families. I detailed the work of scholars who have shown how the rituals, routines, structures, policies, and social interactions within many schools frequently work against students of color by failing to value their cultural capital, identities, and assets.

I have also argued that when principals reject the myth that more accountability and more top-down reform will improve their schools, and when they accept the history of urban school reform failure, they can begin to uncover, challenge, and address the hardened social structures and taken-for-granted practices that continue to marginalize their students. Knowing the history of a community and the shortcomings of traditional approaches to teaching and leadership can initiate inquiry and a search for new opportunities for school transformation. Principals are then able to view their positions not as neutral and apolitical, but rather as moral and political advocates for social justice. Urban schools in low-opportunity communities of color need leaders who:

- acknowledge the pervasiveness of racism in society and political nature of education;
- help students understand, evaluate, and act on their situations;
- generate opportunities for students to value and authentically connect with their community;
- collaborate with families and community-based organizations to collectively learn about the past and work toward a better future.

Such efforts create the networks necessary for accessing opportunities that may have been invisible to schools, families, and students.

Unfortunately, as I have shown, the field of educational administration and leadership has historically privileged a set of leadership approaches that reflect a hidden, vested interest in reinforcing the status quo. Principals operating from a mindset informed by these privileged approaches often fail to recognize the historical context of their schools and communities, the power and pervasiveness of racism and other forms of discrimination, and how unequal power dynamics between the school and students and families will never produce the conditions needed to make a difference. Such approaches have attentively emphasized academic achievement, mastery of basic skills, the general functioning of the school, and the structural and organizational conditions that increase teacher capacity to raise student achievement. These approaches are singularly ineffective in low-opportunity communities because they fail to identify, understand, and work to address the underlying social, economic, and political issues that negatively affect students and families.

Throughout this book, I have argued that knowledge of history is essential to school leadership and understanding the role of the principal. While a small group of critical and social justice-oriented scholars provided alternative approaches that are extremely valuable for re-envisioning leadership, many Black and Latina/o principals were forced to use their knowledge of history to resist the status quo long before scholars in the field documented such efforts. I described the experiences of Black principals leading before and after the *Brown v Board* decision to highlight an alternative approach to school leadership. These principals confronted obvious and hate-inspired obstacles each day, they advocated with and for communities, developed powerful formal and informal networks, and participated in broader social movements with a moral imperative to overcome the barriers of poverty and institutionalized racism in American society. More recently, scholars of color and other critical scholars developed alternative leadership frameworks that emphasize how principals can address racism and the related circumstances that marginalize students of color in low-opportunity communities.

In the final chapters of this book, I provided a discussion of the complexities of social justice. I began with describing the growing body of literature associated with leadership for social justice. I presented a community engaged leadership framework for such work that underscores the importance of personal experiences and commitments, situational awareness, advocacy, critical reflection and praxis, and technical expertise. Then, I offered four case studies of urban principals where I demonstrated how their practice was reflective of the community engaged leadership framework previously presented and highlighted how, in each case, the principal catalyzed meaningful change within their school and community. However, I also detailed how each principal struggled with a range of interrelated issues, made mistakes, and was forced to reflect and make up for their unintentional wrongdoings. These cases demonstrated the reality of principal leadership in low-opportunity communities where injustice is both multifaceted and solidified in the history and culture of the school, district, and unequal social and economic arrangements in the region.

The truth is that community engaged leadership for social justice is often gritty and political, slow-paced when confronted by resistance, and physically and mentally exhausting. The material in this book has been organized and presented to facilitate an argument that urban principals must think and lead differently, but by no means is this work easy. Principals must be concerned with social justice first and foremost and find ways to prioritize the needs of students, families, and communities. They must also be reflective, assume they will struggle and confront dilemmas they cannot avoid, and allow for a collaborative and inclusive dialogue to continually focus and refocus the direction of the school. Some decisions made by principals will be faulty and require reflection and adjustment. Sometimes, leading toward social justice will instigate new and previously unknown forms of resistance. Powerful colleagues and constituents can be offended when disrupting the status quo or the privilege of influential groups. Other times, social justice work will be truly transformative, inspiring, and educative to the community of leaders that seek to improve the lives of all students. Those who may have been resistant early in the process might reconsider their positions and become allies.

I hope that I have been successful in arguing for an alternative approach to leadership and that I have provided the necessary knowledge to extend an important conversation. I also hope that it is clear that I am not suggesting that the field's knowledge base and standards do not have merit or cannot be salvaged. Rather, principals must use whatever knowledge, resources, and skills they have at their disposal to improve their schools. With this new knowledge, I believe further commitments and actions are required. To this end, I conclude this book with a set of insights and recommendations for aspiring and current principals and for those interested in advancing a research agenda in educational administration and leadership that is focused on community engaged leadership for social justice.

Consciousness Through Reflection and Self-Care

A principal who is racially, socially, and politically conscious must have the capacity to engage in ongoing critical inquiry and self-reflection. She or he must be able to see how history shapes their frames of reference, identities, and beliefs about what is possible. Critical inquiry and reflection is central to learning and utilizing history in ways that can promote and sustain a social justice approach to leadership. Critical inquiry has been described as the "consideration of the moral and ethical implications and consequences of schooling practices on students" where self-reflection "adds the dimension of deep examination of personal assumptions, values, and beliefs" (Brown, 2004, p. 89). Cultural biographies and life histories have been used successfully to foster critical inquiry and self-reflection. Cultural biographies foster awareness and acceptance of one's own position in society and helps to reveal how different identities can form unique vantage points through which life's experiences and perceptions are filtered (Brown, 2004). Lisa Delpit (2006) emphasized the importance of investigating one's culture and place in the world, or as she called it, the "unexamined backdrop for everyday living" (p. 92). By exploring and being explicit about one's own culture, language, socioeconomic status, privilege, and other unique characteristics, individuals can develop and question their assumptions, beliefs, and values. Principals can also begin to recognize that other valid alternative interpretations exist and should be valued.

Throughout this book I have argued that principals need an accurate history of schooling as well as an understanding of how racially segregated, low-opportunity communities have been created and maintained. Life-histories can also serve as a means of fostering consciousness within principals because listening to the experiences of an individual who is older than 65 and attended schools in the USA can provide a powerful sense of personal awareness related to the historical context of contemporary education (Brown, 2004). Vanessa Siddle Walker's (Walker & Byas, 2003) historical study of a Black principal (Ulysses Byas) and his leadership experiences as a high school principal in Gainesville, Georgia during the 1960s provided a powerful example of how life histories can raise consciousness and commitments to social justice. The story of Ulysses Byas and how he described leading in a racist social context provided powerful and practical knowledge of how current principals might act against oppression, ignorance, and discriminatory structures within districts and society.

Finally, maintaining a sense of racial, social, and political consciousness requires self-care. Principals need to attend to their emotional and physical health. Much of the actions and expectations that I have placed on principals throughout this book require patience and a commitment to caring for others. These actions and expectations are stressful, especially when students and families must deal with poverty and exposure to community violence. Moreover, the leadership I described in this book requires constant energy, attention, and a willingness to confront resistance collectively and individually.

Many principals experience burnout, emotional exhaustion, depersonalization, and reduced personal accomplishment. Burnout and emotional exhaustion can create a sense of feeling drained and overextended. These feelings contribute to the development of negative and detached attitudes toward other people. It also can add to a sense of hopelessness, which can impact one's ability to do one's job (Stamm, 2010). Thus, principals must heal themselves and be able to make sense of their stress in ways that allow them to move forward (Yamamoto, Gardiner, & Tenuto, 2014).

Self-care has been described as "unbiased observations of one's inner experience and behavior" (Shapiro, Brown, & Biegel, 2007, p. 106). Self-care includes a:

- physical component related to physical activity;
- psychological component related to addressing any type of distress or despair;
- spiritual component that is related to one's sense of purpose and meaning of life;
- support component that includes the relationships associated with one's professional and personal support systems (Richards, Campenni, & Muse-Burke, 2010).

Mindfulness, or an awareness of and attention to one's self and surroundings, is essential to self-care.

Michael Dantley has consistently written about the importance of spirituality in educational leadership, which is related to self-care and leadership persistence. Dantley (2003) argued that principals working with urban youth of color must recognize that they are often in communities deeply grounded in religious and spiritual contexts. The religious foundations within these communities are often powerful sources of hope "as well as resistance to the dehumanizing rituals hegemonically executed against them" (p. 281). Spirituality in educational leadership "rejects the nihilism and justified feelings of despair and hopefulness that pervade communities and schools of color and the marginalized" (p. 289) and, instead, provides a powerful source of strength and commitment to deal with the protracted struggle that is part of creating more socially just schools and communities. When principals are emotionally exhausted, they can also look to the powerful religious and spiritual contexts of their communities for renewal and hope.

From Critique to Action

For many principals, the knowledge of persistent inequality within schools and society does not build confidence, but instead contributes to burnout, lower expectations, and a sense of hopelessness. As more principals and teachers feel this sense of hopelessness, schools become increasingly powerless to resist and address injustices within their own confines. Therefore, hopelessness and an inability to see a way through the challenges reinforce a negative and downward cycle that solidifies inequality in schools and communities. To break this cycle, principals need to be hopeful.

Freire (2014) described hope as an "ontological need" and hopelessness as "hope that has lost its bearings, and become a distortion of that ontological need" (p. 2). Freire (2014) stated, "We need critical hope the way a fish needs unpolluted water" (p. 2). I too take the position that hope is a human need and is an essential component of our human condition. While hope is not sufficient for meaningful change or eradicating inequality in schools or society, it is certainly a precursor to change and related to the power to transform reality. Any struggle or form of leadership without hope will be weak. For Freire, hope and education were inextricably tied, because education is grounded in the recognition of our incompleteness as humans and in a constant search for developing our consciousness. Thus, those who claim to be leaders and educators must seek out opportunities for hope despite the challenges that may seem incontrovertible.

Hope is also about the future and a belief that we can transform the dehumanizing conditions that make life difficult. Principals must be able to imagine a new picture of their schools and communities. They need to share this hope, because hope can be contagious and can provide a foundation for school and community inquiry and collective problem-solving. Sometimes, the conditions of inequality within schools and communities require principals and teachers to catalyze hope and bring hope forward. One way of advancing hope is helping to unveil the structures of oppression that exist within schools and in society. While principals and educators are confronted with a crushing and immobilizing high-stakes accountability context, they may find sources of hope by studying their schools, calling out the taken-for-granted structures and approaches that maintain inequality, and then collectively problem-solving. Equity audits within schools are one way to initiate critique, action, and a revitalized sense of hope.

Audits in education have been used in combination with curriculum audits and as part of state accountability and reform efforts for the past 50 years (Skrla, Scheurich, Garcia, & Nolly, 2004). In contrast to these usages, a set of equity audits for principals and teachers have been developed to recognize strong and persistent patterns of inequality within schools (McKenzie & Skrla, 2011; Skrla, McKenzie, & Scheurich, 2009). Specifically, equity audits can help uncover systemic inequities embedded within schools and how they unjustly allocate resources and learning opportunities, how policies are implemented unevenly, and the ways teachers and principals value the cultural and linguistic diversity of students and families. Equity audits are described as a systematic approach to assess the presence of inequality in programs, teacher quality, and achievement (Skrla, McKenzie, & Scheurich, 2009). These auditing tools allow for a critical consideration of teacher quality, programmatic quality, and achievement quality.

- Teacher quality considers how teachers are dispersed in a school in ways that maximizes equity.
- Programmatic quality is related to special education, gifted and talent, bilingual education, and student discipline.
- Achievement quality is related to state achievement test results and achievement gaps, dropout rates, high school graduation tracks, and SAT, ACT, Advanced Placement (AP), and International Baccalaureate (IB) results and placements.

By auditing these areas, principals and teachers can learn about how their schools are structured and the ways equity is promoted or constrained. Moreover, equity audits can be used to assess the competency of teachers to meet the diverse needs of all students, to embrace a self-reflective approach to teaching and leadership, to critically evaluate and assess student achievement from an equity-perspective, and to further develop the teaching skills and consciousness to advance student achievement for all.

Building Community Capacity and Networks

Creating hope amongst educators and creating more equitable systems and practices within schools is important, but insufficient. Principals also need to consider community outcomes and foster solidarity amongst educators and a range of stakeholders. As I have previously noted in this book, most school-community approaches focus narrowly on achieving district- and school-related priorities such as test scores but disregard broader social concerns within neighborhoods. For example, Standard 8 of the Professional Standards in Educational Leadership (PSEL) (National Policy Board for Educational Administration (NPBEA), 2015) is the primary standard focused on family and community engagement. The standard emphasizes a reciprocal and mutually beneficial relationship that promotes each student's academic success and well-being, but mostly stresses the need to work with families to eliminate external barriers to school improvement and student achievement. Consequently, many principals leave their preparation programs and work in districts that provide limited guidance for understanding the needs of low-opportunity communities and families. Moreover, few principals are equipped with the knowledge to understand institutional racism, unequal access to housing and healthcare, systemic poverty, and community violence. Given their position as principals, they are in an advantageous position to build or extend partnerships and relationships with local communities.

Community audits and community-based participatory research (CBPR) have long been approaches used by social movements, non-profit organizations, research–community partnerships, and various government agencies. They have been used to hear "people's views, opinions, needs, or what resources are available" (Packham, 1998, p. 250). Community audits and CBPR value community participation which is used to empower people to work on issues that directly impact their lives (Packham, 1998). These processes should also attend to issues of gender, class, race, and culture and maintain an emancipatory focus that uses new information to change the lives of stakeholders. Community auditing and research processes are designed to provide all stakeholders with a sense of joint ownership over the process and the information that is collected and gleaned. Often, audit and research facilitators are not from the community and may have specific areas of expertise, but they maintain a co-facilitator role and challenge the notion that they are the sole leader or knowledge-holder. Moreover, external stakeholders who value community in the auditing process "start where people are" and put effort into fostering a dialogical process through which community concerns profoundly shape the issues explored and the challenges that should be addressed (Minkler & Hancock, 2003).

One way to build school-community capacity to take advantage of the resources within a neighborhood is to utilize a community-based equity audit (CBEA). CBEAs have been described by Green (2017) as an "instrument, strategy, process, and approach to guide educational leaders in supporting equitable school-community outcomes" (p. 5). Green articulated six key aspects of CBEAs:

- CBEAs are flexibly applied to develop context-specific strategies for school-community challenge. No step-by-step, linear, or one-size-fits-all approach or process must be followed.
- CBEAs are not quick fixes to short-term problems, but instead are used to address systemic problems that require long-term investment, time, trust-development, and collective problem-solving.
- CBEAs can be used in tandem with school-based equity audits.
- Principals are not the only educational leaders nor should they be the only ones engaged in co-facilitating CBEAs.
- CBEAs are built and implemented on the premise that families of color living in low-opportunity communities are not hard to reach, but that traditional approaches to family engagement have been ineffective and culturally incongruent.
- All stakeholders engaged in CBEAs must anchor their practice in a commitment to equity and social justice.

Green (2017) emphasized the critical role of the principal as a co-leader and co-facilitator and described four primary phases of CBEA. I will briefly summarize these phases as they are of tremendous importance for principals seeking to make a difference. First, CBEAs work to disrupt deficit views of the community. Principals can initiate this work by creating a school-based team of diverse stakeholders that are proportionally representative of the population in which the school is located, which might include administrators, teachers, staff, parents, and students. Members of the committee should work to define and discuss current school practices, problematize existing approaches, and consider an asset-based approach to working in low-opportunity communities of color. This phase requires principals and other team members to work to collectively understand the assets of families and communities and reject deficit perspectives that impede progress. Such actions help to facilitate the defining of core beliefs and non-negotiables. Then, teams can work to assess the effectiveness of current school-community practices and begin to align them with their new core beliefs and non-negotiables.

The second phase is centered on an initial community inquiry where principals and their teams develop relationships with community-based organizations and leaders. The teams can also conduct local asset mapping to identify community assets that can serve as "sites of connection, places of engagement, and avenues for social capital development" (Green, 2017, p. 21). Next, teams can identify at least five assets (non-profits, places of worship, businesses, universities) and create a profile that describes each organization's mission, proximity and embeddedness in the community, and potential avenues of partnership. Asset maps and profiles can then serve as a driver identifying and interviewing community leaders to understand the power structure in communities and learn more about the community's history, resources, and challenges. These interviews also help to develop relationships, provide learning opportunities to understand the realities within the community, and can uncover potential benefits of solidarity and mutual participation. Mapping and interviews can provide the team with a shared sense of community experience that can afford new avenues for being proactive about challenging and working to address the structures that marginalize students and communities.

The third phase is focused on the establishment of a community leadership team (CLT), which might consist of formal and informal community leaders who live in the area. This team should value an asset- and equity-based approach to decision-making and action, and serve as an intermediator between the school and community. The CLT is tasked with gathering data to promote school-community change. The CLT should also be open to new ideas and processes that encourage local solidarity and school-community equity.

The fourth phase of the audit involves several steps. First, the CLT works to collect data on school-community history to develop an understanding of "how the community and school has changed over time, and for developing critical thinking about how the current economic, political, and social histories shape community inequity" (Green, 2017, p. 26). The CLT should interview a representative sample of community members who have a broad historical perspective on the community. CLTs should also analyze and discuss archived documents, including neighborhood plans, newspapers, and other school-community documents. Next, the CLT should examine community opportunity and demographic factors, such as total population disaggregated by race, income, employment, and educational attainment levels. These data should be critically analyzed to understand the conditions within communities and understand how opportunities and resources are dispersed geographically. These data should also be combined with the information gleaned from interviews to develop a comprehensive understanding of life in the community. These data are crucial to establishing a critical community dialogue, which is not a one-time meeting, but, instead, an ongoing conversation where the group can dream about what the school and community should be like, develop consensus on causes of inequality, and propose potential solutions and shared approaches to action. Relatedly, drawing on all the data and information previously collected, the CLT and community dialogue provides an opportunity to identify one to three goals that can be achieved through partnership and solidarity. Finally, this group can work to collectively develop an equity focused vision statement, host a community forum with invited politicians and other community leaders, and solidify an ongoing plan of cooperation that identifies resources, benchmarks, accountability systems, and a commitment to continuous engagement.

Final Words

The principal can be instrumental in bringing about change in schools and communities, but they must see the world differently and lead in ways that build hope, community solidarity, and an unwavering commitment to reflection and inquiry. The school leadership needed in low-opportunity communities requires a commitment to taking a position with students and families and a frame of mind that is flexible, critical, and rooted in the historical, social, economic, and political context of inequality within schools and society. When principals are critical, they must not only critique, but also create and propose with teachers, staff, families, students, and community members. Principals must be perpetually hopeful, caring, and inclusive. They may need to catalyze a new vision for the school and facilitate discussions on how things might be done differently in the future. Sometimes, they may need to step back and let others lead. Rather than focusing solely on district and school priorities, principals must build meaning, work with people and not on people, and demonstrate a profound love and faith in the people they serve. They must lead with humility, recognize that they do not have all the answers, and commit to the idea that "we know more collectively than any of us know in isolation."

Principals will undoubtedly face challenges and resistance when they work and lead collaboratively with teachers, staff, families, students, and communities. Dilemmas and resistance will arise. Mistakes will be made. Unseen obstacles will surface and slow the pace of transformation. Social, political, and economic issues will arise and some will remain beyond the control of a principal, school, and community. Despite these challenges, when principals lead with deep wells of hope and love, they can empower others to view a school as a community hub and as a place of possibility. Principals are in one of the most important and advantageous positions for social transformation in our society and when they share their schools with all stakeholders they can find amazing success. Together with families and communities, principals and their schools can help rewrite the history of low-opportunity communities and have a profound impact on their students.

References

Brown, K. M. (2004). Leadership for social justice and equity: Weaving a transformative framework and pedagogy. *Educational Administration Quarterly, 40*(1), 77–108.

Dantley, M. E. (2003). Purpose-driven leadership: The spiritual imperative to guiding schools beyond high-stakes testing and minimum proficiency. *Education and Urban Society, 35*(3), 273–291.

Delpit, L. (2006). *Other people's children: Cultural conflict in the classroom.* New York: New Press.

Freire, P. (2014). *Pedagogy of hope: Reliving pedagogy of the oppressed.* New York: Bloomsbury Academic.

Green, T. L. (2017). Community-based equity audits: A practical approach for educational leaders to support equitable community-school improvements. *Educational Administration Quarterly, 53*(1), 3–39.

McKenzie, K. B., & Skrla, L. (2011). *Equity audits in the classroom to reach and teach all students.* Thousand Oaks, CA: Corwin.

Minkler, M., & Hancock, T. (2003). Community-driven asset identification and issue selection. In M. Minkler & N. Wallerstein (Eds.), *Community-based participatory research for health* (pp. 135–154). San Francisco, CA: Jossey-Bass.

NPBEA. (2015). *Professional standards for educational leaders 2015.* Reston, VA: Author.

Packham, C. (1998). Community auditing as community development. *Community Development Journal, 33*, 249–259.

Richards, K. C., Campenni, C. E., & Muse-Burke, J. (2010). Self-care and well-being in mental health professionals: The mediating effects of self-awareness and mindfulness. *Journal of Mental Health Counseling, 32*(3), 247–264.

Shapiro, S. L., Brown, K. W., & Biegel, G. M. (2007). Teaching self-care to caregivers: Effects of mindfulness-based stress reduction on the mental health of therapists in training. *Training and Education in Professional Psychology, 1*(2), 105.

Skrla, L., McKenzie, K. B., Scheurich, J. J. (2009). *Using equity audits to create equitable and excellent schools.* Thousand Oaks, CA: Corwin.

Skrla, L., Scheurich, J. J., Garcia, J., & Nolly, G. (2004). Equity audits: A practical leadership tool for developing equitable and excellent schools. *Educational Administration Quarterly, 40*(1), 133–161.

Stamm, B. H. (2010). *The concise ProQOL manual* (2nd ed.). Pocatello, ID: ProQOL.org.

Walker, V. S., & Byas, U. (2003). The architects of black schooling in the segregated south: The case of one principal leader. *Journal of Curriculum & Supervision, 19*(1), 54–72.

Yamamoto, J. K., Gardiner, M. E., & Tenuto, P. L. (2014). Emotion in leadership: Secondary school administrators' perceptions of critical incidents. *Educational Management Administration & Leadership, 42*(2), 165–183.

INDEX

Note: References in *italics* are to figures, those in **bold** to tables.